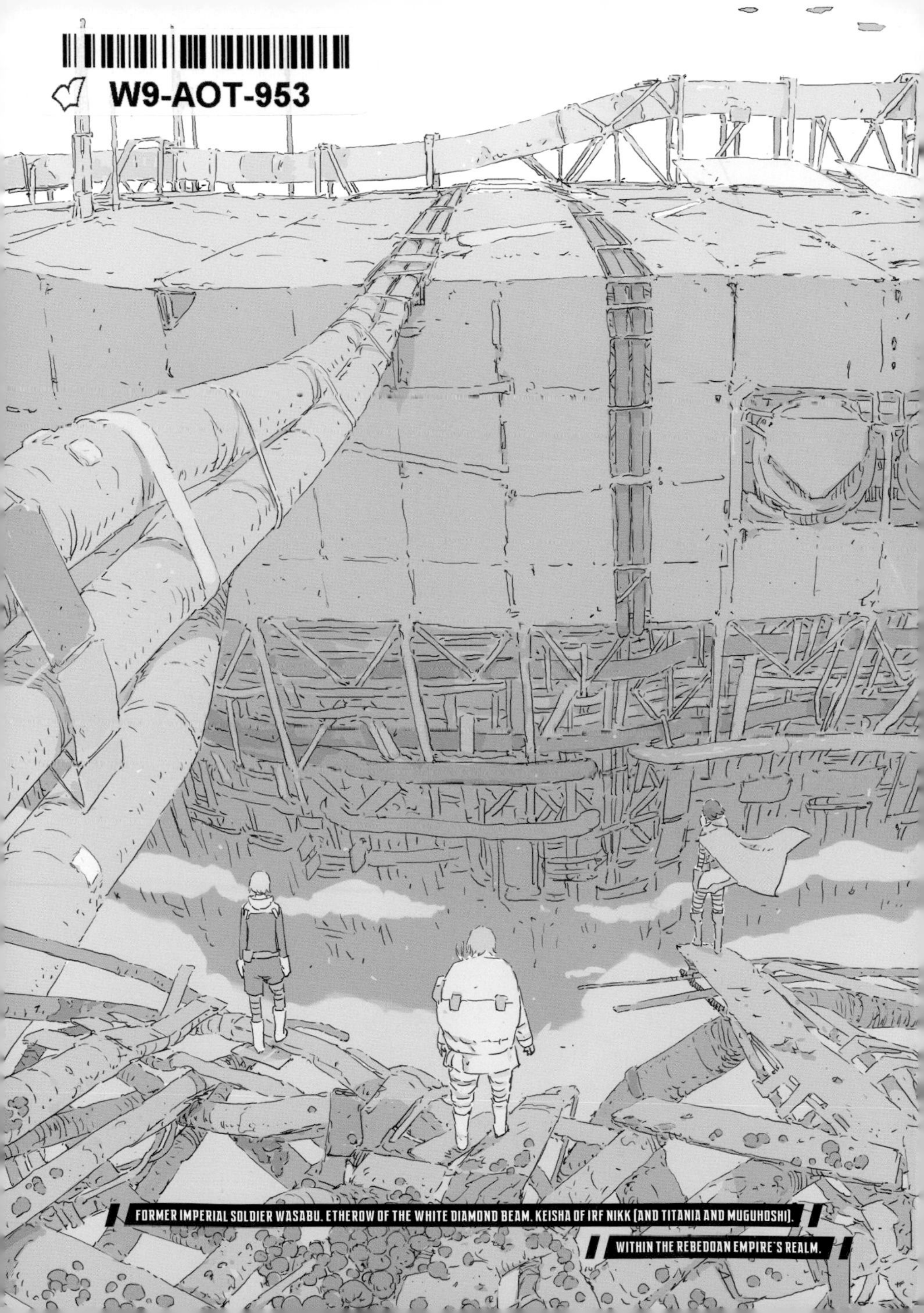
FORMER IMPERIAL SOLDIER WASABU. ETHEROW OF THE WHITE DIAMOND BEAM. KEISHA OF IRF NIKK (AND TITANIA AND MUGUHOSHI).
WITHIN THE REBEDOAN EMPIRE'S REALM.

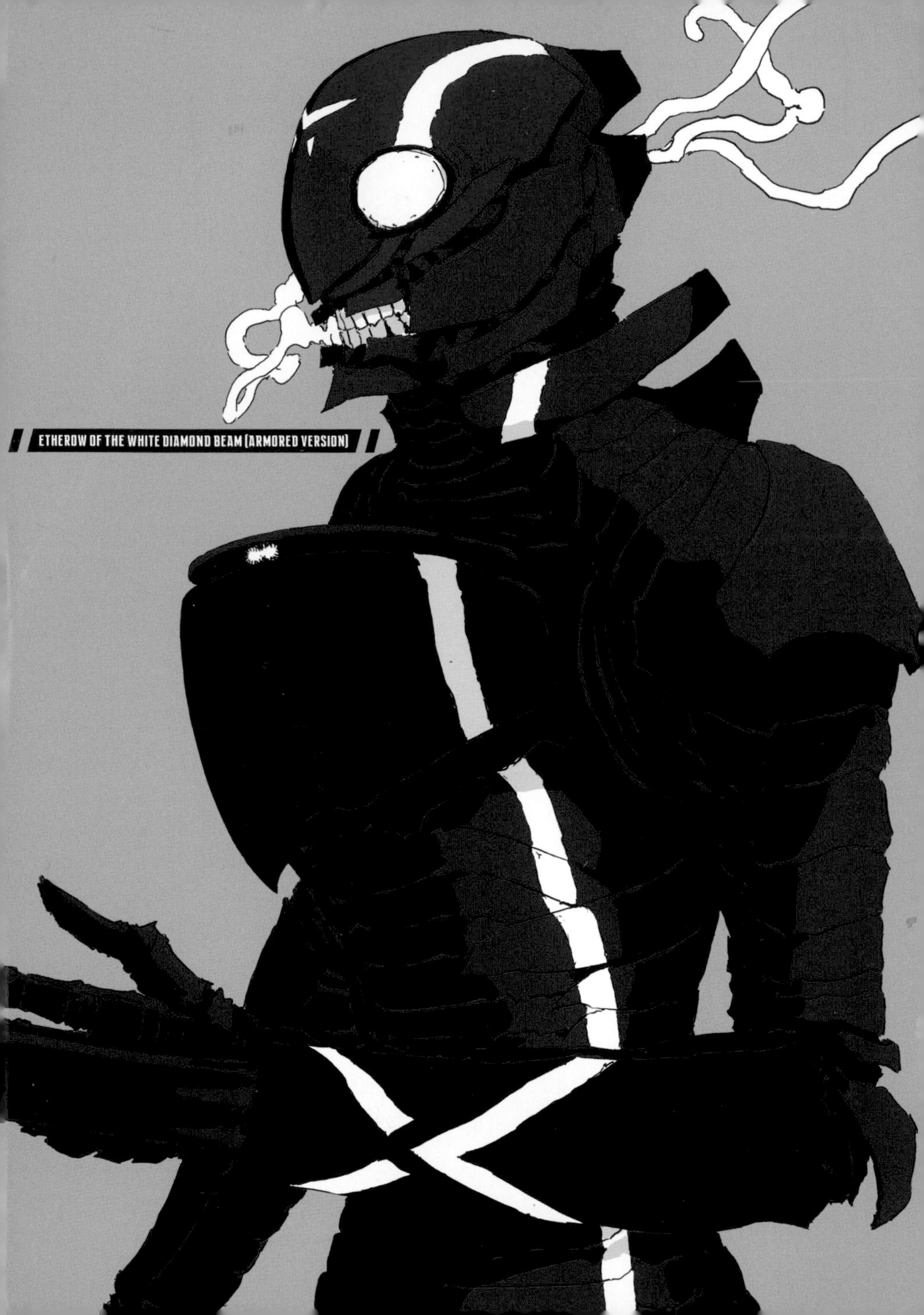
ETHEROW OF THE WHITE DIAMOND BEAM (ARMORED VERSION)

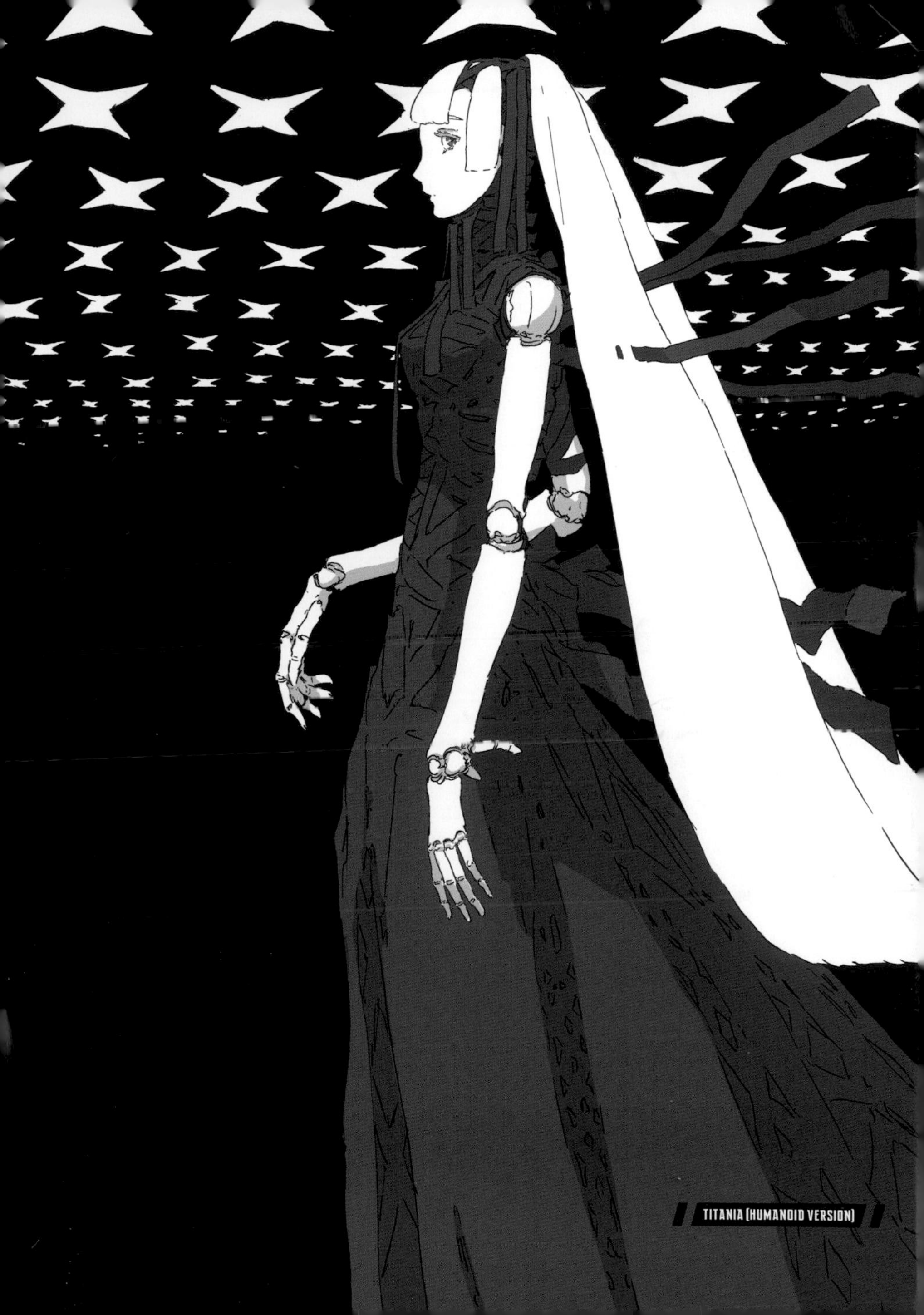

TITANIA (HUMANOID VERSION)

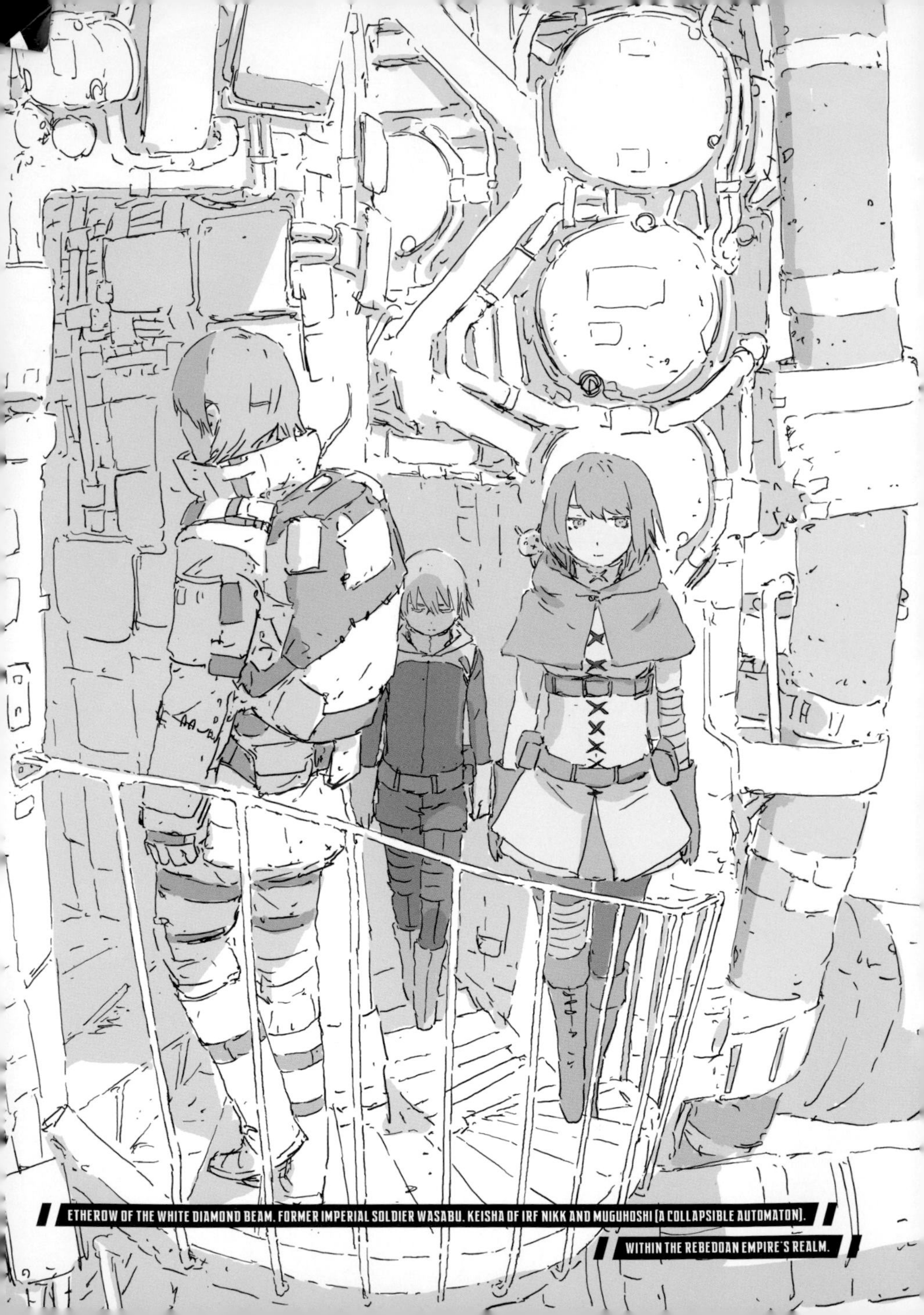

ETHEROW OF THE WHITE DIAMOND BEAM. FORMER IMPERIAL SOLDIER WASABU. KEISHA OF IRF NIKK AND MUGUHOSHI (A COLLAPSIBLE AUTOMATON).

WITHIN THE REBEDDAN EMPIRE'S REALM.

APOSIMZ

08

TSUTOMU
NIHEI

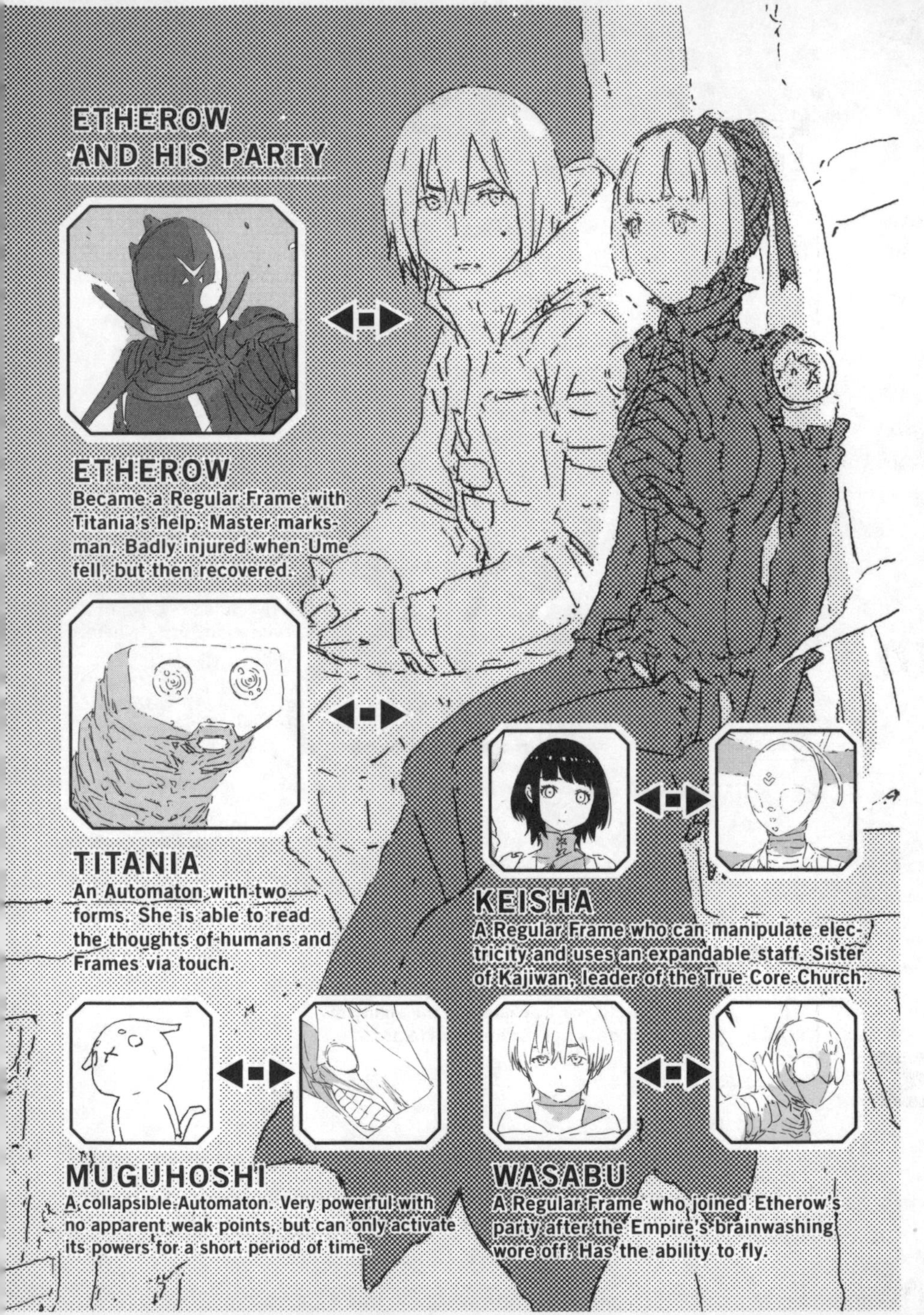
ETHEROW AND HIS PARTY
ETHEROW
Became a Regular Frame with Titania's help. Master marksman. Badly injured when Ume fell, but then recovered.
TITANIA
An Automaton with two forms. She is able to read the thoughts of humans and Frames via touch.
KEISHA
A Regular Frame who can manipulate electricity and uses an expandable staff. Sister of Kajiwan, leader of the True Core Church.
MUGUHOSHI
A collapsible Automaton. Very powerful with no apparent weak points, but can only activate its powers for a short period of time.
WASABU
A Regular Frame who joined Etherow's party after the Empire's brainwashing wore off. Has the ability to fly.

APOSIMZ

PLOT AND CHARACTER INTRO

REBEDOAN EMPIRE

A militant state with powerful, heavily-armed forces that continues to invade various regions. Has many Regular Frames in its ranks.

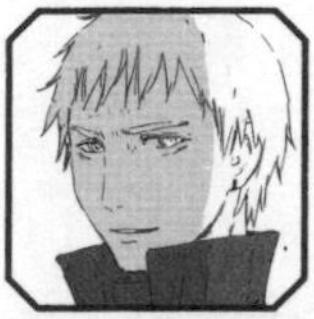

NICHIKO SUOU

The Emperor of Rebedoa. Has the ability to predict the future.

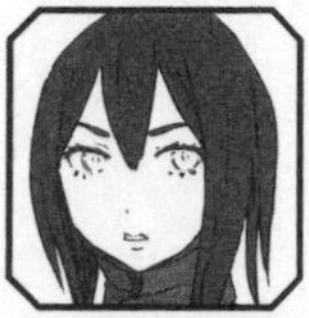

JATE

A high-level Reincarnated of the Rebedoan Empire. Has the ability to manipulate Automatons.

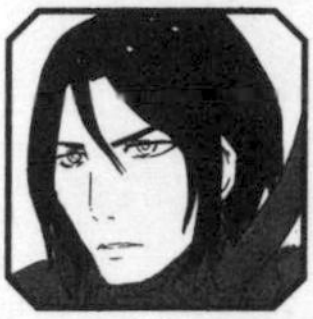

TOSU

A high-level Reincarnated of the Rebedoan Empire. Has the ability to manipulate metal.

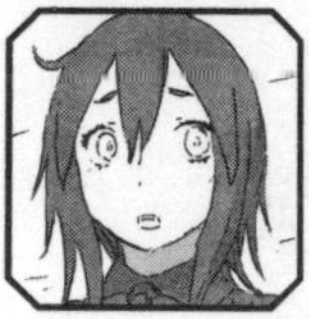

AJATE

A clone of Jate created via artificial Code. She looks like a giant version of Jate.

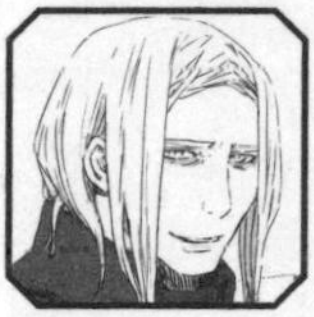

RINAI

Reincarnated.
An old friend of Jate's.
Has the ability to transfer matter.

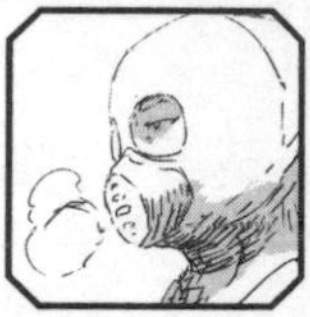

TASHITSUMA

Member of the Imperial Science Division. Successfully created a Regular Frame clone of Jate named Ajate.

TRUE CORE CHURCH

Organization created by Kajiwan to gather those afflicted with Frame disease. Bestows certain sufferers with knowledge and power, turning them into "Regenerateds." Views both the Empire and humans as enemies.

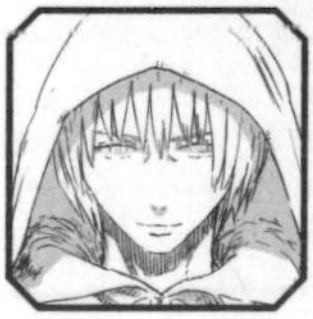

KAJIWAN

The last King of Irf Nikk. Using the powers of the mysterious Frame created from Titania's stolen arm, he became a Regular Frame himself. Has the ability to produce fireballs.

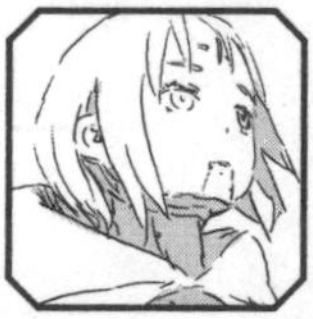

JINATA

Regenerated member of the True Core Church. Her only power is the ability to fight back against Regular Frames.

Previously

In order to fulfill their mission of taking down Nichiko Suou, Etherow and his party press further into the Empire. Kajiwan, having lost most of his followers, has ended up in the Northern Composite Slab Region to collect holy relics and grow more "hosts." Meanwhile, the city of Rutohmero, near the Empire's border, has seen a mass outbreak of Frame disease sufferers...

APOSIMZ

CHAPTER 43

KEISHA OF IRF NIKK (HUMAN FORM)

ETHEROW OF THE WHITE DIAMOND BEAM (HUMAN FORM)

FORMER IMPERIAL SOLDIER WASABU (HUMAN FORM)

> By using "Codes," humans are transformed into Regular Frames. A Regular Frame has powerful physical abilities, has no need for breathing or nutrition (exceptions exist), and does not age. A Regular Frame will not die unless their brain is destroyed.

KEISHA'S FRAME FORM
Uses an electric shock element. An extendible staff (which can also be split apart) is her main weapon.

ETHEROW'S FRAME FORM
Has the projectile firing "EBTG" ability, with which he can fire diverse bullets. Can also handle AMBs.

WASABU'S FRAME FORM
Doesn't have any unique abilities, but can fly.

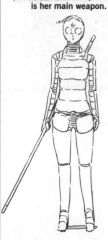

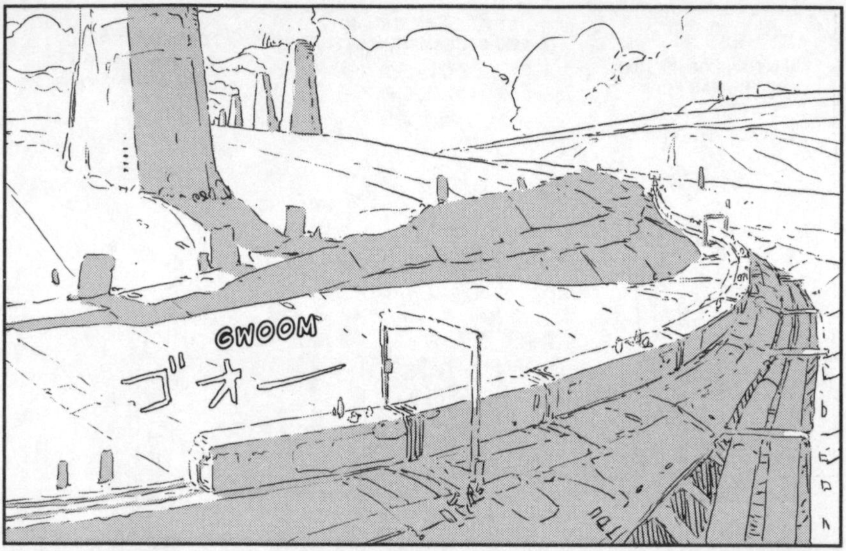
GWOOM
ゴオー

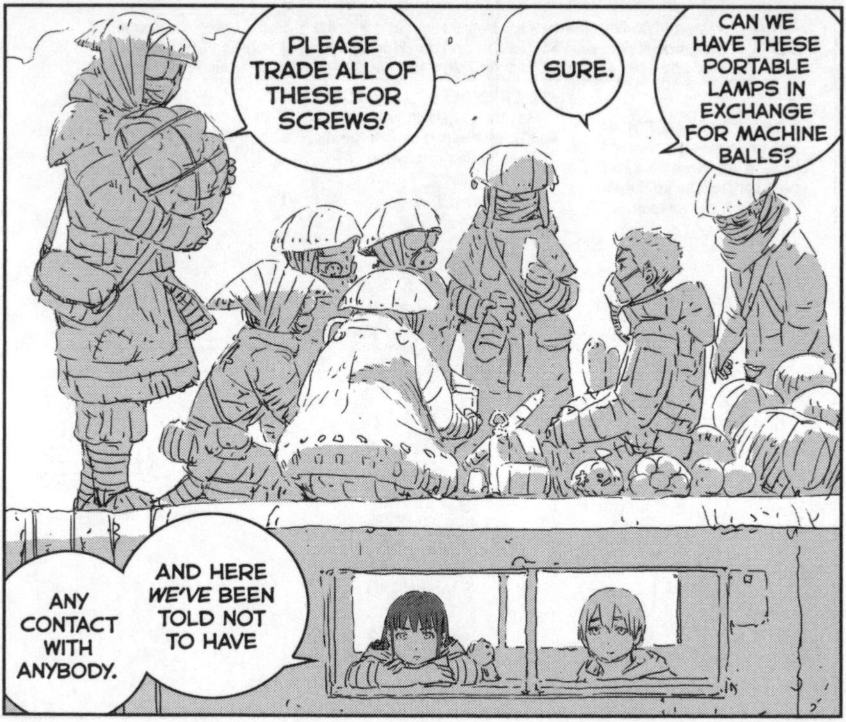
CAN WE HAVE THESE PORTABLE LAMPS IN EXCHANGE FOR MACHINE BALLS?
SURE.
PLEASE TRADE ALL OF THESE FOR SCREWS!
AND HERE *WE'VE* BEEN TOLD NOT TO HAVE
ANY CONTACT WITH ANYBODY.

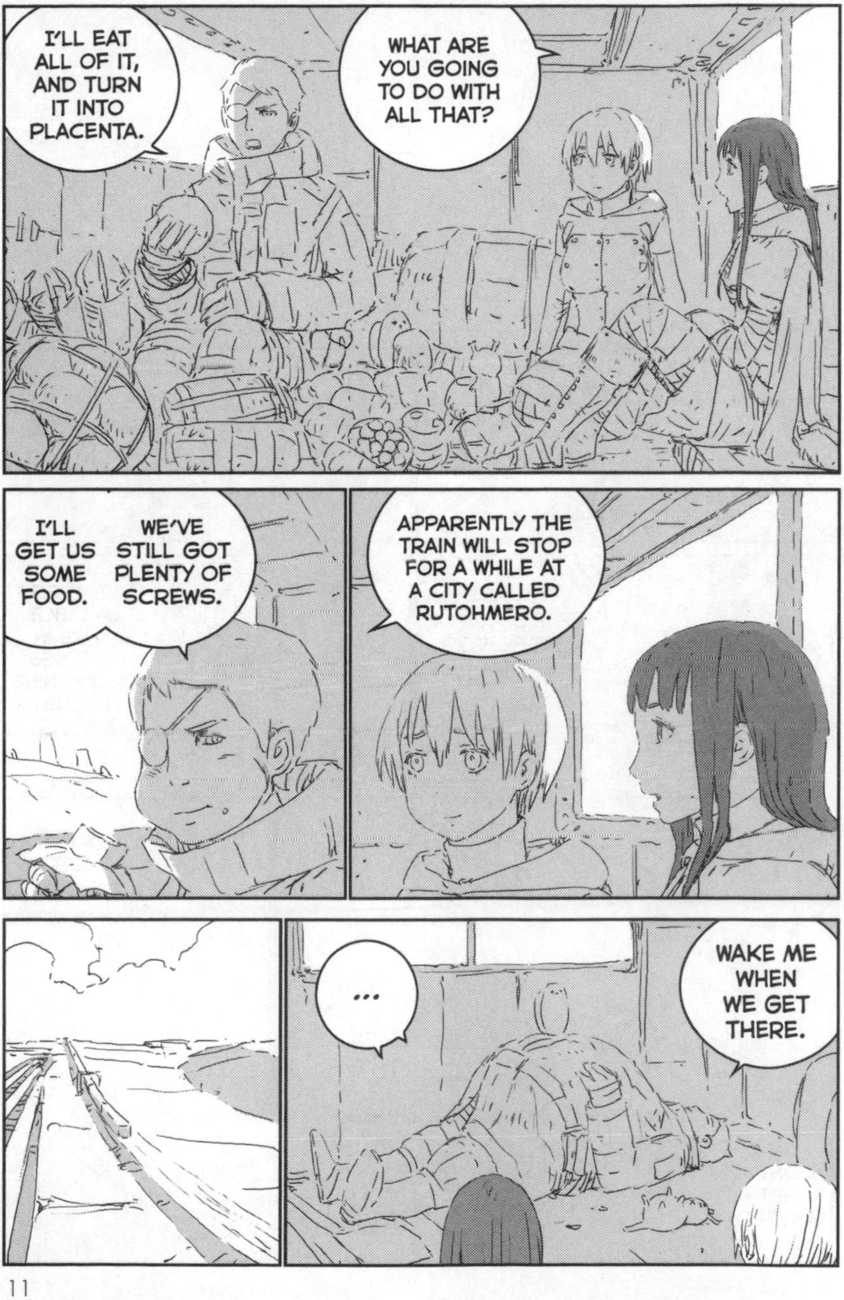
WHAT ARE YOU GOING TO DO WITH ALL THAT?
I'LL EAT ALL OF IT, AND TURN IT INTO PLACENTA.
APPARENTLY THE TRAIN WILL STOP FOR A WHILE AT A CITY CALLED RUTOHMERO.
WE'VE STILL GOT PLENTY OF SCREWS.
I'LL GET US SOME FOOD.
WAKE ME WHEN WE GET THERE.
...

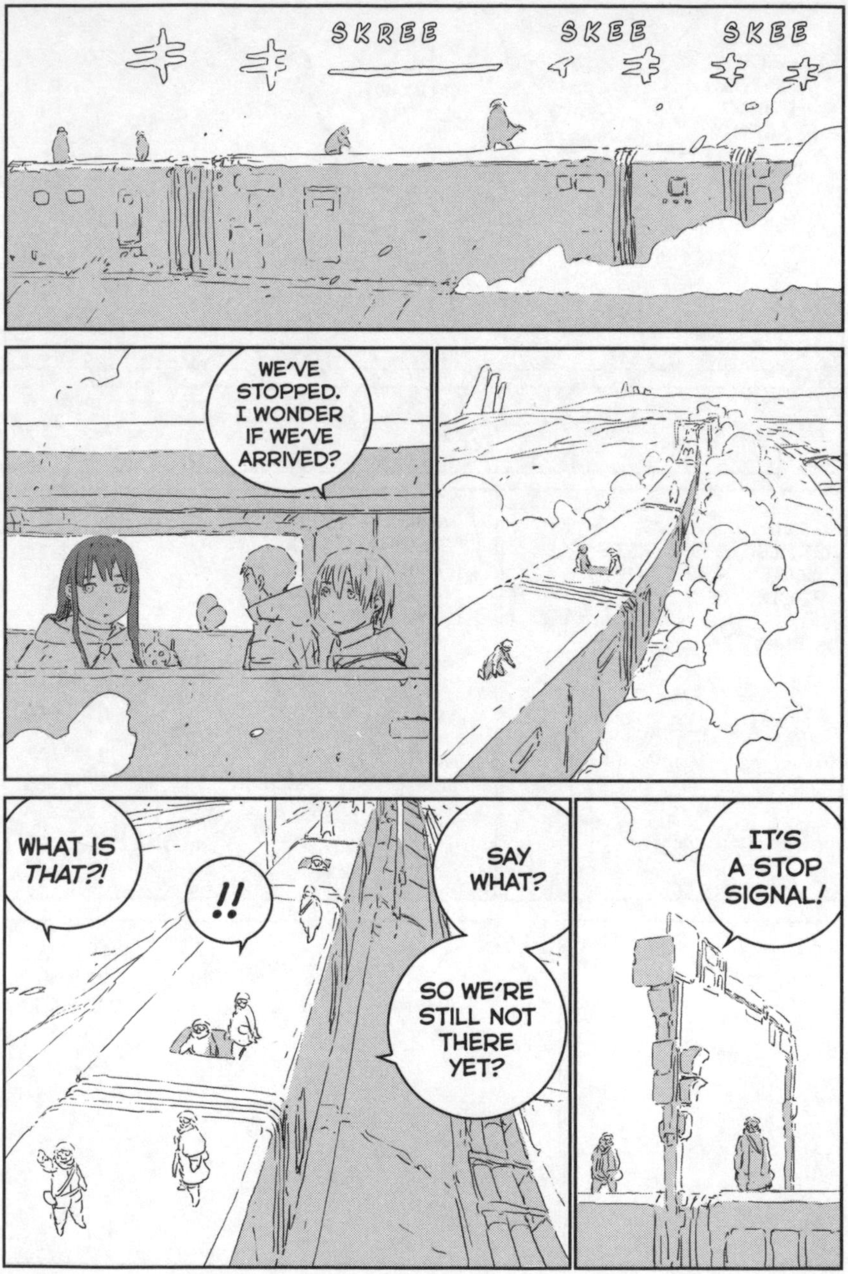
SKREE
SKEE
SKEE
キキーーィキキキ
WE'VE STOPPED. I WONDER IF WE'VE ARRIVED?
IT'S A STOP SIGNAL!
SAY WHAT?
SO WE'RE STILL NOT THERE YET?
!!
WHAT IS *THAT?!*

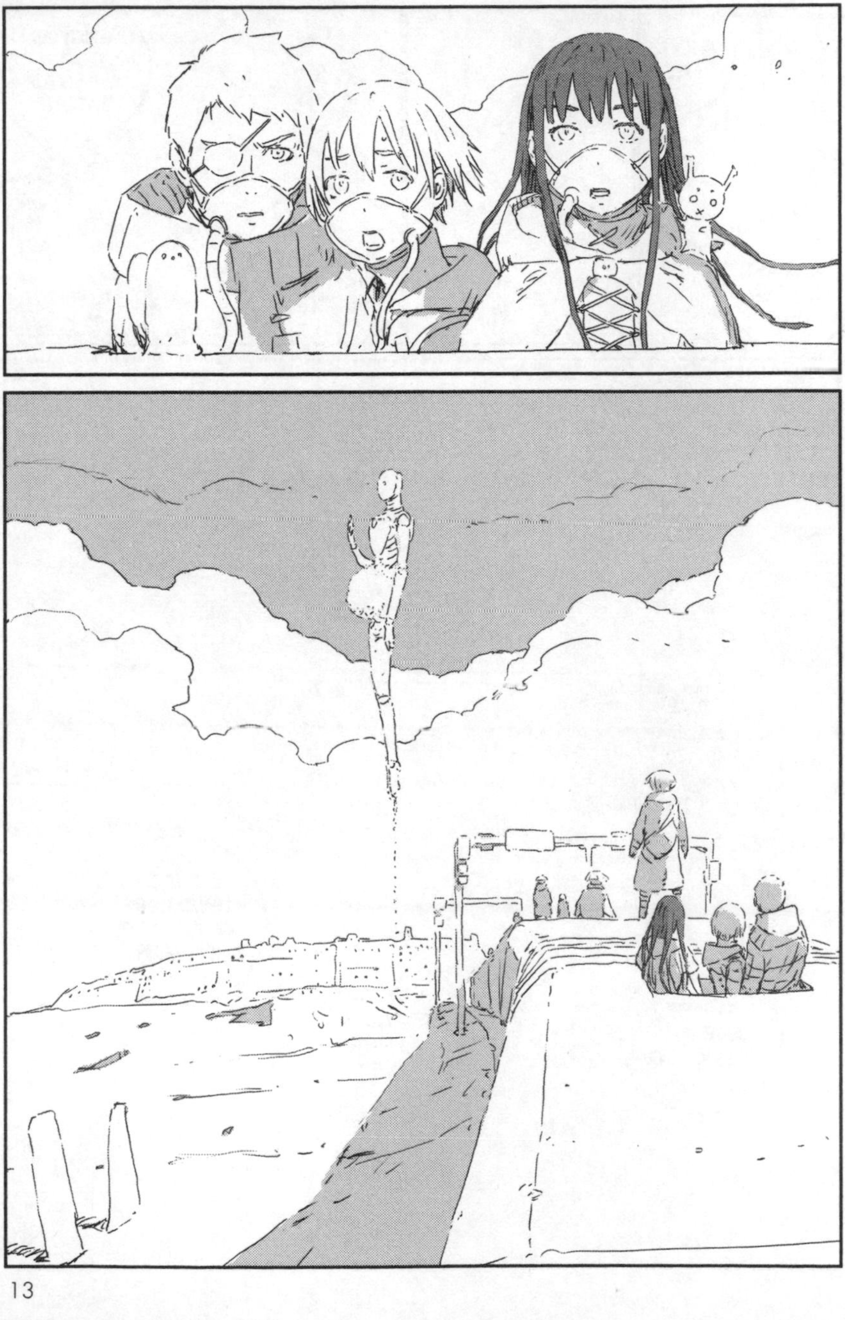

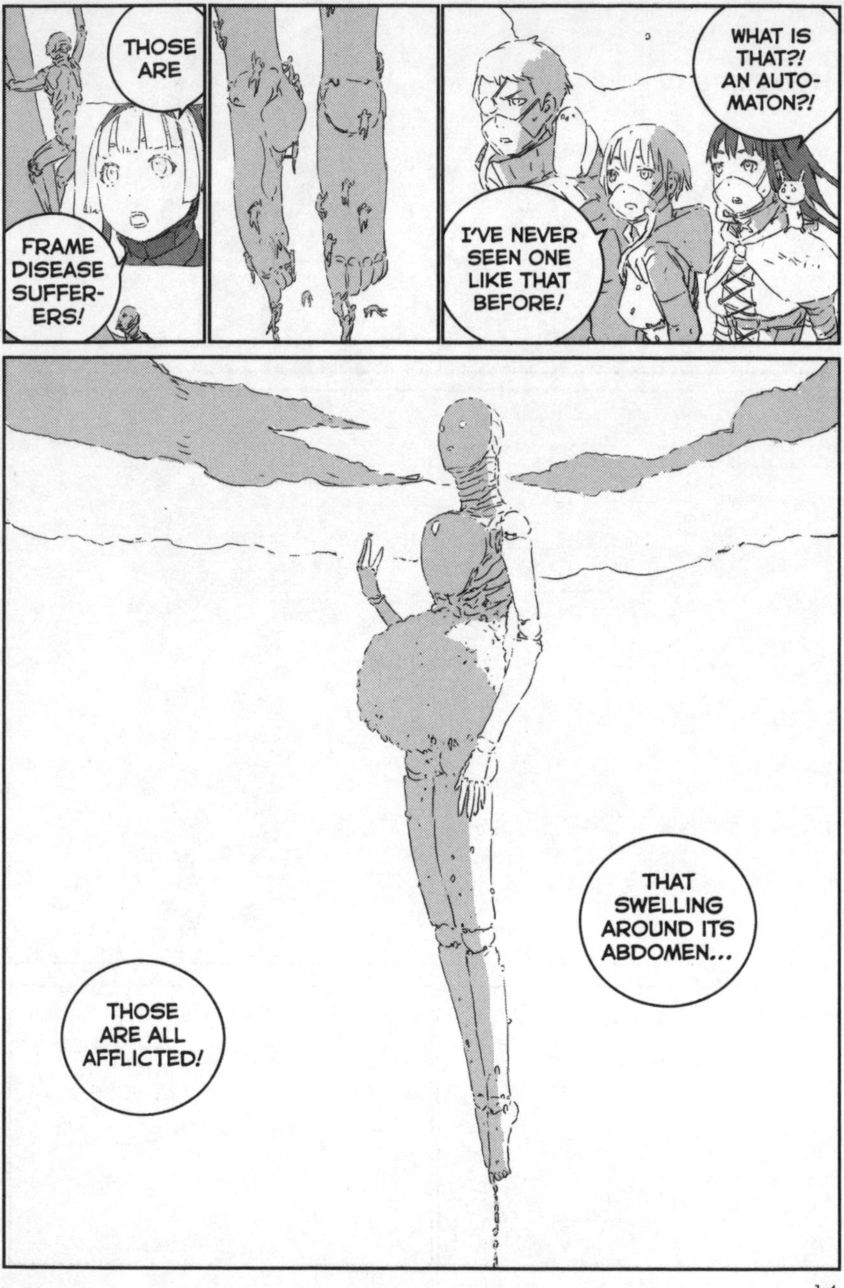
WHAT IS THAT?! AN AUTO-MATON?!
I'VE NEVER SEEN ONE LIKE THAT BEFORE!
THOSE ARE
FRAME DISEASE SUFFER-ERS!
THAT SWELLING AROUND ITS ABDOMEN...
THOSE ARE ALL AFFLICTED!

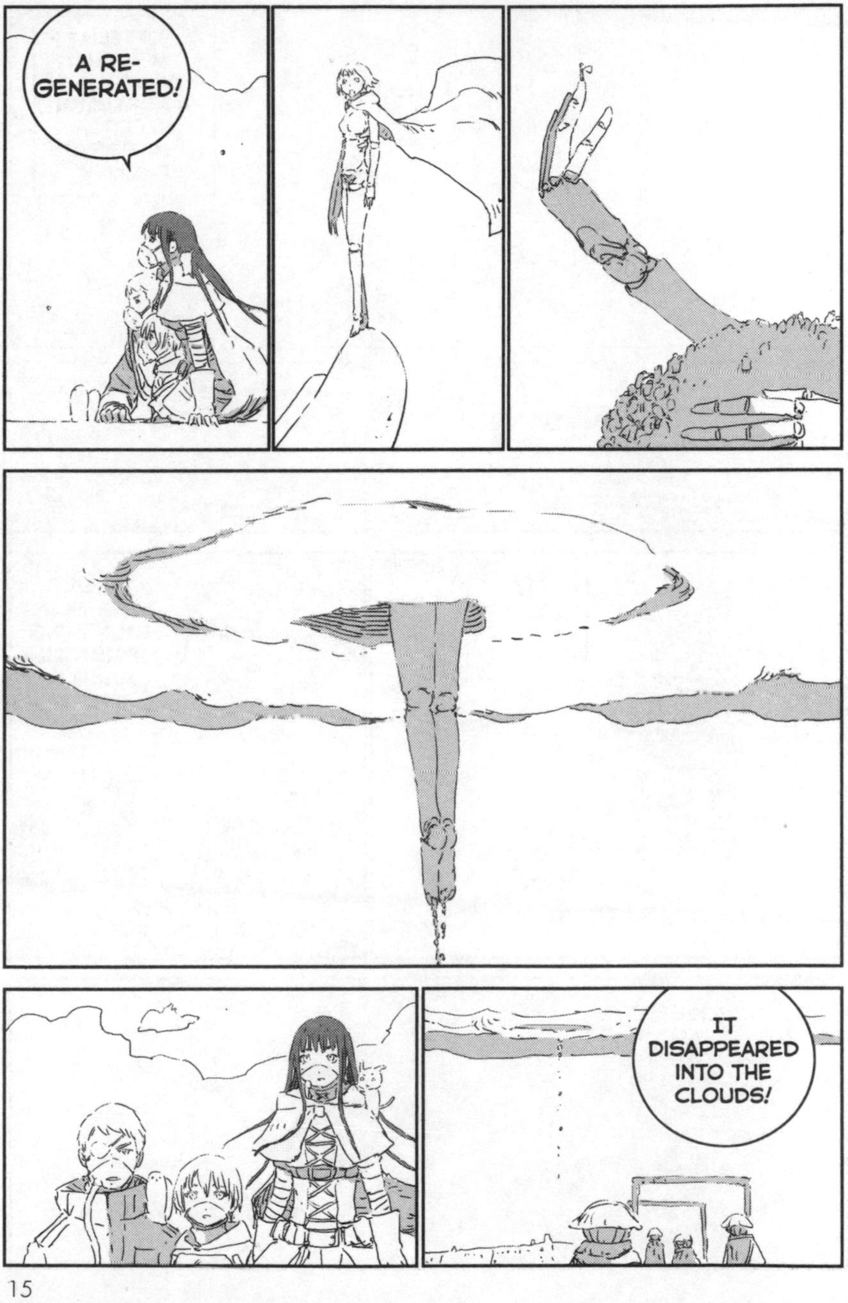
A RE-GENERATED!
IT DISAPPEARED INTO THE CLOUDS!

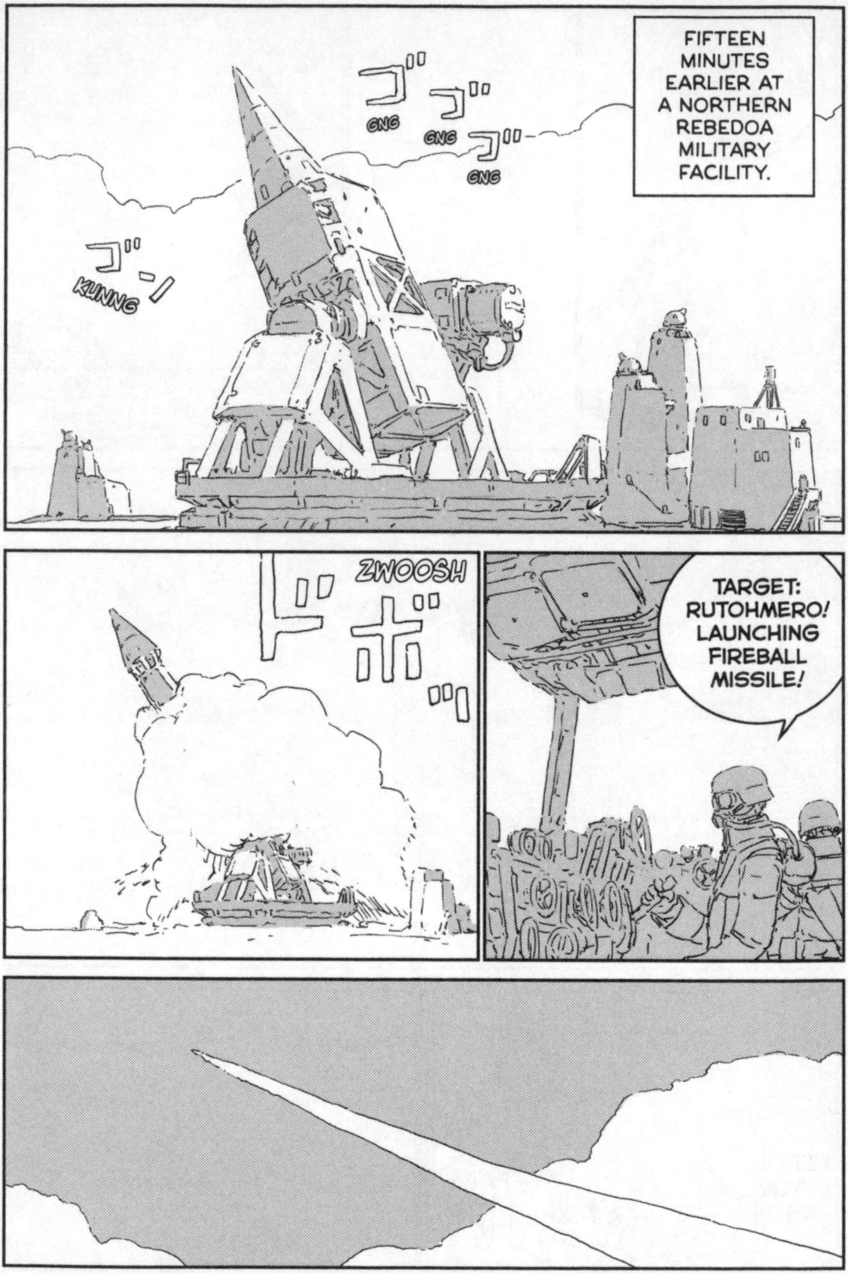
FIFTEEN MINUTES EARLIER AT A NORTHERN REBEDOA MILITARY FACILITY.
GNG
GNG
GNG
KUNNG
TARGET: RUTOHMERO! LAUNCHING FIREBALL MISSILE!
ZWOOSH

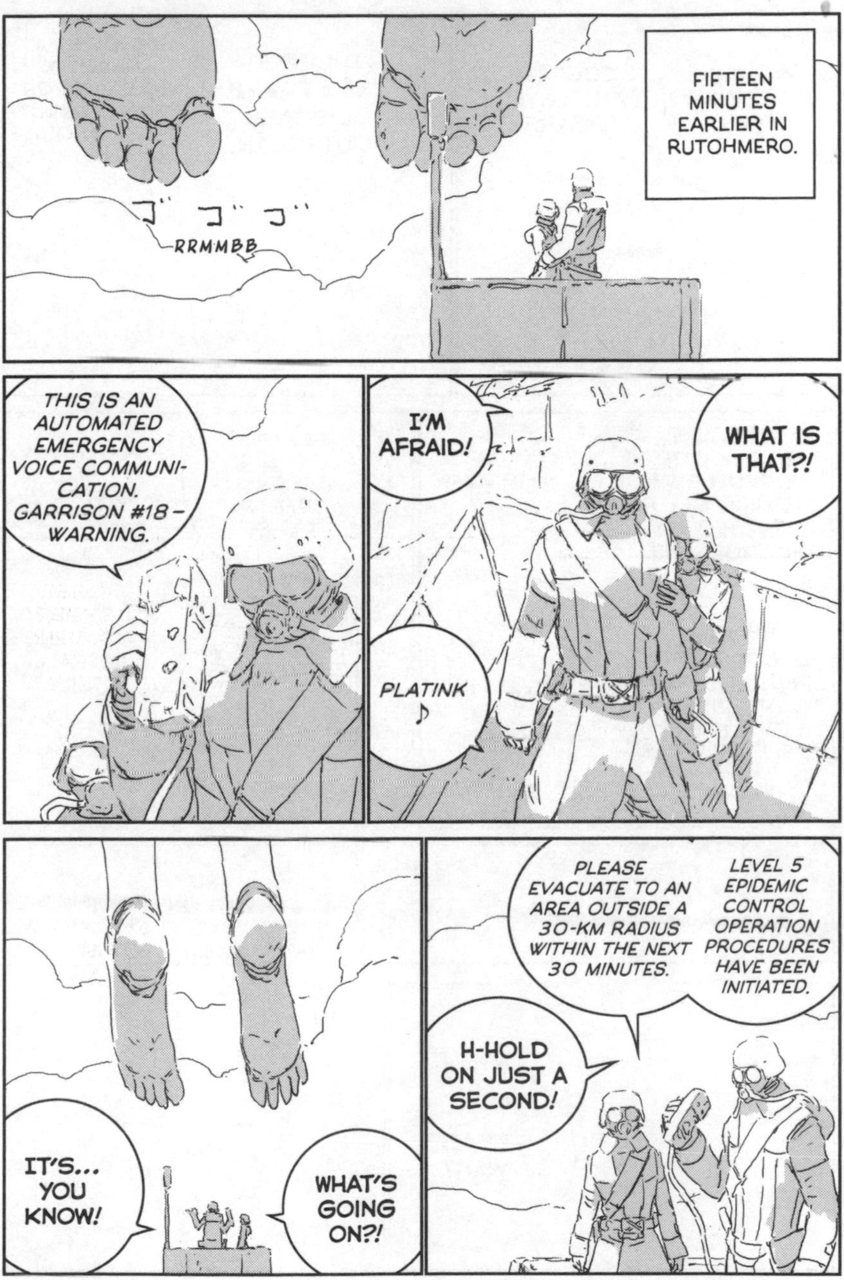
FIFTEEN MINUTES EARLIER IN RUTOHMERO.
ゴゴゴ
RRMMBB
WHAT IS THAT?!
I'M AFRAID!
PLATINK ♪
THIS IS AN AUTOMATED EMERGENCY VOICE COMMUNI-CATION. GARRISON #18 – WARNING.
LEVEL 5 EPIDEMIC CONTROL OPERATION PROCEDURES HAVE BEEN INITIATED.
PLEASE EVACUATE TO AN AREA OUTSIDE A 30-KM RADIUS WITHIN THE NEXT 30 MINUTES.
H-HOLD ON JUST A SECOND!
WHAT'S GOING ON?!
IT'S... YOU KNOW!

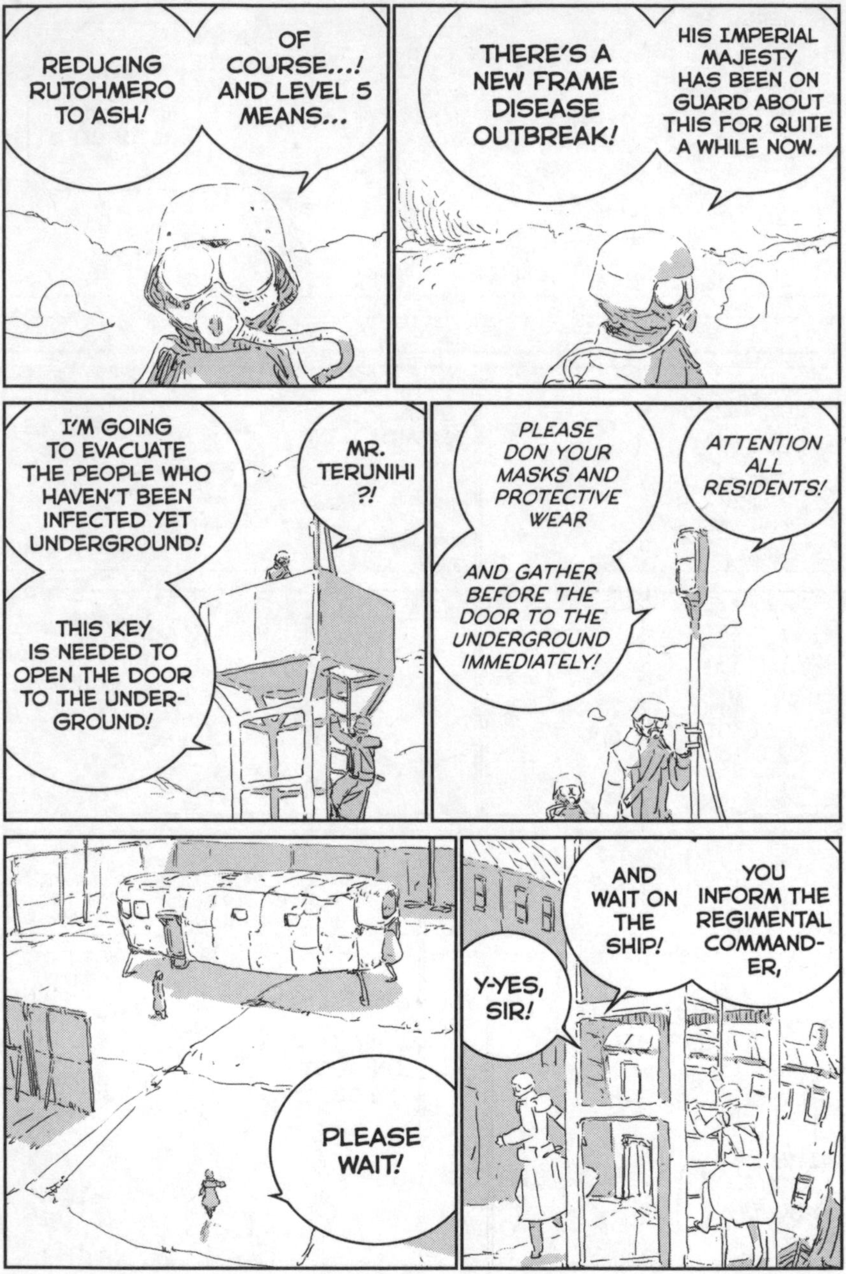
HIS IMPERIAL MAJESTY HAS BEEN ON GUARD ABOUT THIS FOR QUITE A WHILE NOW.
THERE'S A NEW FRAME DISEASE OUTBREAK!
OF COURSE...! AND LEVEL 5 MEANS...
REDUCING RUTOHMERO TO ASH!
ATTENTION ALL RESIDENTS!
PLEASE DON YOUR MASKS AND PROTECTIVE WEAR
AND GATHER BEFORE THE DOOR TO THE UNDERGROUND IMMEDIATELY!
MR. TERUNIHI ?!
I'M GOING TO EVACUATE THE PEOPLE WHO HAVEN'T BEEN INFECTED YET UNDERGROUND!
THIS KEY IS NEEDED TO OPEN THE DOOR TO THE UNDER-GROUND!
YOU INFORM THE REGIMENTAL COMMAND-ER,
AND WAIT ON THE SHIP!
Y-YES, SIR!
PLEASE WAIT!

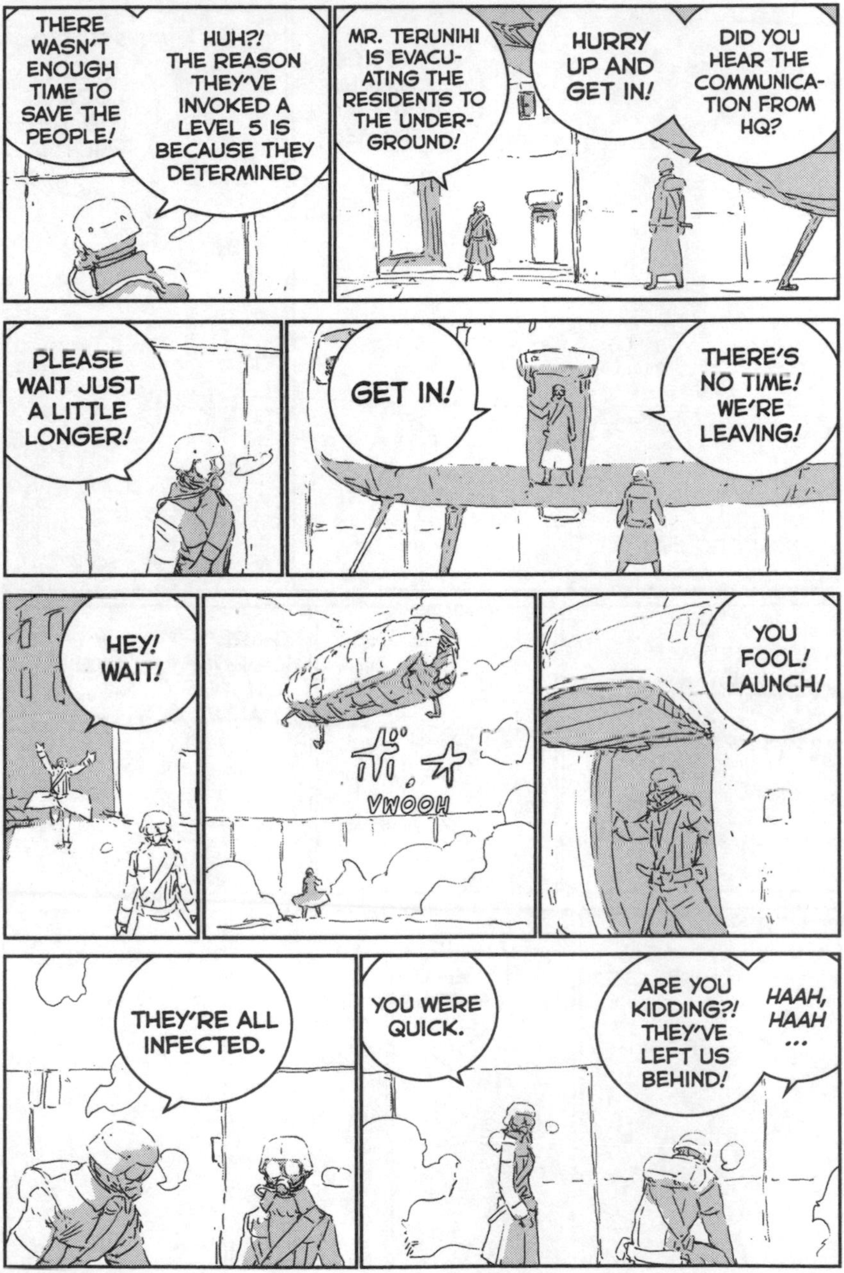
DID YOU HEAR THE COMMUNICATION FROM HQ?
HURRY UP AND GET IN!
MR. TERUNIHI IS EVACUATING THE RESIDENTS TO THE UNDERGROUND!
HUH?! THE REASON THEY'VE INVOKED A LEVEL 5 IS BECAUSE THEY DETERMINED
THERE WASN'T ENOUGH TIME TO SAVE THE PEOPLE!
THERE'S NO TIME! WE'RE LEAVING!
GET IN!
PLEASE WAIT JUST A LITTLE LONGER!
YOU FOOL! LAUNCH!
VWOOH
HEY! WAIT!
HAAH, HAAH ...
ARE YOU KIDDING?! THEY'VE LEFT US BEHIND!
YOU WERE QUICK.
THEY'RE ALL INFECTED.

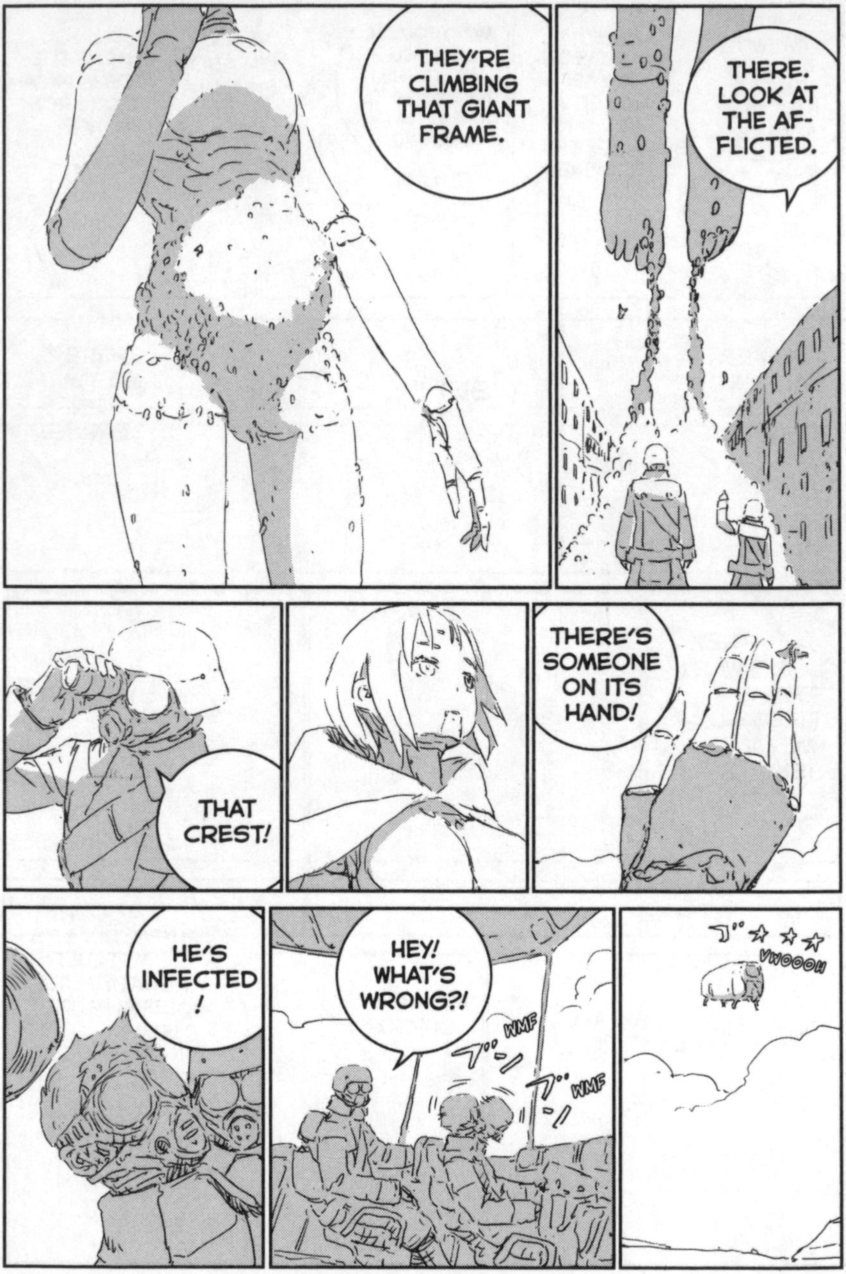
THERE. LOOK AT THE AF- FLICTED.
THEY'RE CLIMBING THAT GIANT FRAME.
THERE'S SOMEONE ON ITS HAND!
THAT CREST!
VWOOOH
HEY! WHAT'S WRONG?!
WMF
WMF
HE'S INFECTED!

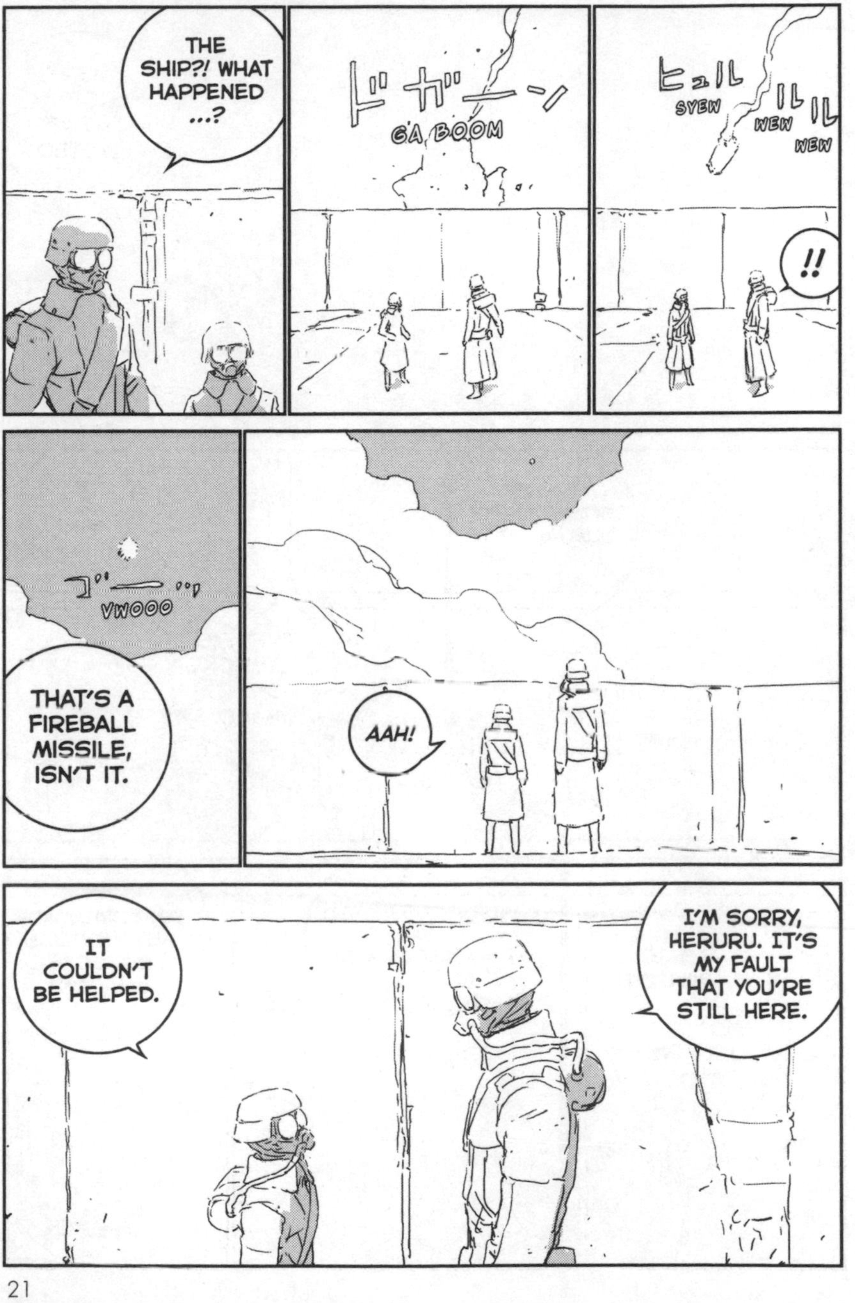
ヒュルルル
SYEW
WEW
WEW
!!
ドガーーン
GA BOOM
THE SHIP?! WHAT HAPPENED ...?
AAH!
ゴー…
VWOOO
THAT'S A FIREBALL MISSILE, ISN'T IT.
I'M SORRY, HERURU. IT'S MY FAULT THAT YOU'RE STILL HERE.
IT COULDN'T BE HELPED.

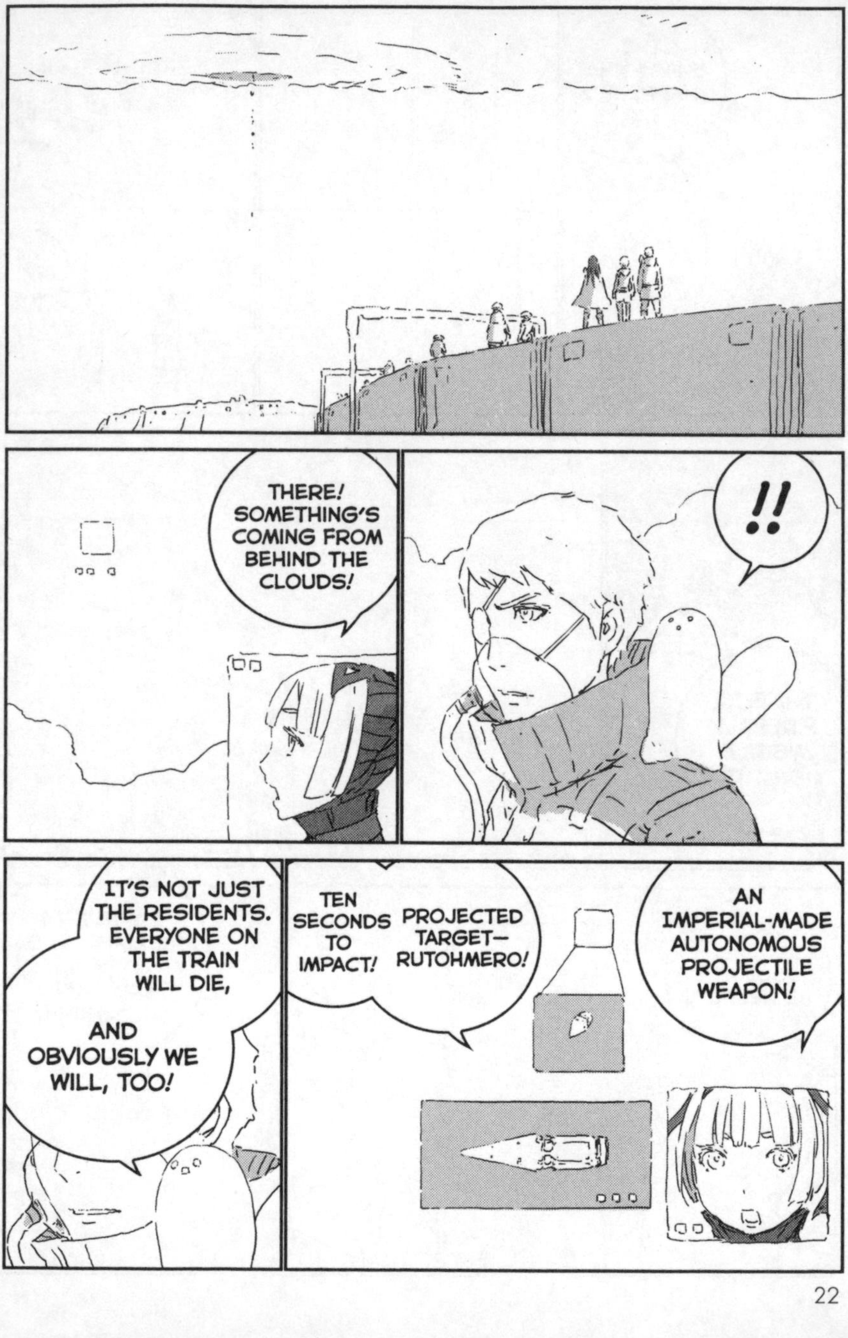
!!
THERE! SOMETHING'S COMING FROM BEHIND THE CLOUDS!
AN IMPERIAL-MADE AUTONOMOUS PROJECTILE WEAPON!
PROJECTED TARGET—RUTOHMERO!
TEN SECONDS TO IMPACT!
IT'S NOT JUST THE RESIDENTS. EVERYONE ON THE TRAIN WILL DIE,
AND OBVIOUSLY WE WILL, TOO!

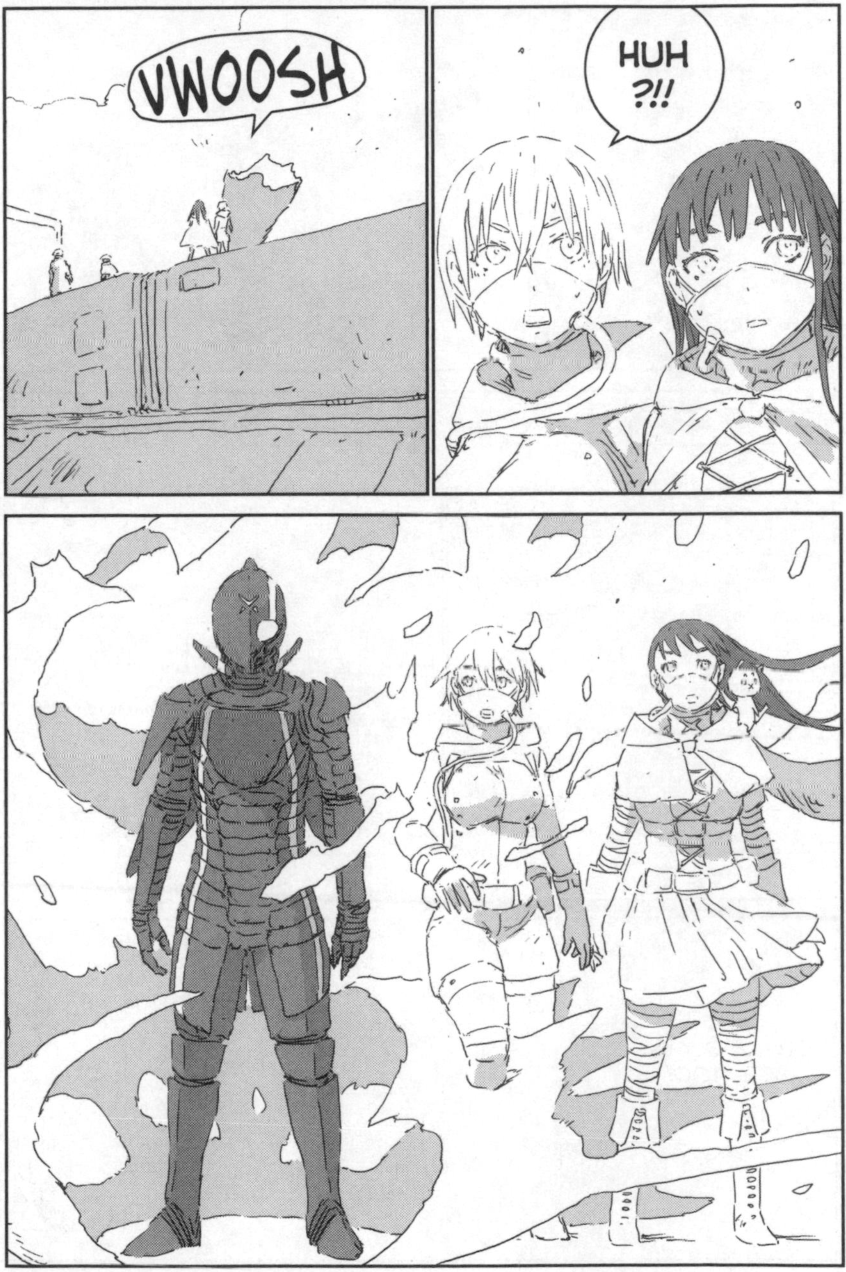
HUH ?!!
VWOOSH

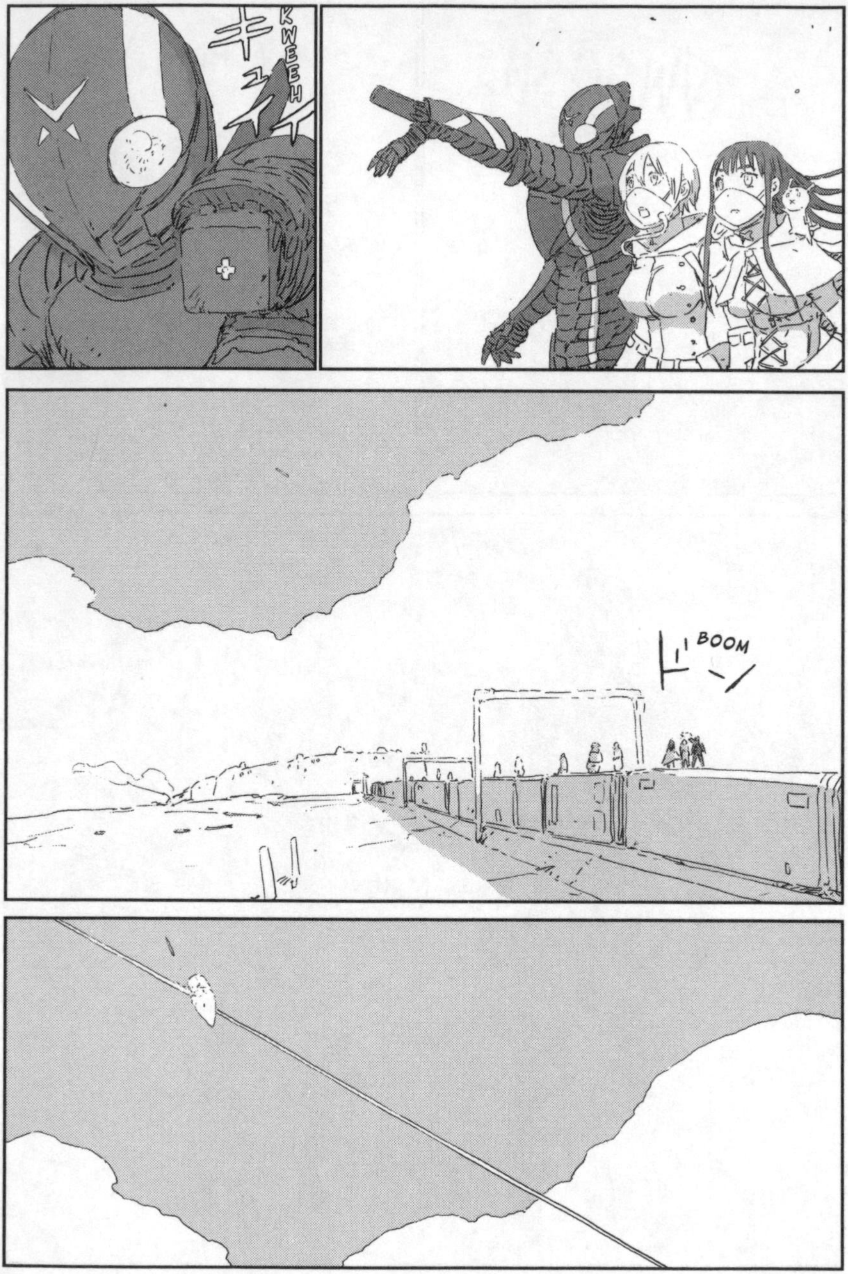
KWEEH
BOOM

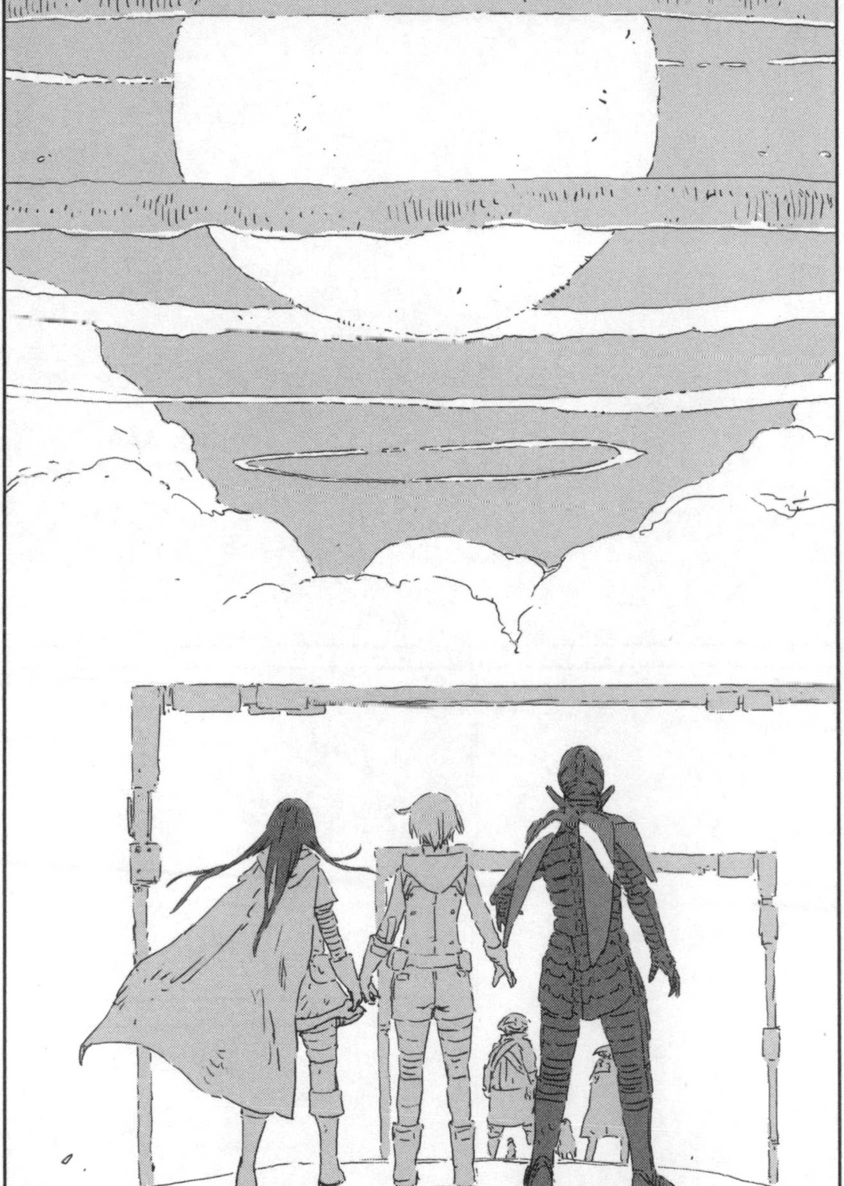

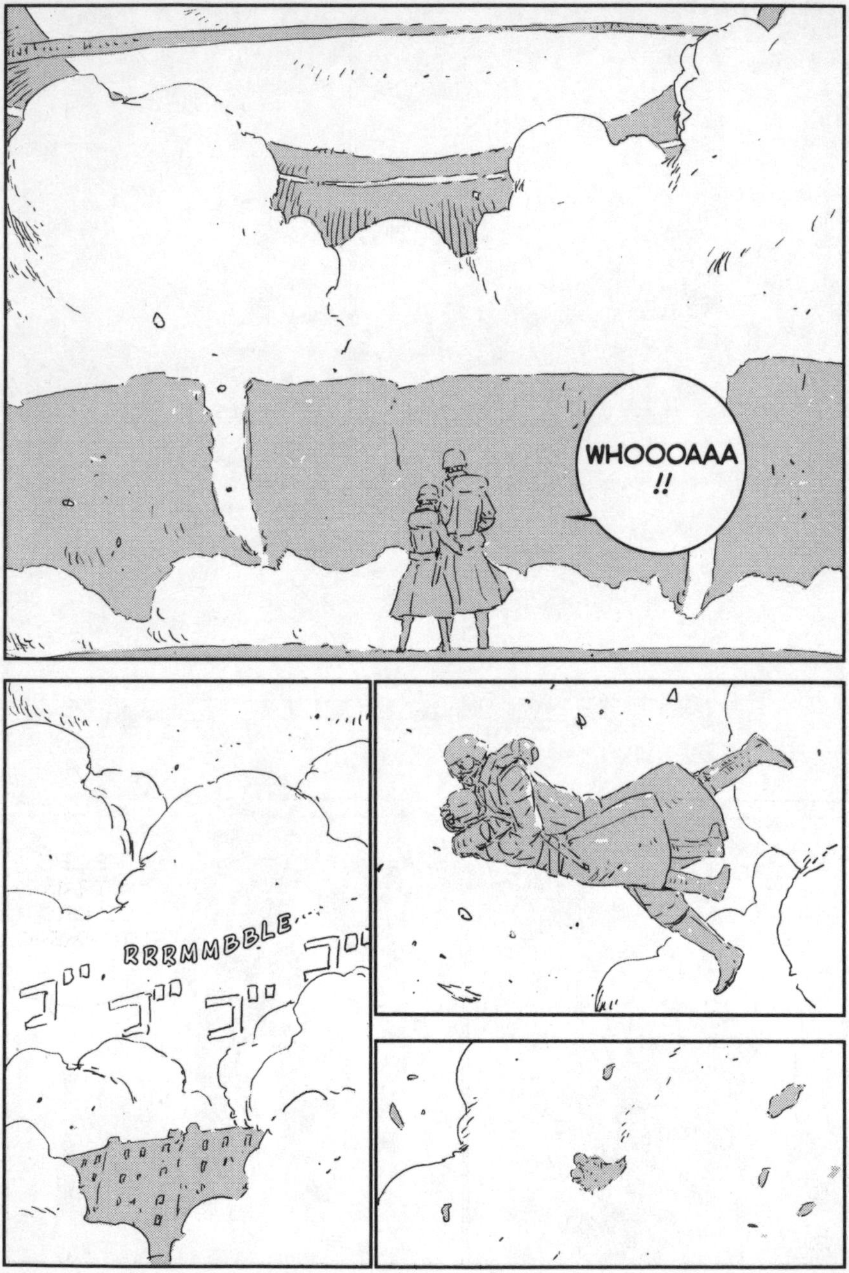
WHOOOAAA !!
RRRMMBBLE.....
ゴ ゴ ゴ ゴ

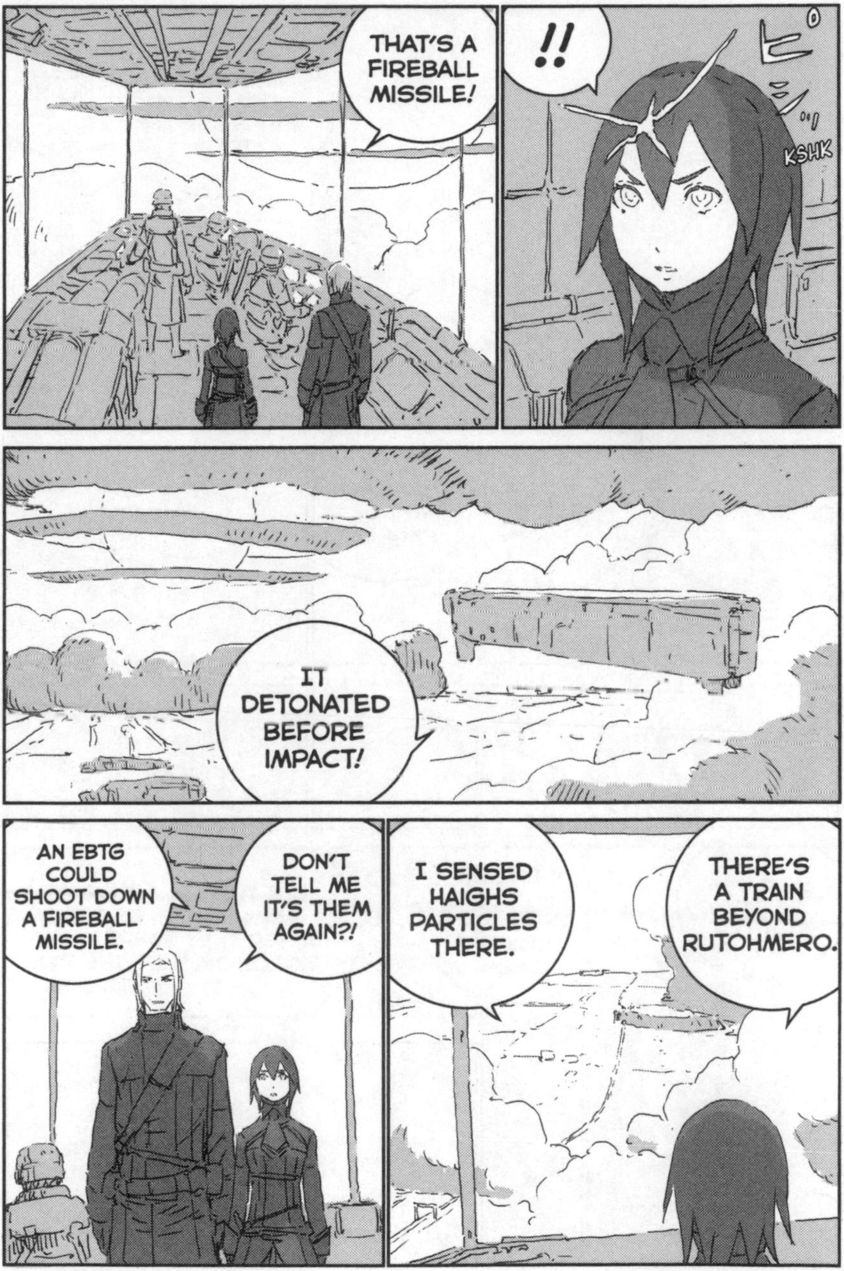
!!
KSHK
THAT'S A FIREBALL MISSILE!
IT DETONATED BEFORE IMPACT!
THERE'S A TRAIN BEYOND RUTOHMERO.
I SENSED HAIGHS PARTICLES THERE.
DON'T TELL ME IT'S THEM AGAIN?!
AN EBTG COULD SHOOT DOWN A FIREBALL MISSILE.

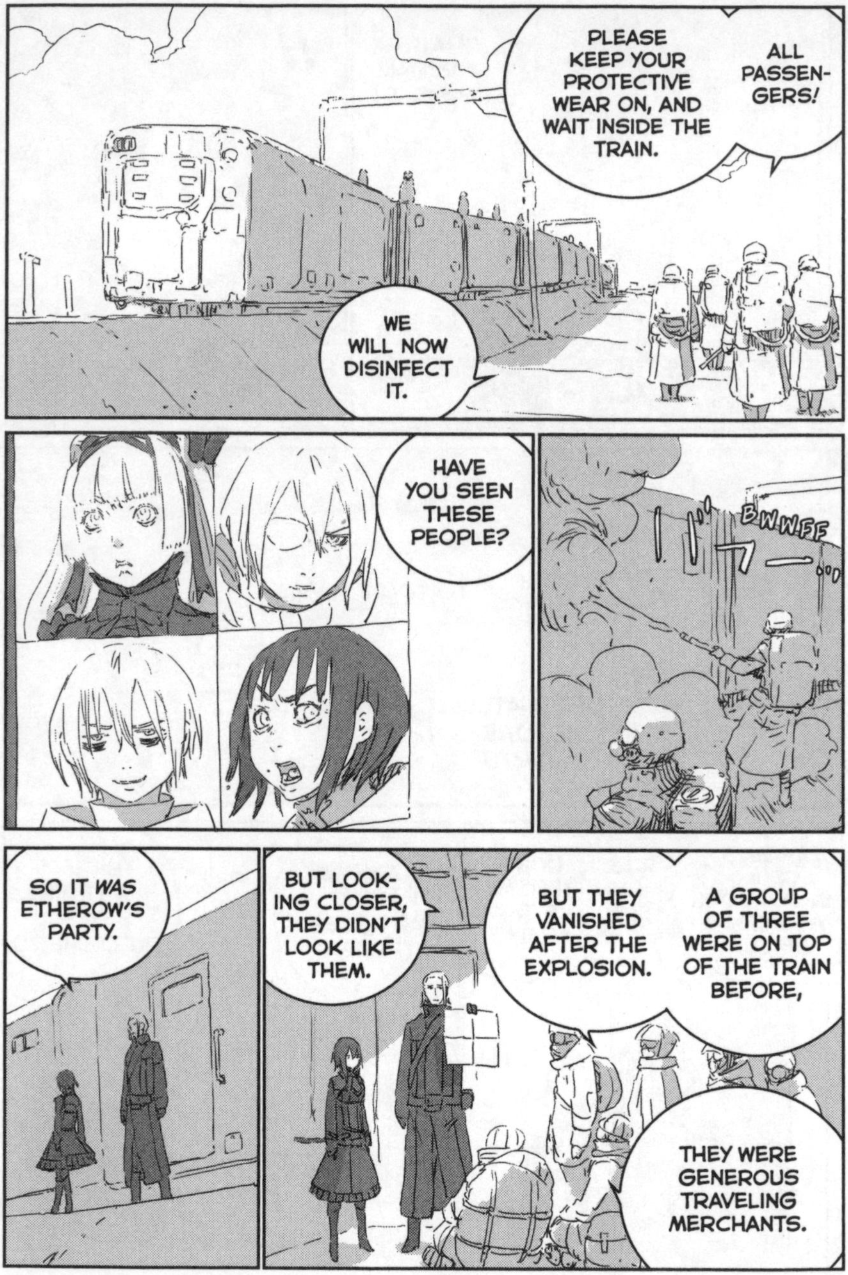
ALL PASSENGERS!
PLEASE KEEP YOUR PROTECTIVE WEAR ON, AND WAIT INSIDE THE TRAIN.
WE WILL NOW DISINFECT IT.
BWWFF
HAVE YOU SEEN THESE PEOPLE?
A GROUP OF THREE WERE ON TOP OF THE TRAIN BEFORE,
BUT THEY VANISHED AFTER THE EXPLOSION.
THEY WERE GENEROUS TRAVELING MERCHANTS.
BUT LOOKING CLOSER, THEY DIDN'T LOOK LIKE THEM.
SO IT WAS *ETHEROW'S* PARTY.

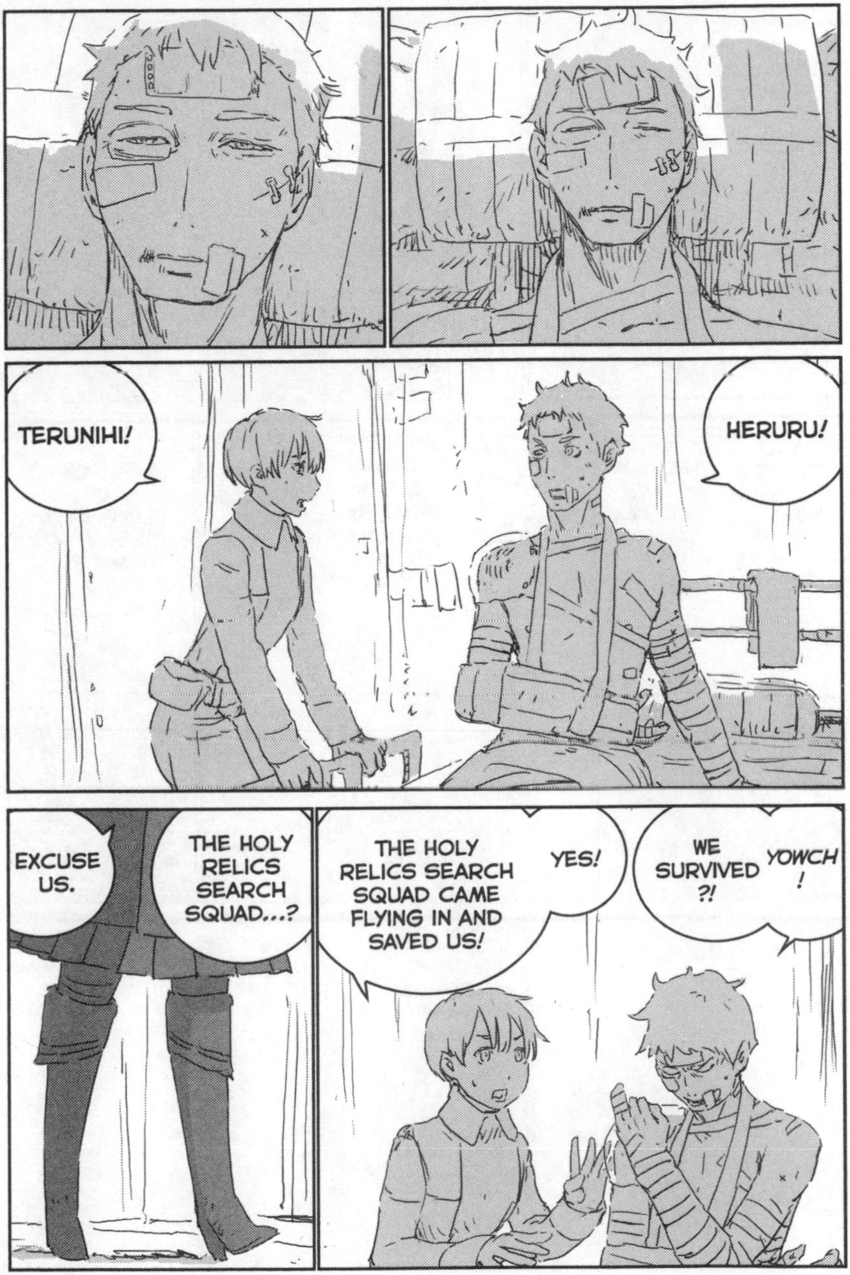
HERURU!
TERUNIHI!
YOWCH!
WE SURVIVED?!
YES!
THE HOLY RELICS SEARCH SQUAD CAME FLYING IN AND SAVED US!
THE HOLY RELICS SEARCH SQUAD...?
EXCUSE US.

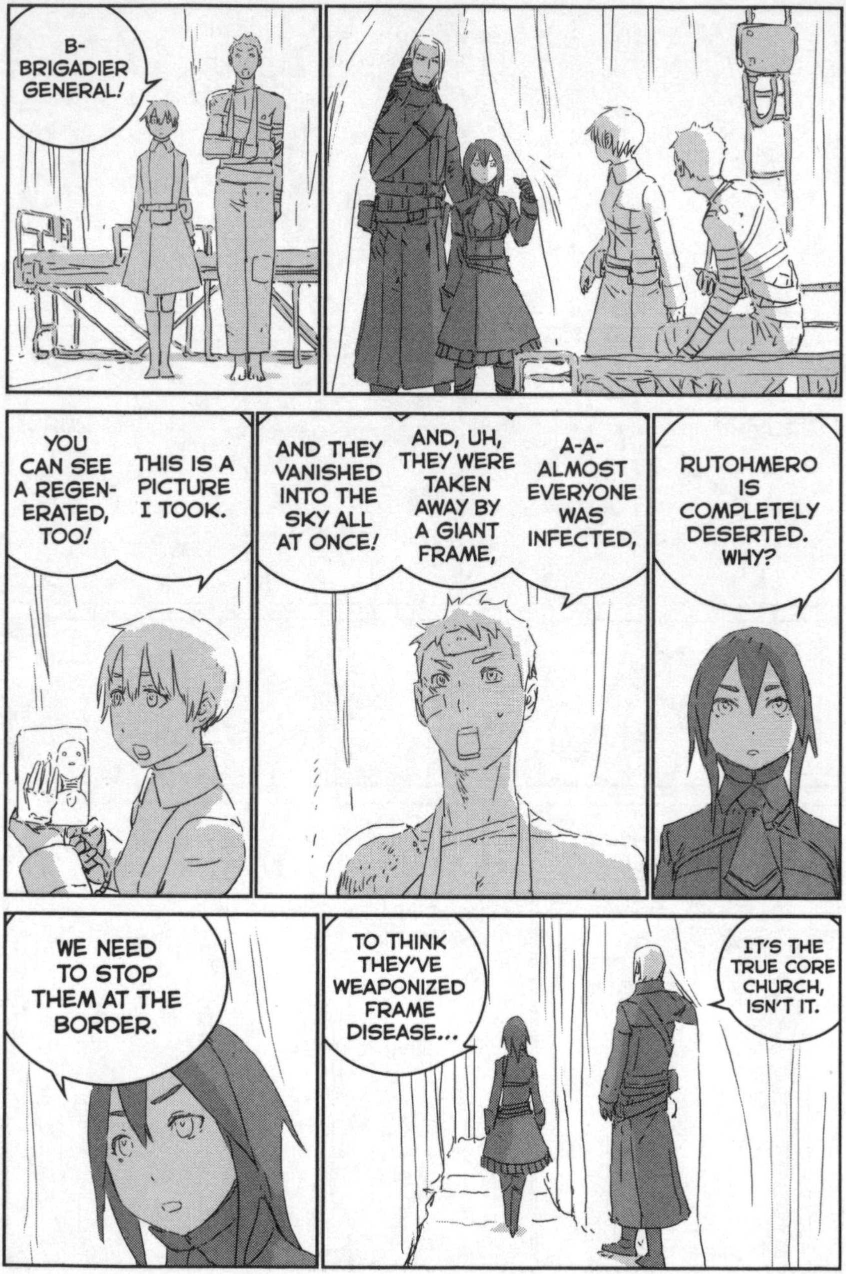
B-BRIGADIER GENERAL!
RUTOHMERO IS COMPLETELY DESERTED. WHY?
A-A-ALMOST EVERYONE WAS INFECTED,
AND, UH, THEY WERE TAKEN AWAY BY A GIANT FRAME,
AND THEY VANISHED INTO THE SKY ALL AT ONCE!
THIS IS A PICTURE I TOOK.
YOU CAN SEE A REGEN-ERATED, TOO!
IT'S THE TRUE CORE CHURCH, ISN'T IT.
TO THINK THEY'VE WEAPONIZED FRAME DISEASE...
WE NEED TO STOP THEM AT THE BORDER.

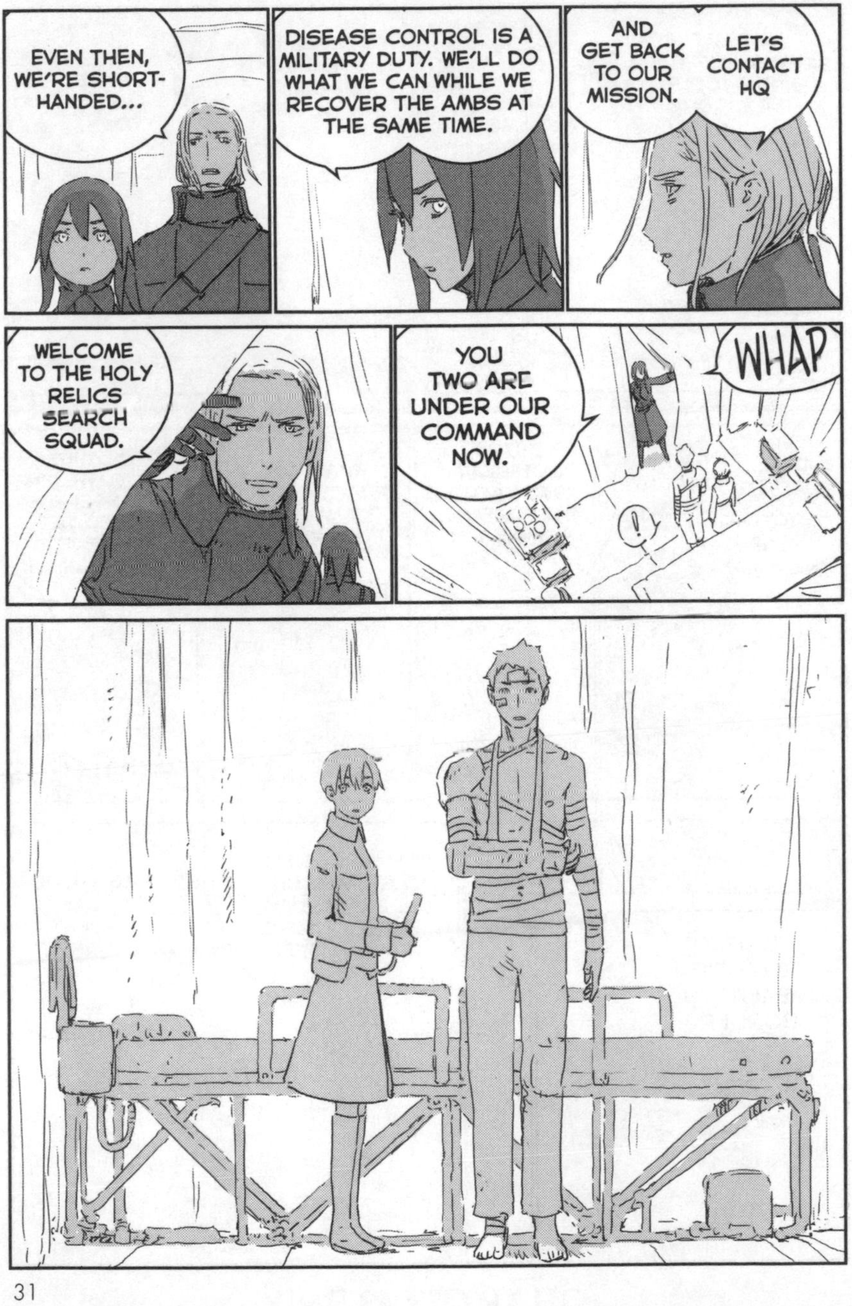
LET'S CONTACT HQ
AND GET BACK TO OUR MISSION.
DISEASE CONTROL IS A MILITARY DUTY. WE'LL DO WHAT WE CAN WHILE WE RECOVER THE AMBS AT THE SAME TIME.
EVEN THEN, WE'RE SHORT-HANDED...
WHAP
YOU TWO ARE UNDER OUR COMMAND NOW.
!
WELCOME TO THE HOLY RELICS SEARCH SQUAD.

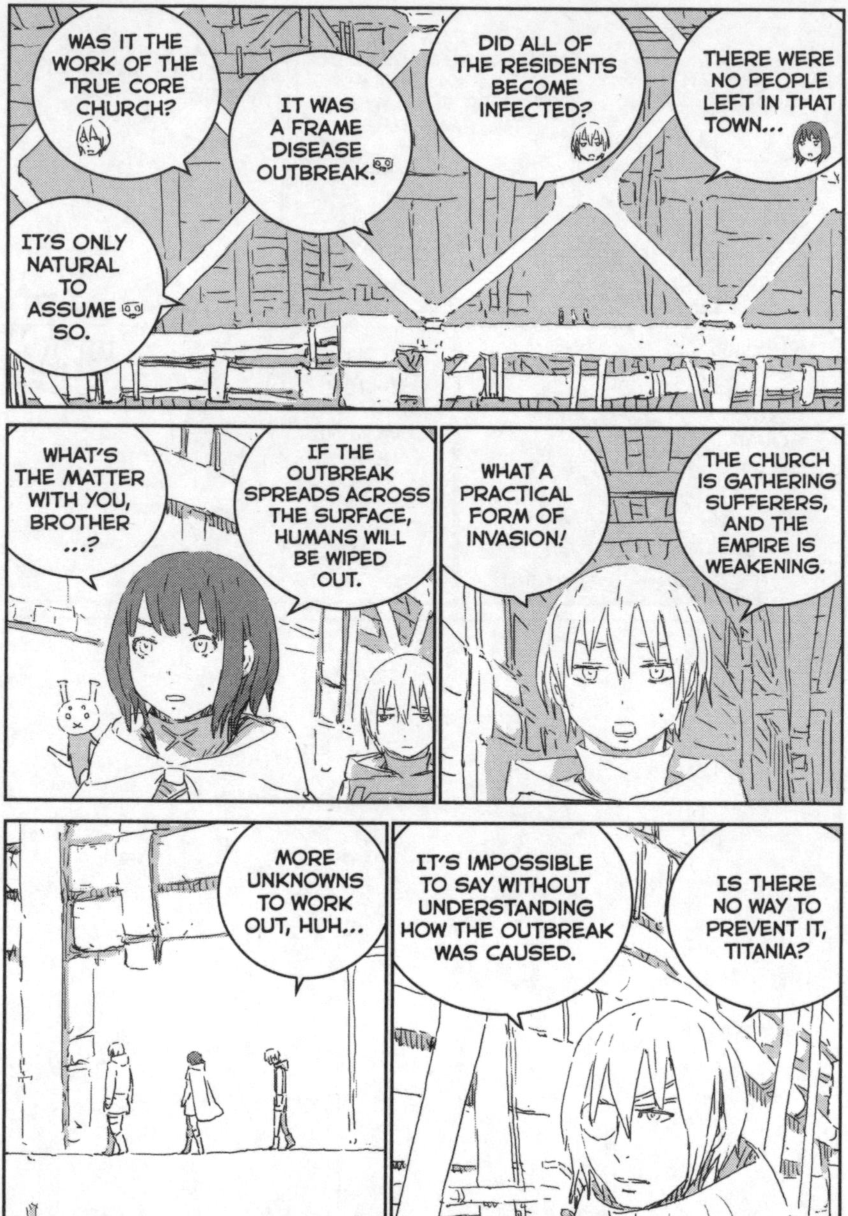
THERE WERE NO PEOPLE LEFT IN THAT TOWN...
DID ALL OF THE RESIDENTS BECOME INFECTED?
IT WAS A FRAME DISEASE OUTBREAK.
WAS IT THE WORK OF THE TRUE CORE CHURCH?
IT'S ONLY NATURAL TO ASSUME SO.
THE CHURCH IS GATHERING SUFFERERS, AND THE EMPIRE IS WEAKENING.
WHAT A PRACTICAL FORM OF INVASION!
IF THE OUTBREAK SPREADS ACROSS THE SURFACE, HUMANS WILL BE WIPED OUT.
WHAT'S THE MATTER WITH YOU, BROTHER ...?
IS THERE NO WAY TO PREVENT IT, TITANIA?
IT'S IMPOSSIBLE TO SAY WITHOUT UNDERSTANDING HOW THE OUTBREAK WAS CAUSED.
MORE UNKNOWNS TO WORK OUT, HUH...

CHAPTER 43 END

APOSIMZ

CHAPTER 44

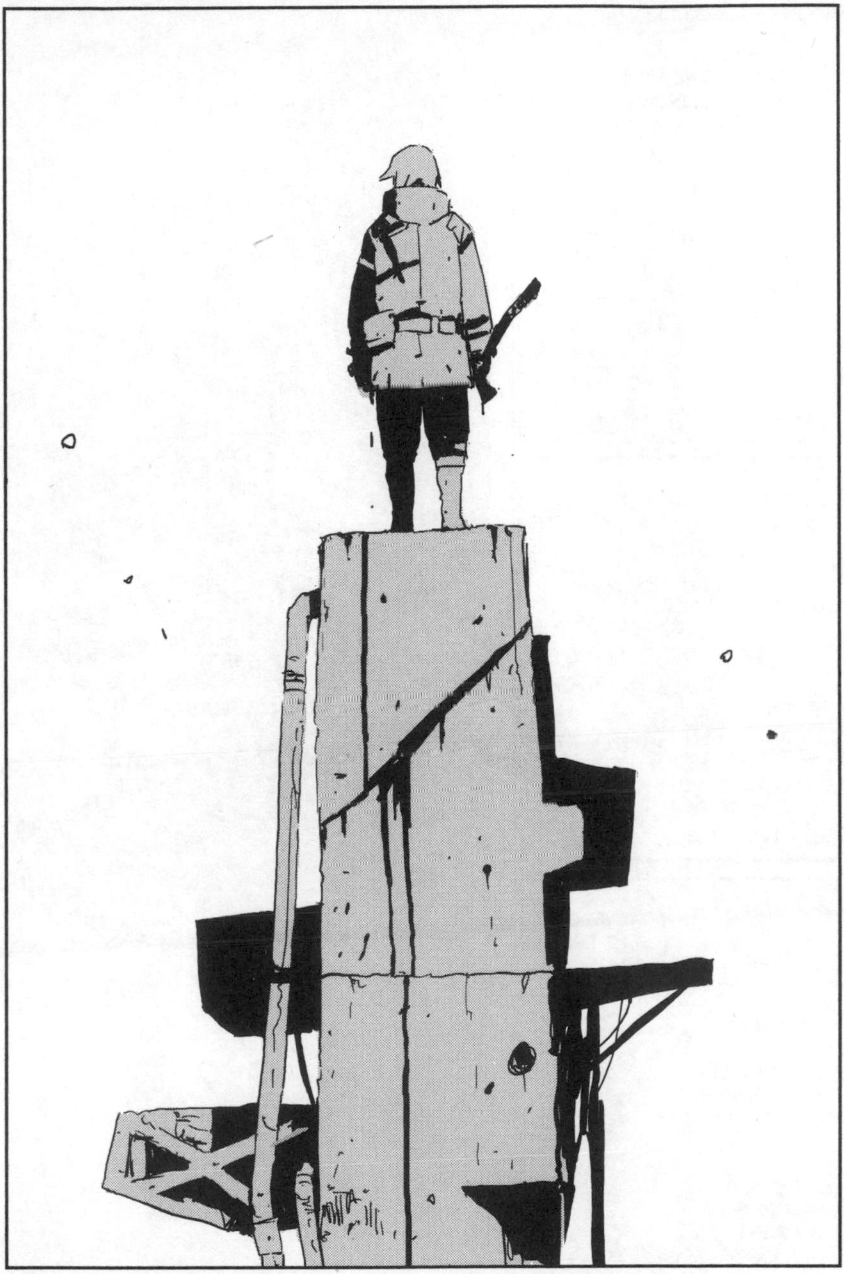

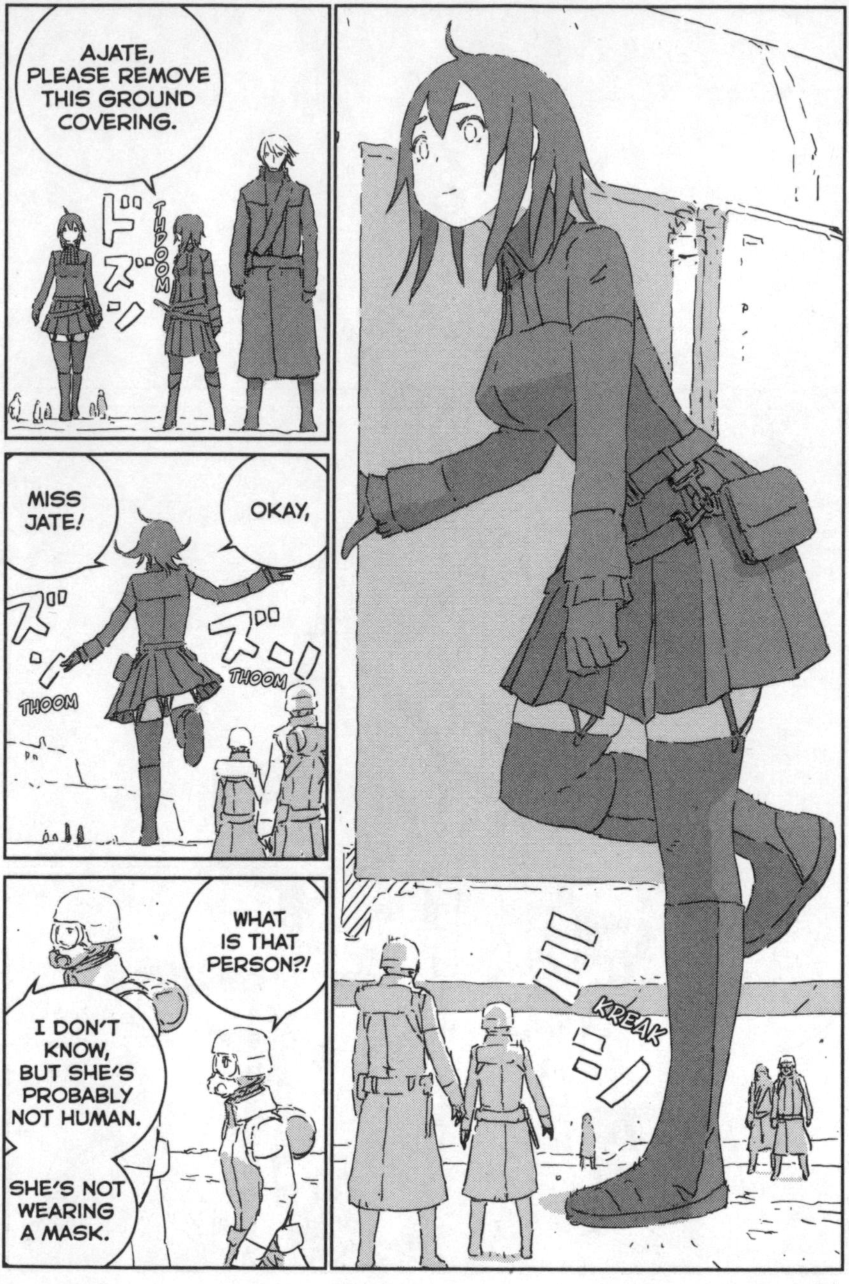
KREAK
AJATE, PLEASE REMOVE THIS GROUND COVERING.
ドズン
THDOOM
OKAY,
MISS JATE!
ズン
THOOM
ズン
THOOM
WHAT IS THAT PERSON?!
I DON'T KNOW, BUT SHE'S PROBABLY NOT HUMAN.
SHE'S NOT WEARING A MASK.

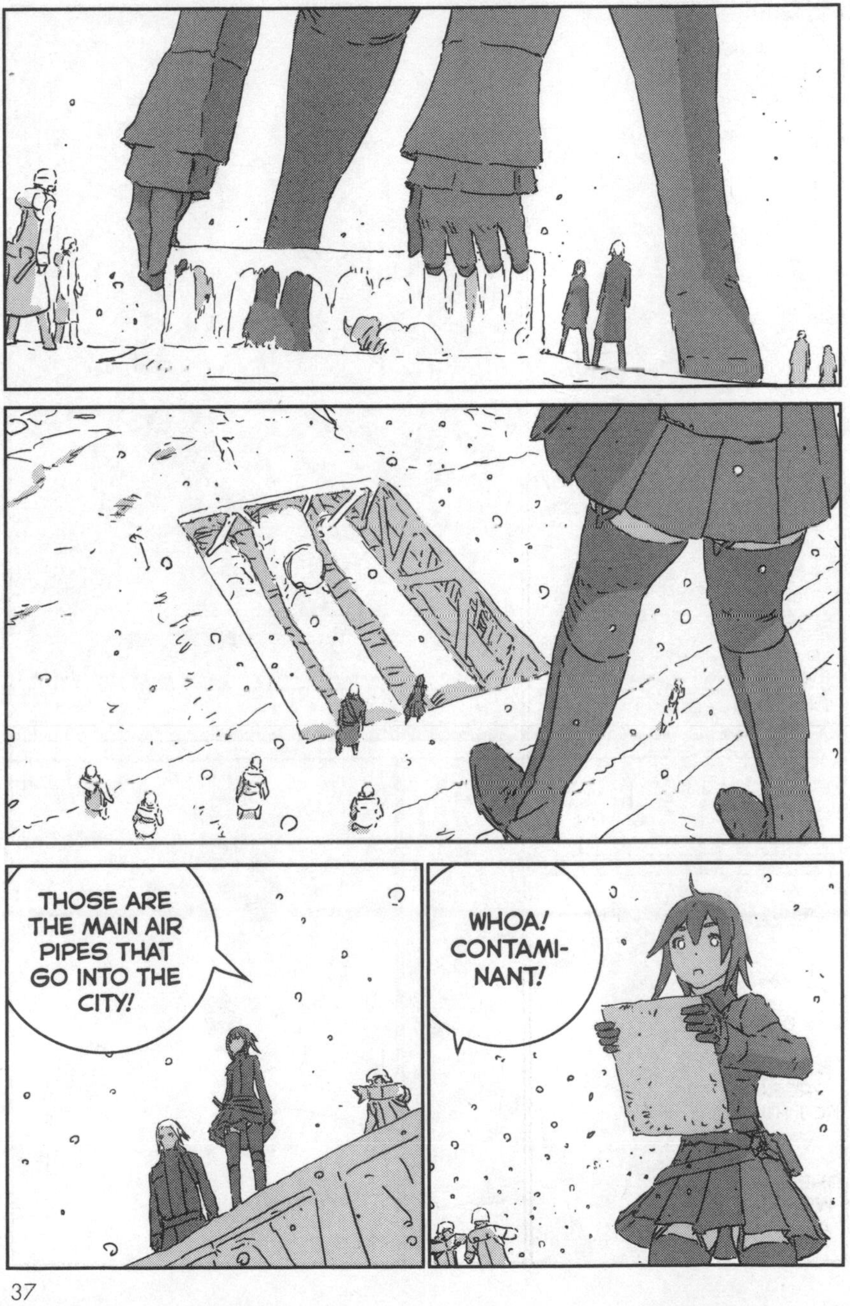
WHOA! CONTAMI-NANT!
THOSE ARE THE MAIN AIR PIPES THAT GO INTO THE CITY!

BAKANG

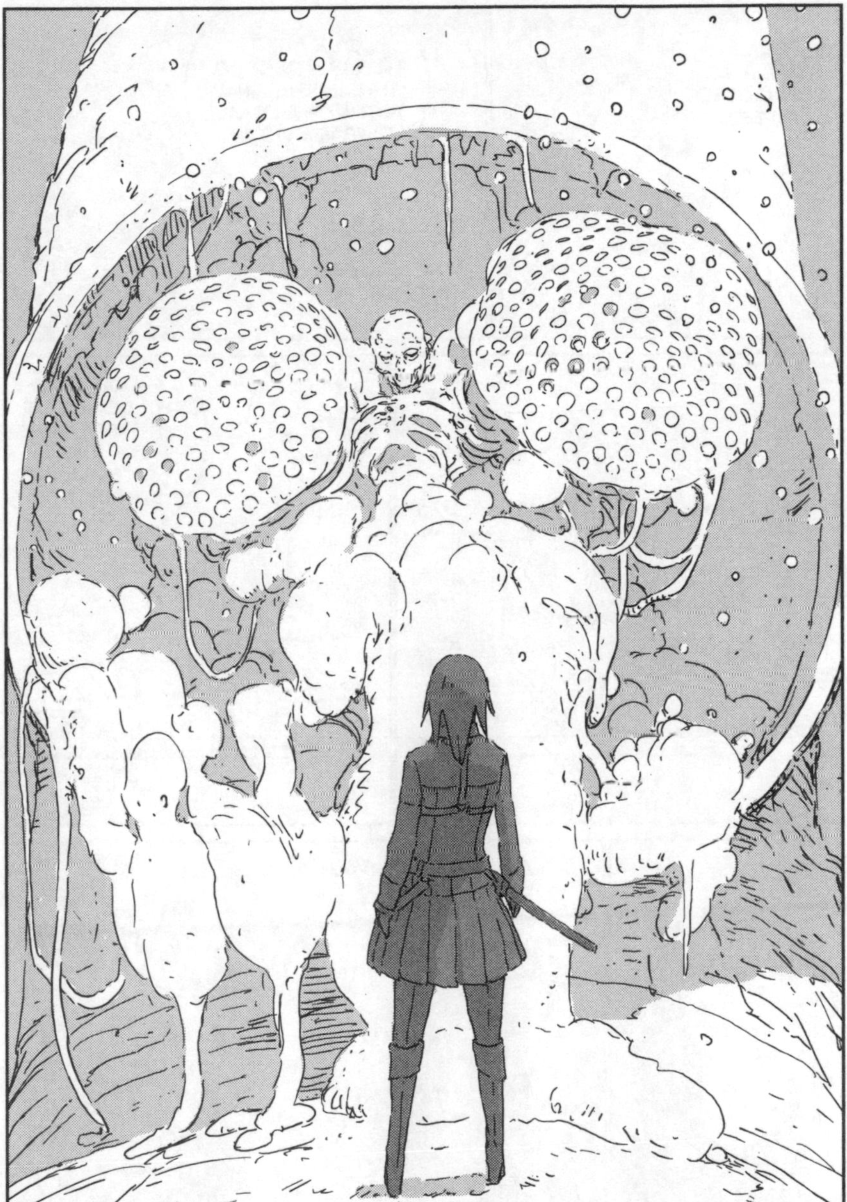

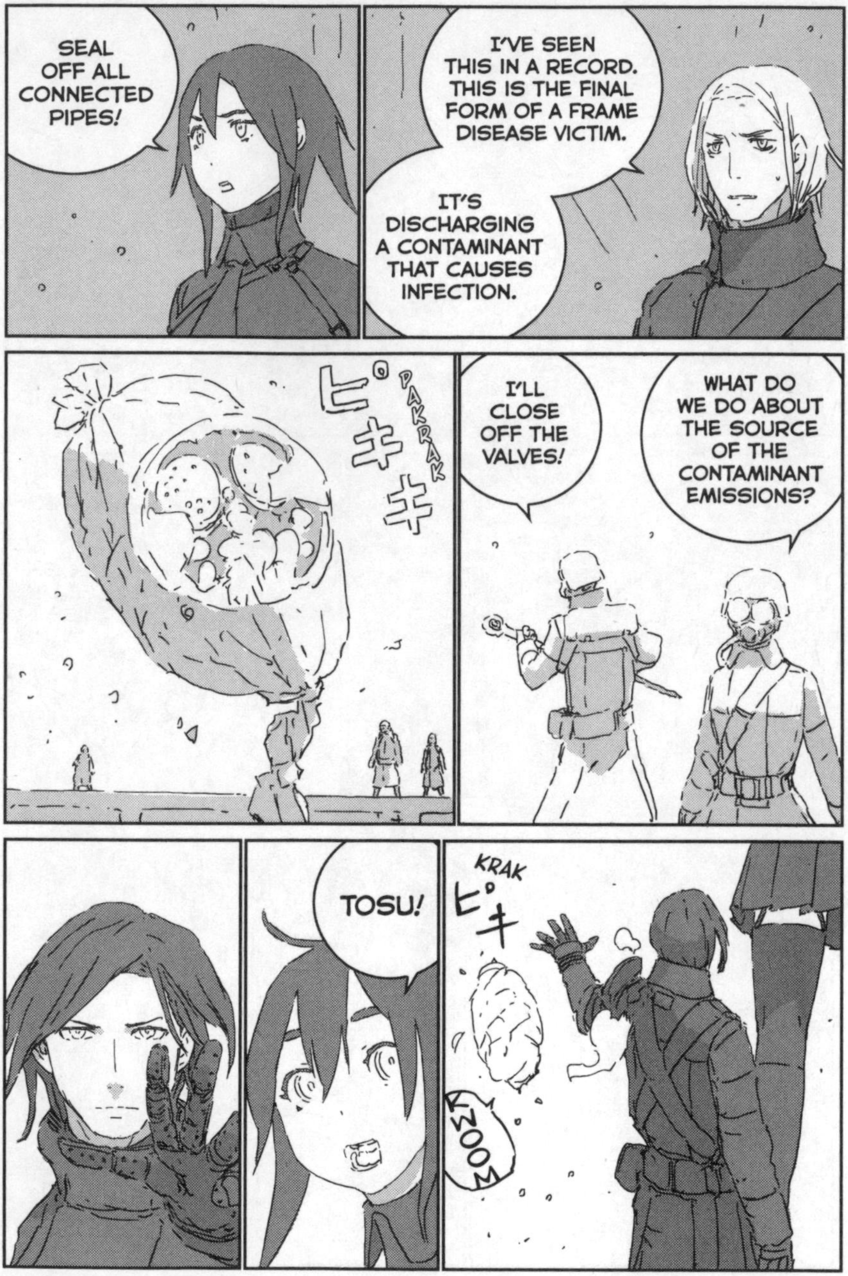
I'VE SEEN THIS IN A RECORD. THIS IS THE FINAL FORM OF A FRAME DISEASE VICTIM.
IT'S DISCHARGING A CONTAMINANT THAT CAUSES INFECTION.
SEAL OFF ALL CONNECTED PIPES!
WHAT DO WE DO ABOUT THE SOURCE OF THE CONTAMINANT EMISSIONS?
I'LL CLOSE OFF THE VALVES!
ピキキ
PAKRAK
KRAK
ピキ
KWOOM
TOSU!

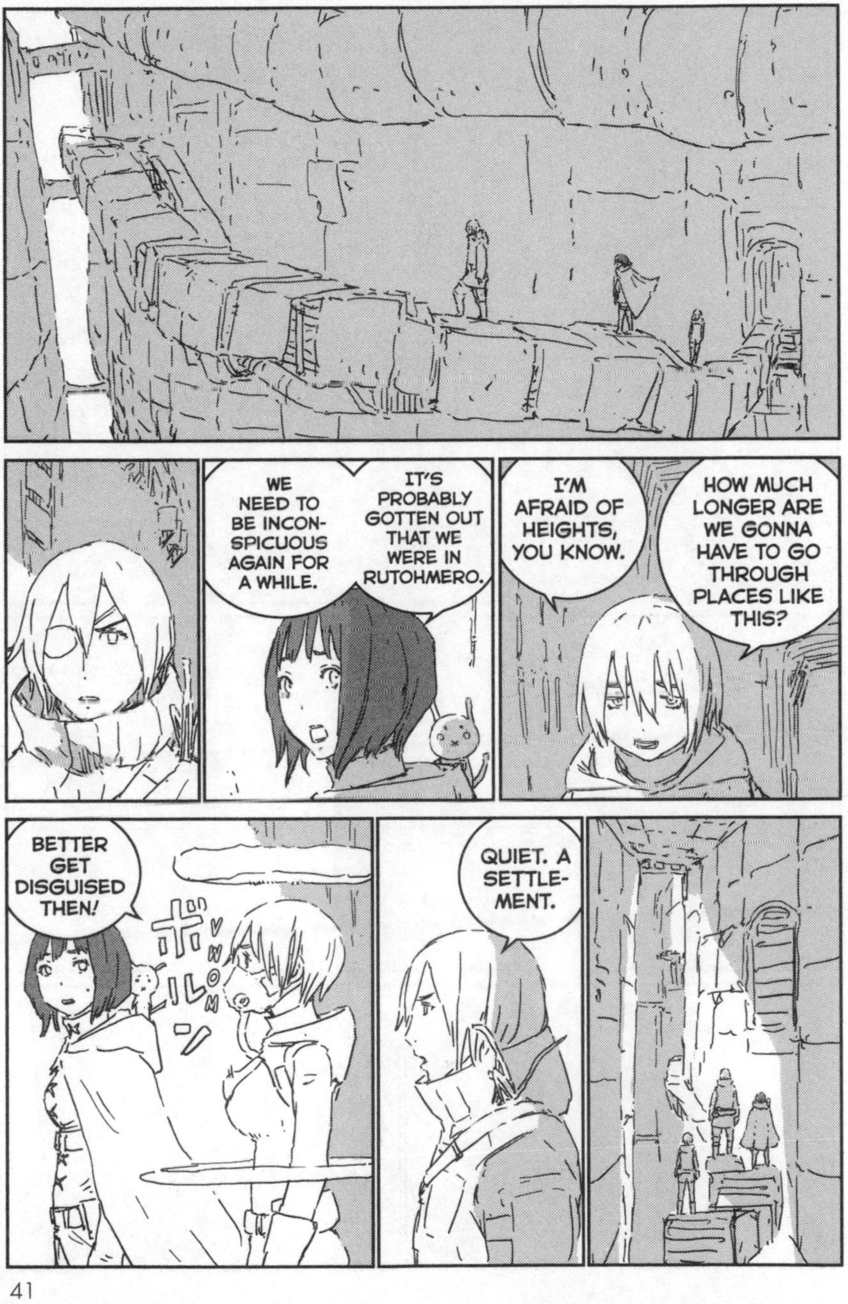
HOW MUCH LONGER ARE WE GONNA HAVE TO GO THROUGH PLACES LIKE THIS?
I'M AFRAID OF HEIGHTS, YOU KNOW.
IT'S PROBABLY GOTTEN OUT THAT WE WERE IN RUTOHMERO.
WE NEED TO BE INCONSPICUOUS AGAIN FOR A WHILE.
QUIET. A SETTLE-MENT.
BETTER GET DISGUISED THEN!
VWOM

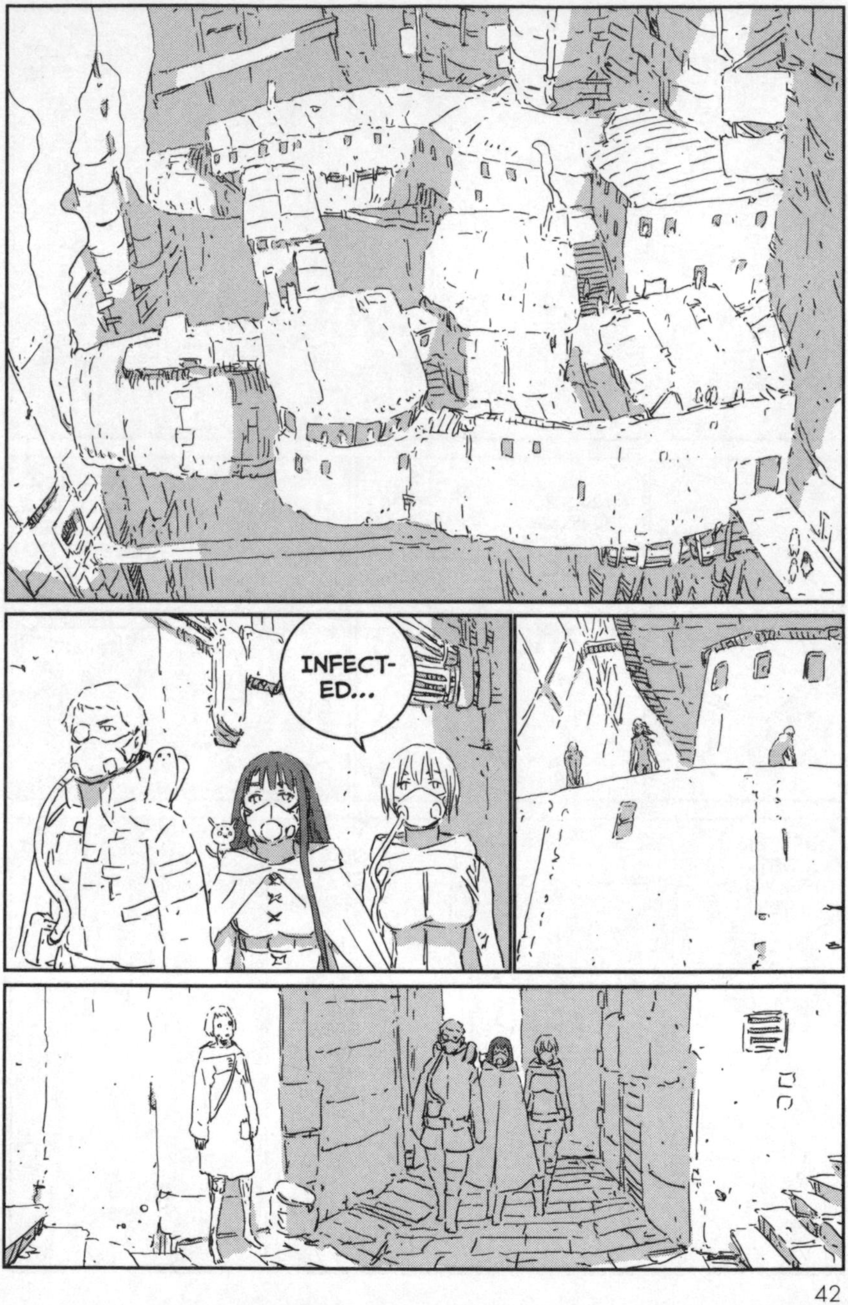
INFECT-
ED...

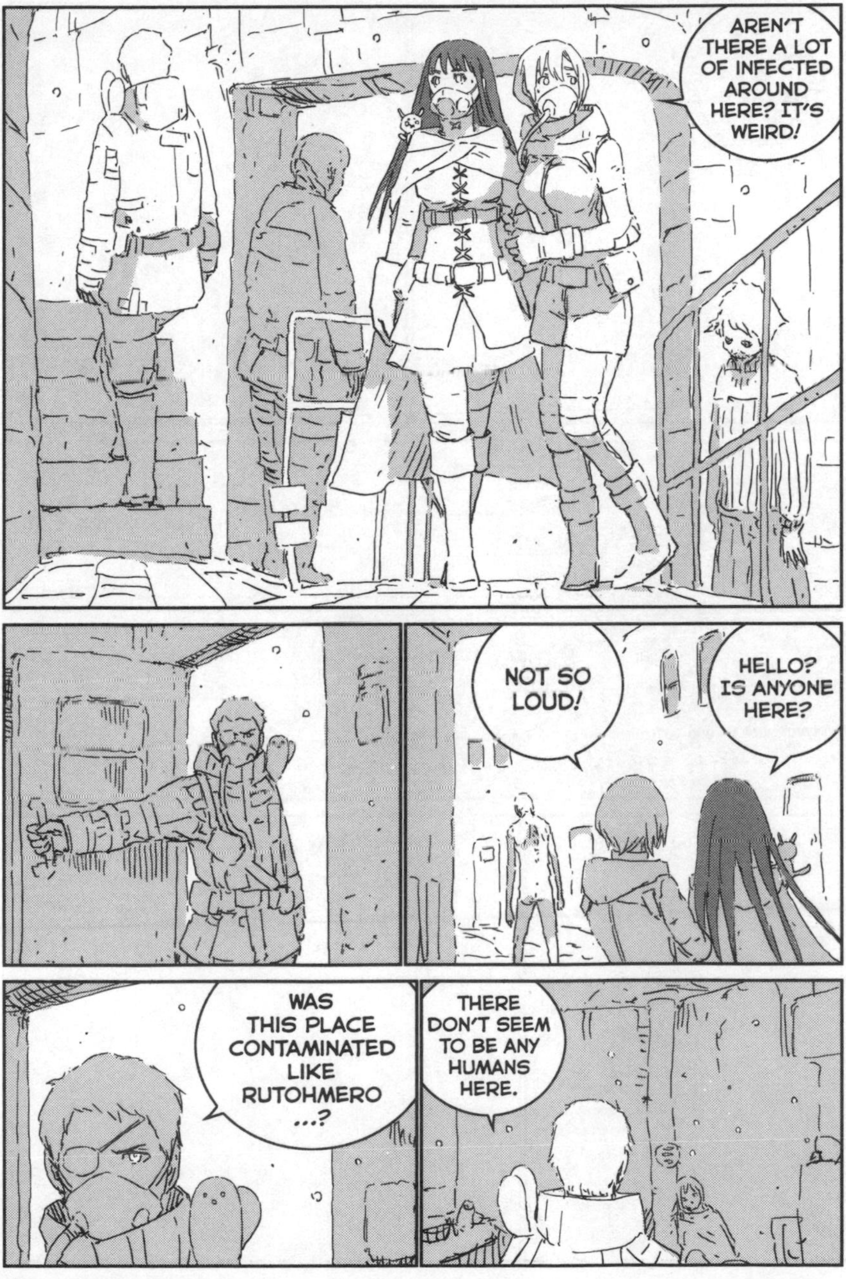
AREN'T THERE A LOT OF INFECTED AROUND HERE? IT'S WEIRD!
HELLO? IS ANYONE HERE?
NOT SO LOUD!
THERE DON'T SEEM TO BE ANY HUMANS HERE.
WAS THIS PLACE CONTAMINATED LIKE RUTOHMERO ...?

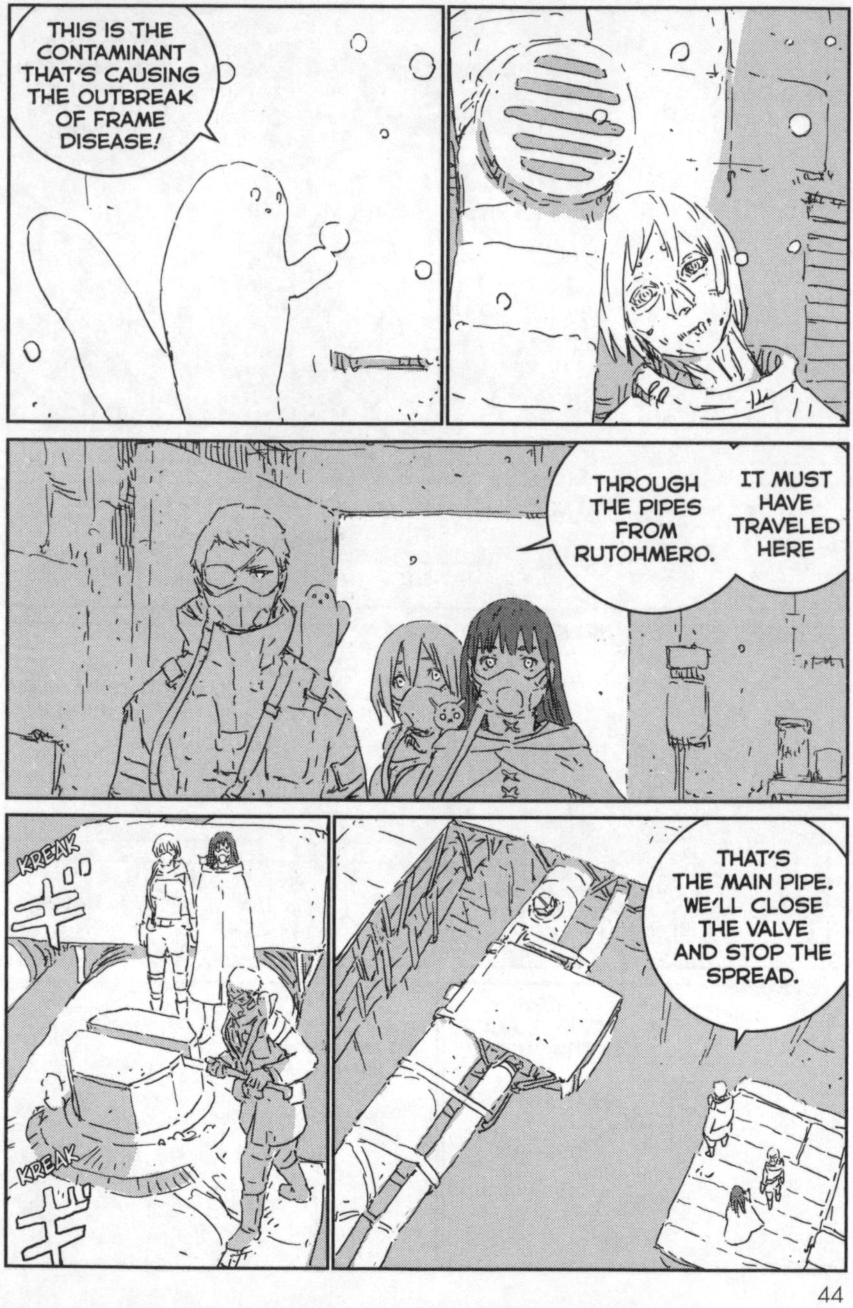
THIS IS THE CONTAMINANT THAT'S CAUSING THE OUTBREAK OF FRAME DISEASE!
IT MUST HAVE TRAVELED HERE
THROUGH THE PIPES FROM RUTOHMERO.
THAT'S THE MAIN PIPE. WE'LL CLOSE THE VALVE AND STOP THE SPREAD.
KREAK
KREAK

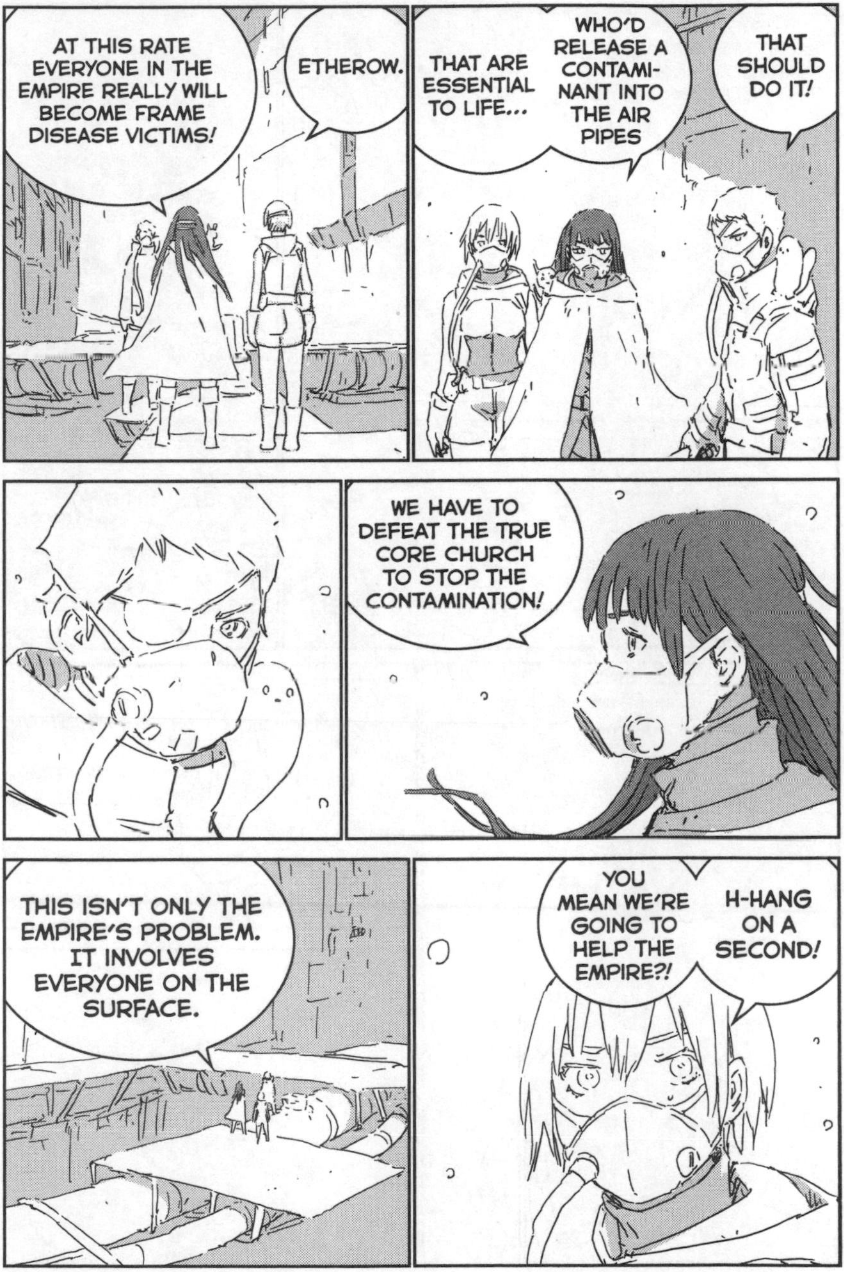
THAT SHOULD DO IT!
WHO'D RELEASE A CONTAMI- NANT INTO THE AIR PIPES
THAT ARE ESSENTIAL TO LIFE...
ETHEROW.
AT THIS RATE EVERYONE IN THE EMPIRE REALLY WILL BECOME FRAME DISEASE VICTIMS!
WE HAVE TO DEFEAT THE TRUE CORE CHURCH TO STOP THE CONTAMINATION!
H-HANG ON A SECOND!
YOU MEAN WE'RE GOING TO HELP THE EMPIRE?!
THIS ISN'T ONLY THE EMPIRE'S PROBLEM. IT INVOLVES EVERYONE ON THE SURFACE.

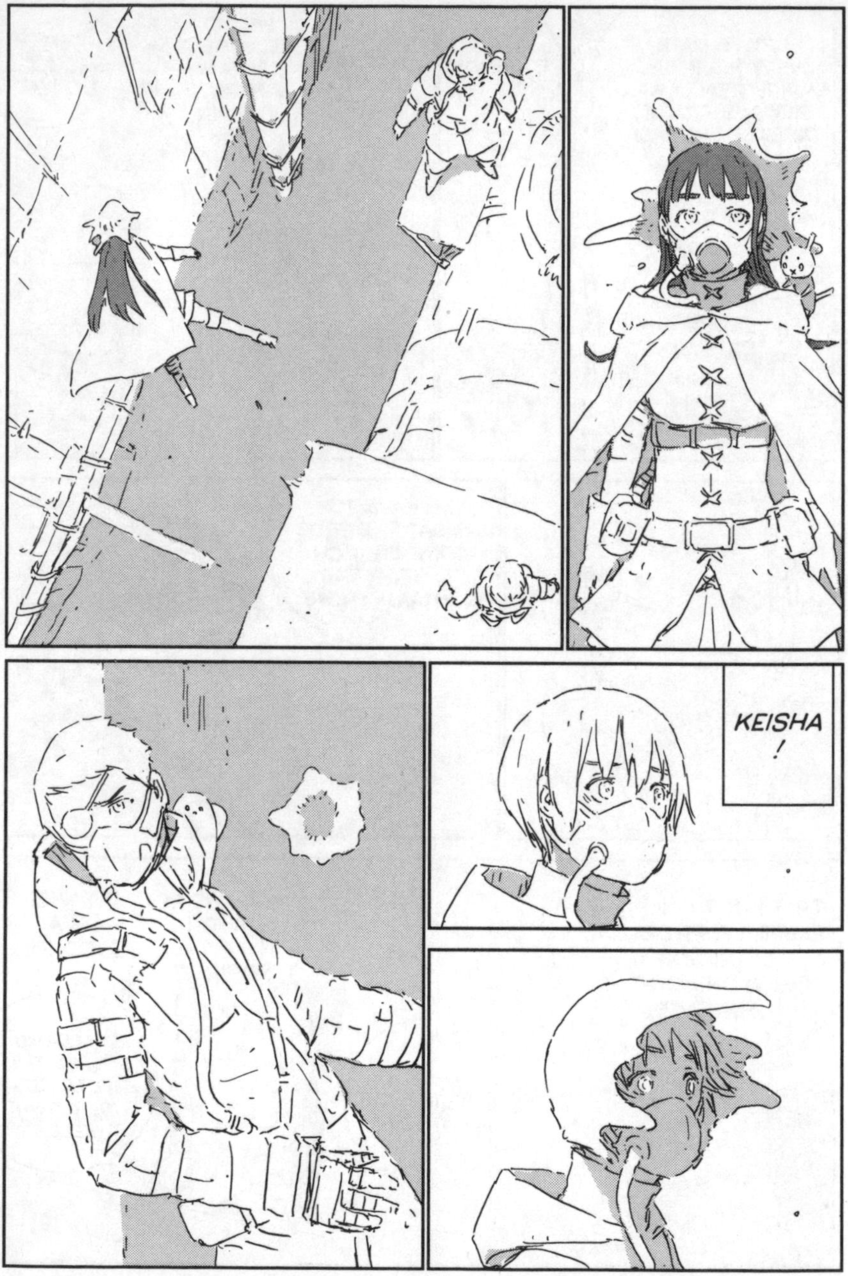
KEISHA !

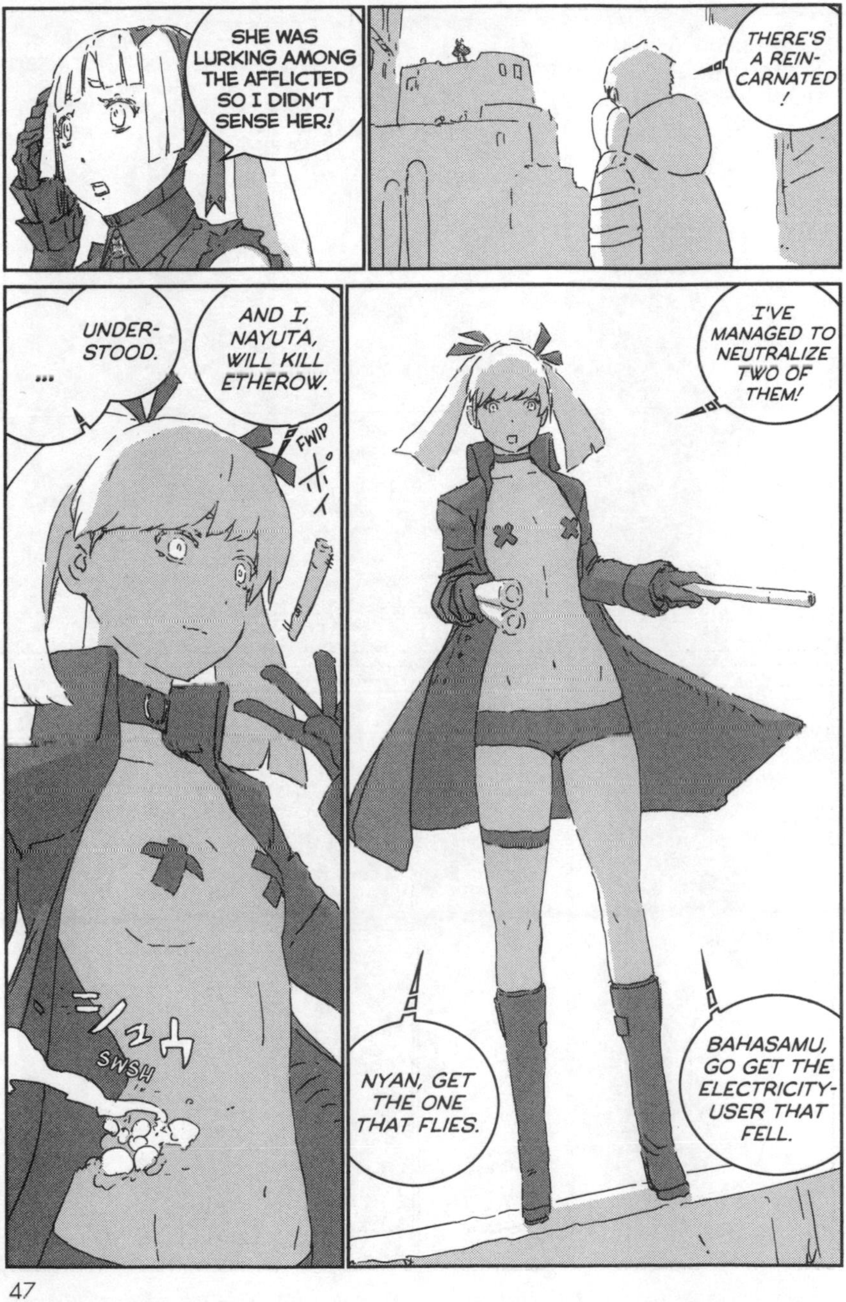
THERE'S A REIN-CARNATED!
SHE WAS LURKING AMONG THE AFFLICTED SO I DIDN'T SENSE HER!
I'VE MANAGED TO NEUTRALIZE TWO OF THEM!
BAHASAMU, GO GET THE ELECTRICITY-USER THAT FELL.
NYAN, GET THE ONE THAT FLIES.
AND I, NAYUTA, WILL KILL ETHEROW.
FWIP
ポイ
UNDER-STOOD.
...
SWSH

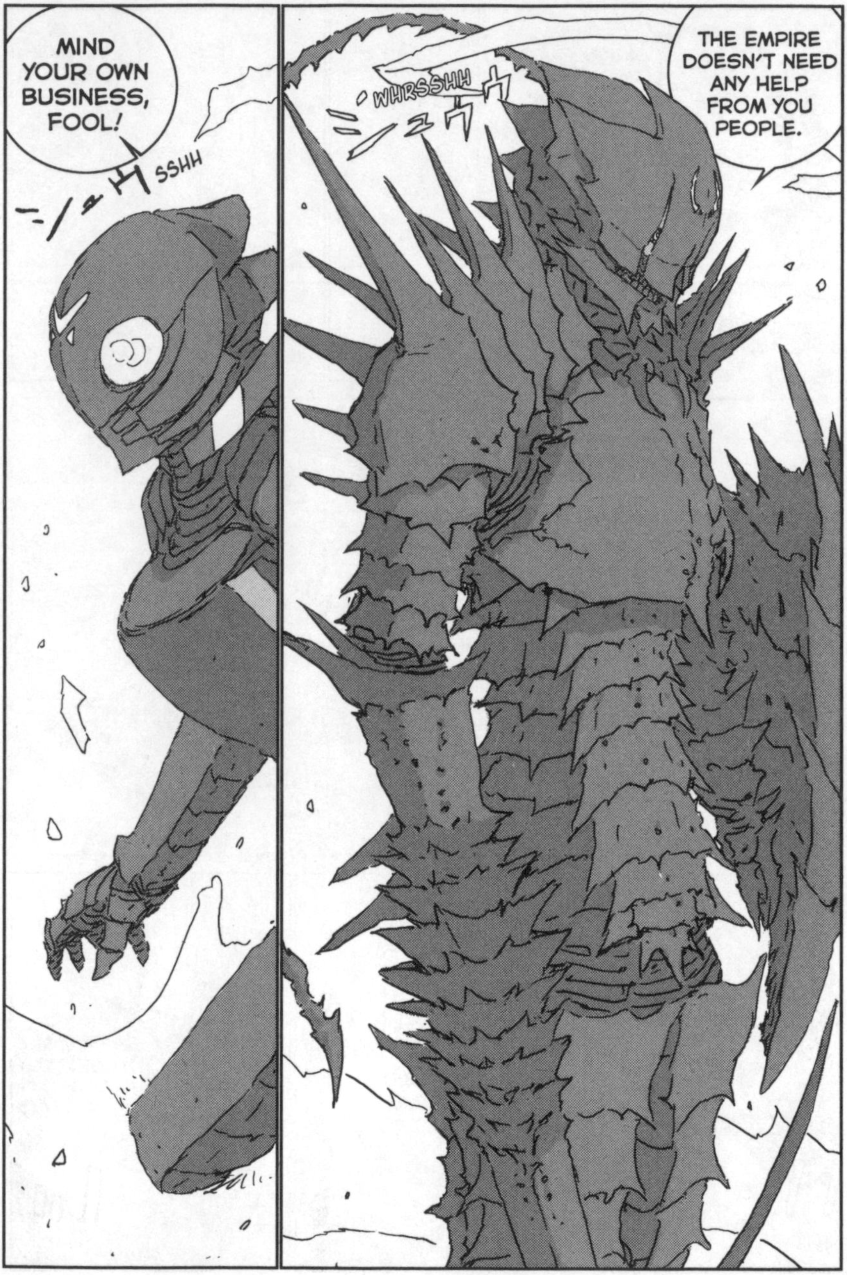
THE EMPIRE DOESN'T NEED ANY HELP FROM YOU PEOPLE.
WHRSSHH
MIND YOUR OWN BUSINESS, FOOL!
SSHH

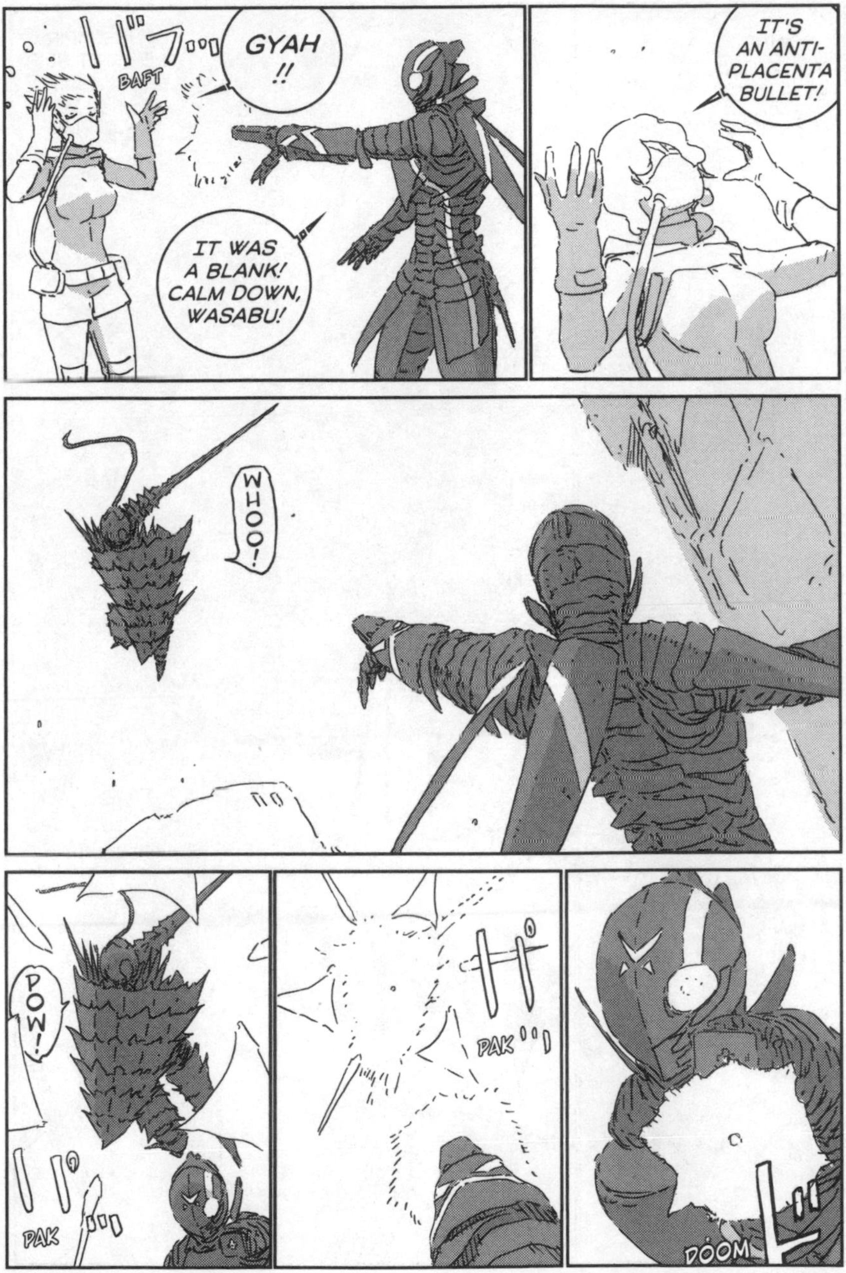

IT'S AN ANTI-PLACENTA BULLET!
GYAH !!
BAFT
IT WAS A BLANK! CALM DOWN, WASABU!
WHOO!
DOOM
PAK
POW!
PAK

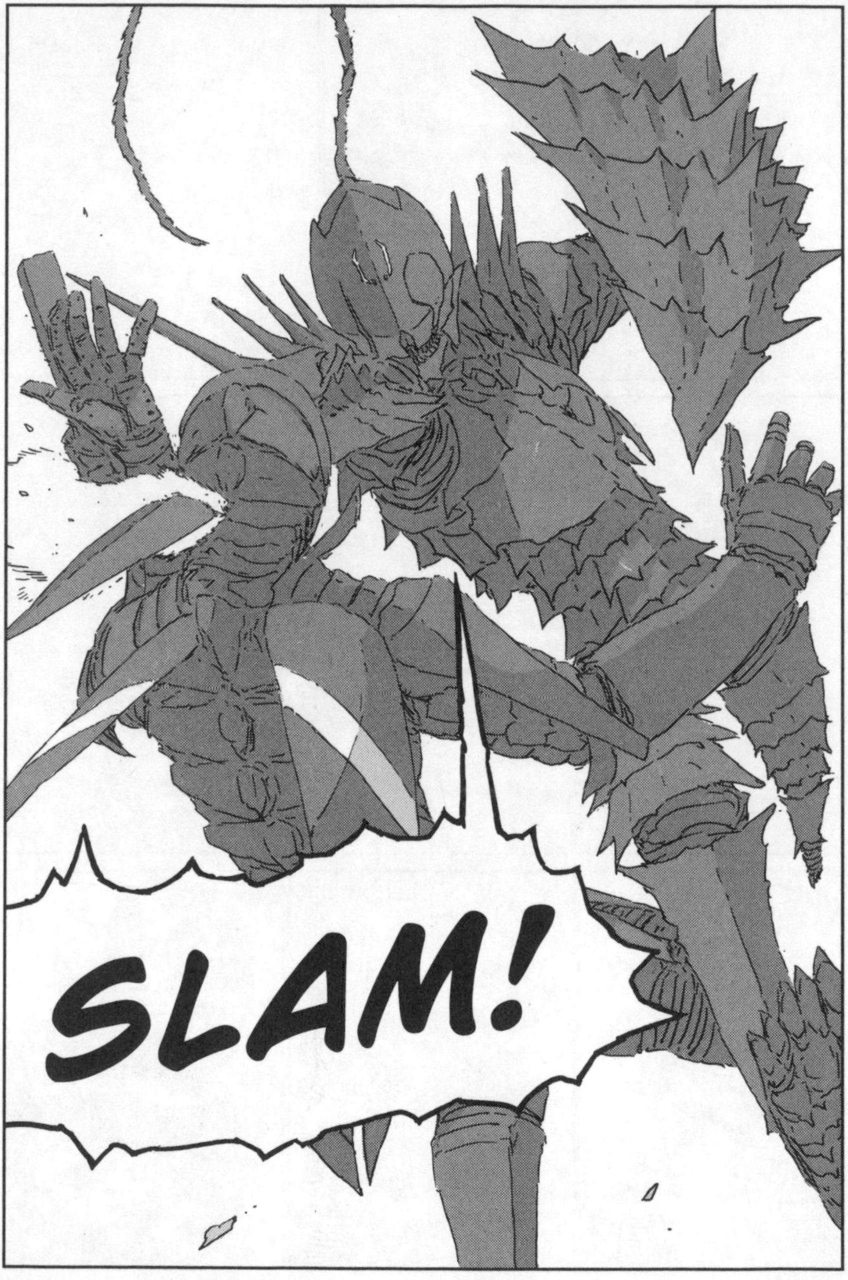
SLAM!

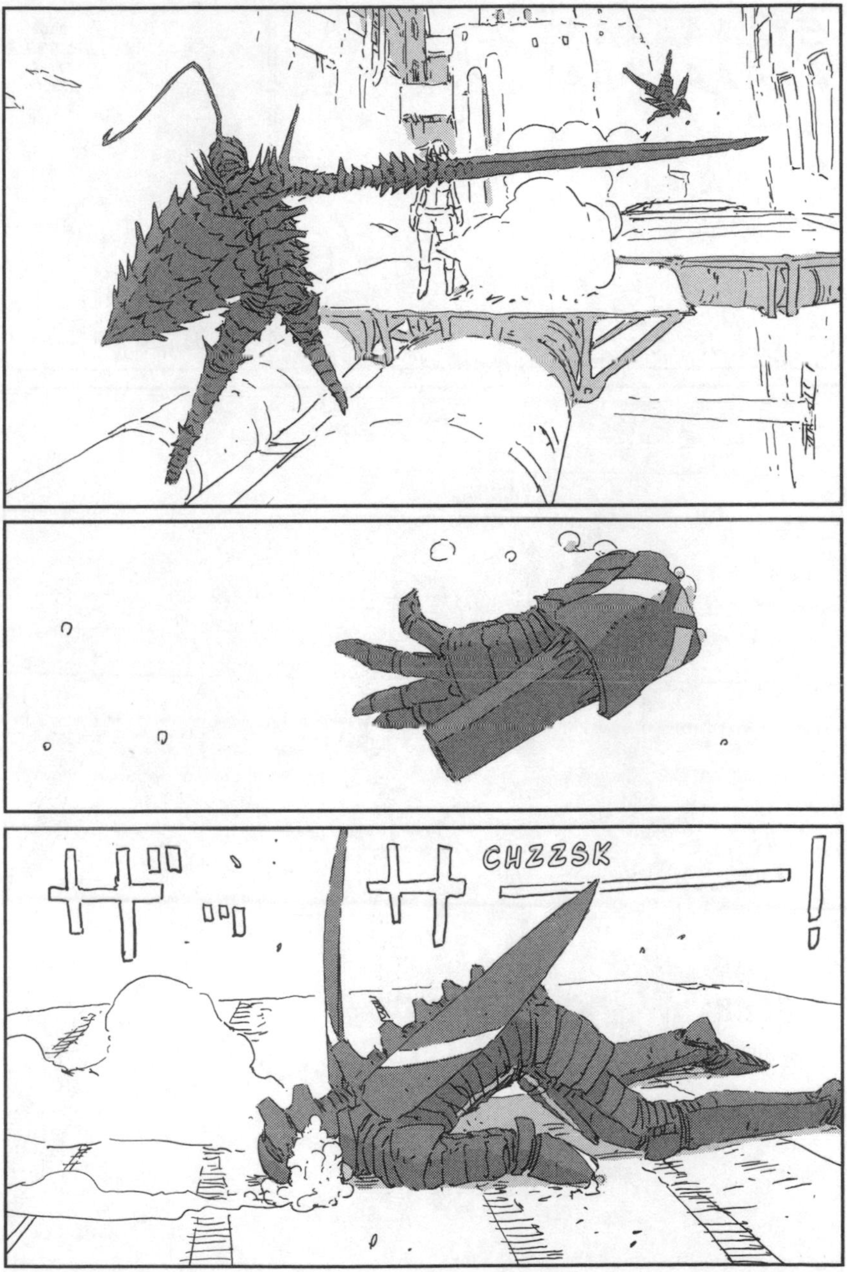
CHZZSK

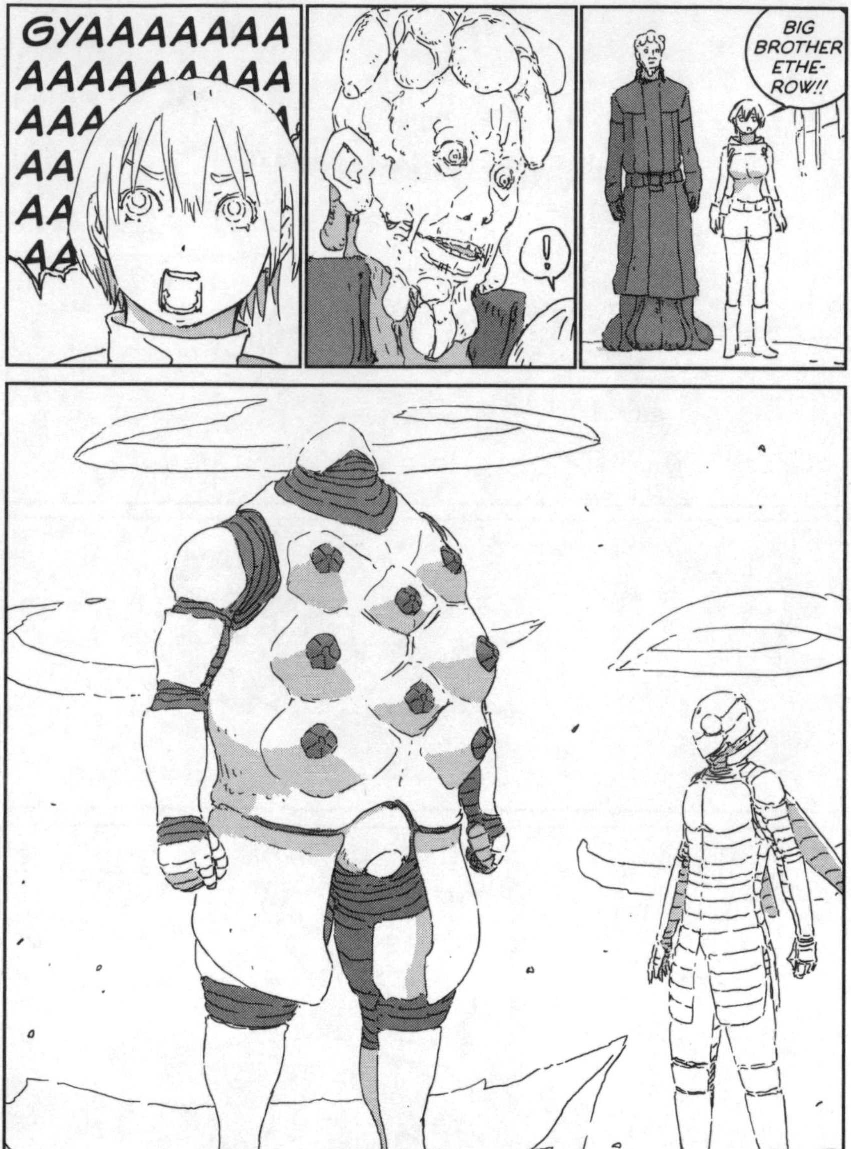
BIG BROTHER ETHE-ROW!!
!
GYAAAAAAAA AAAAAAAAAA AAA AA AA AA

ポ
DOOF
ポ
DOOF
ポ
DOOF
ポ
DOOF
ビュ——
SHWOOOOOO——
!

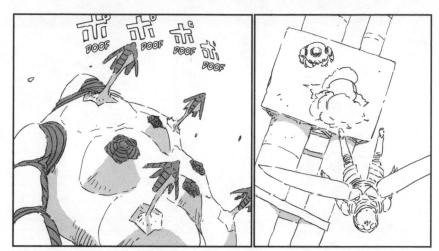

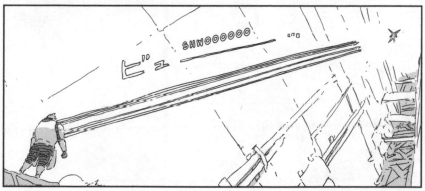

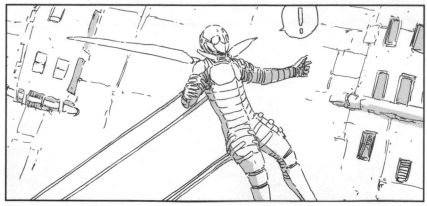

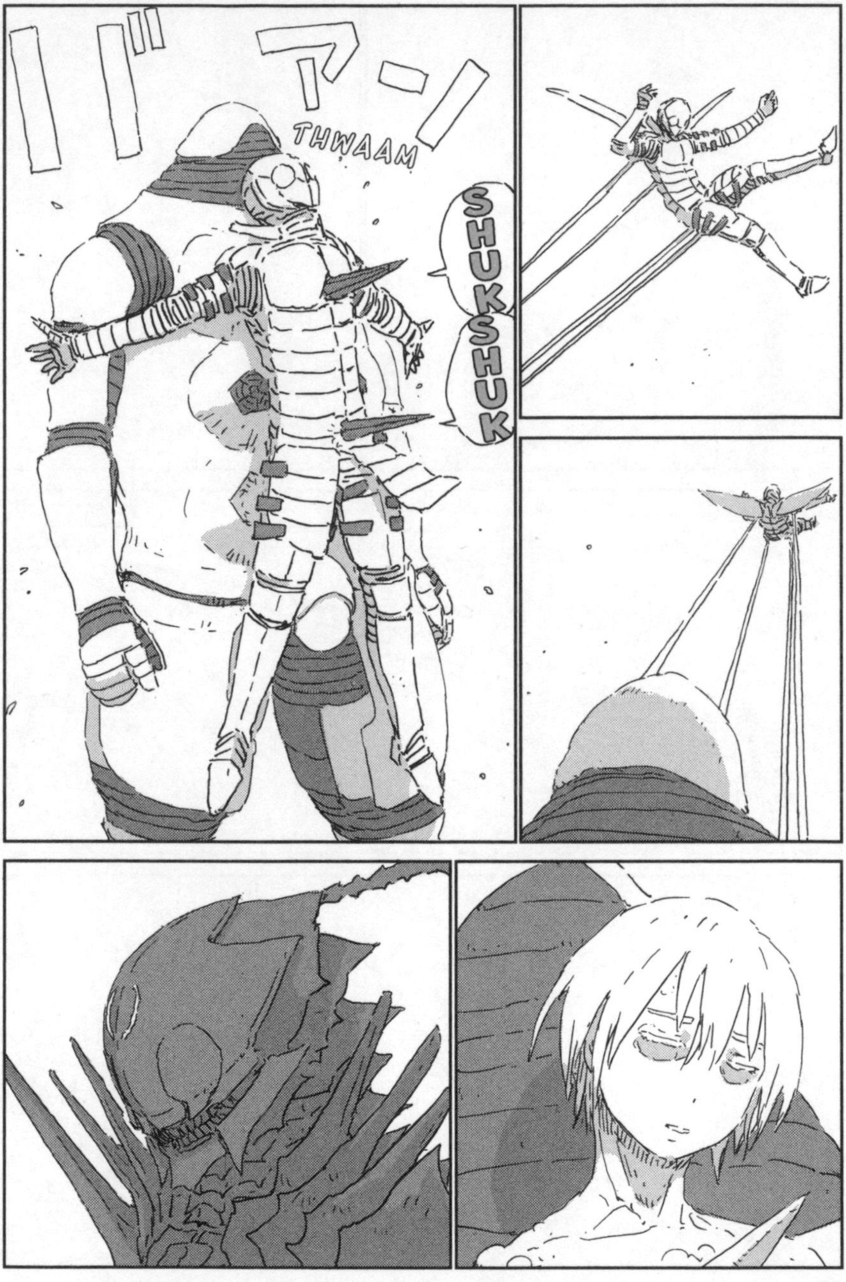
バアーン
THWAAM
SHUKSHUKSHUK

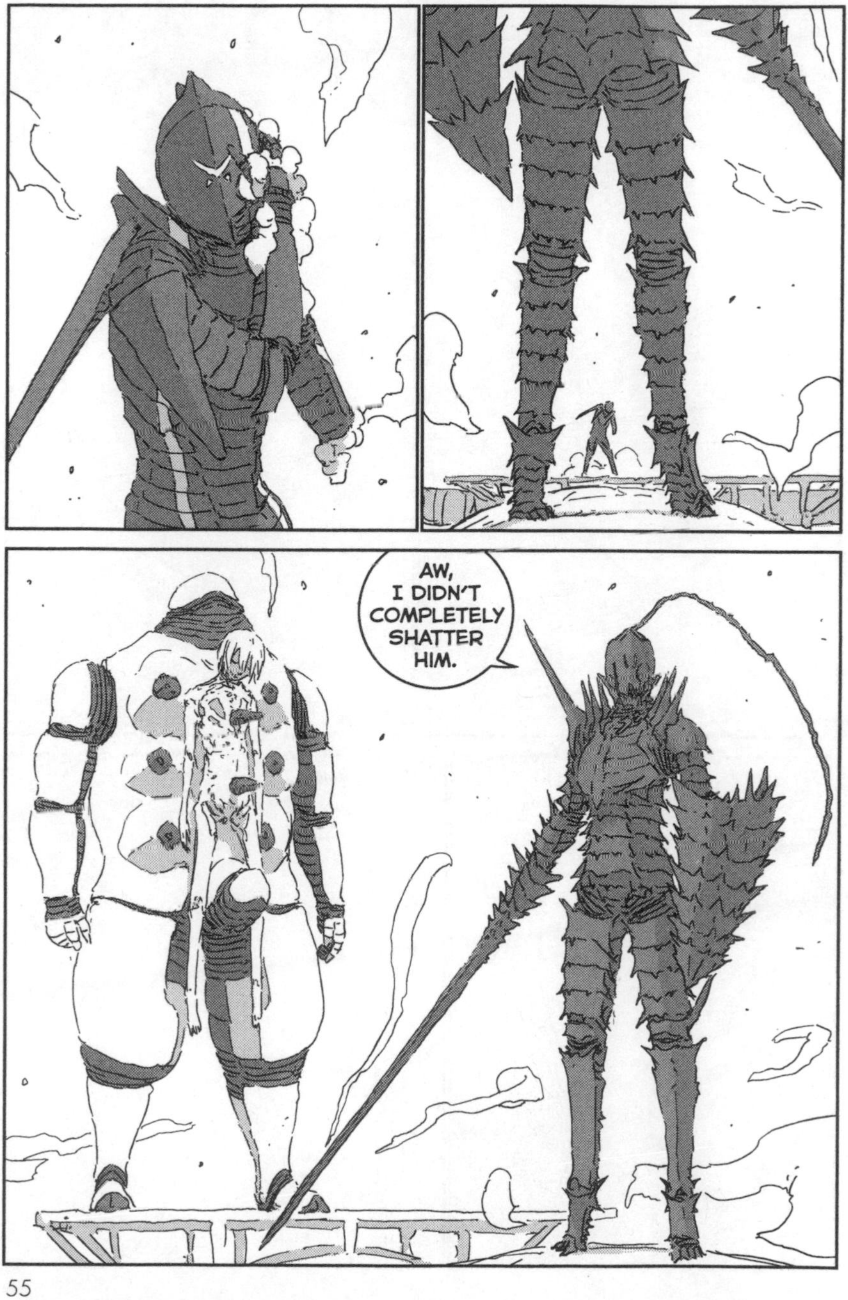
AW, I DIDN'T COMPLETELY SHATTER HIM.

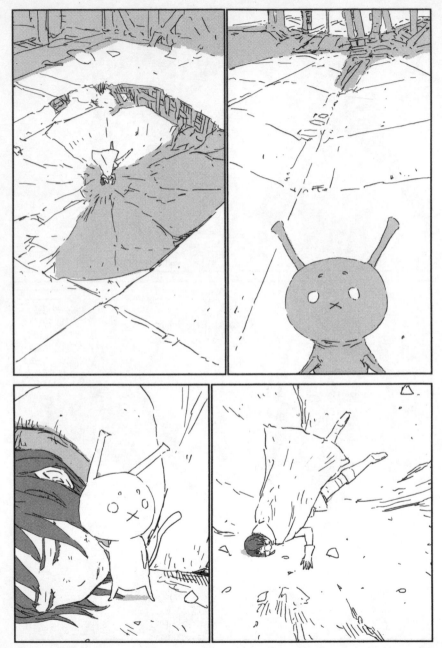

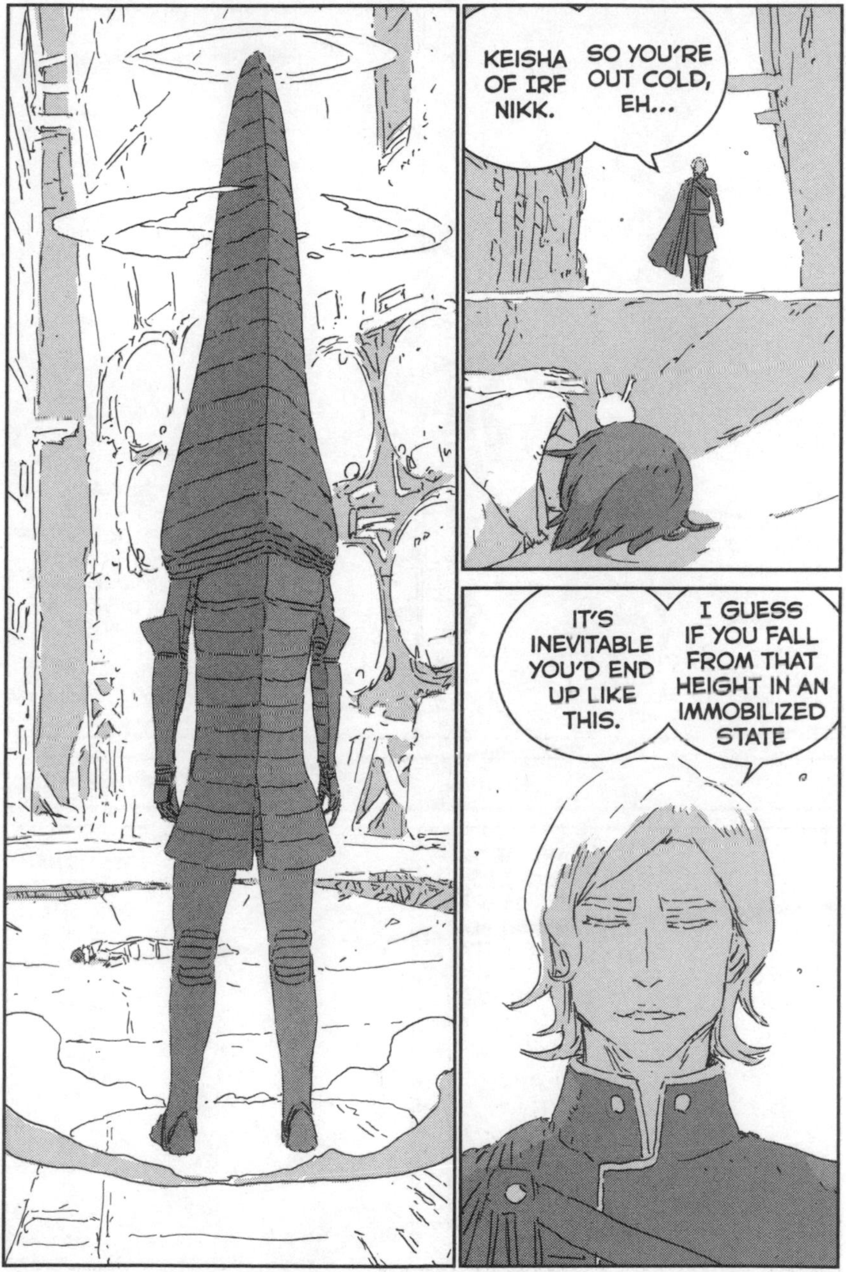
SO YOU'RE OUT COLD, EH...
KEISHA OF IRF NIKK.
I GUESS IF YOU FALL FROM THAT HEIGHT IN AN IMMOBILIZED STATE
IT'S INEVITABLE YOU'D END UP LIKE THIS.

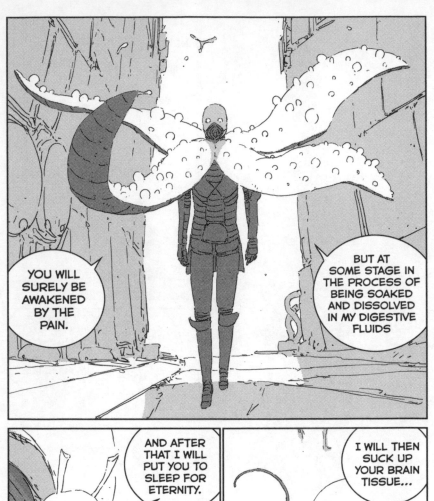

BUT AT SOME STAGE IN THE PROCESS OF BEING SOAKED AND DISSOLVED IN MY DIGESTIVE FLUIDS
YOU WILL SURELY BE AWAKENED BY THE PAIN.
I WILL THEN SUCK UP YOUR BRAIN TISSUE...
AND AFTER THAT I WILL PUT YOU TO SLEEP FOR ETERNITY.

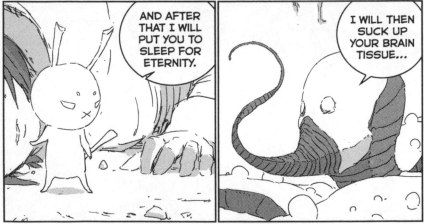

CHAPTER 44 END

APOSIMZ

CHAPTER 45

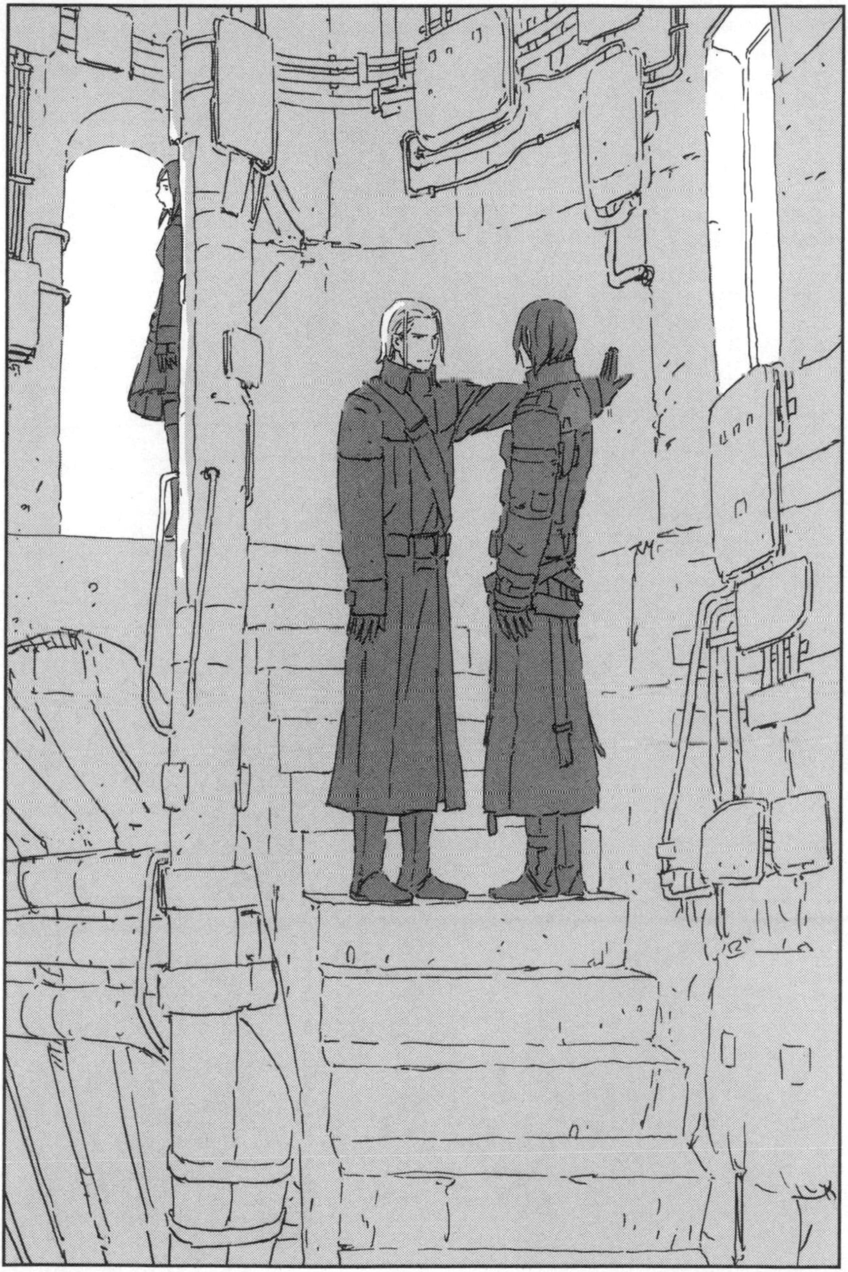

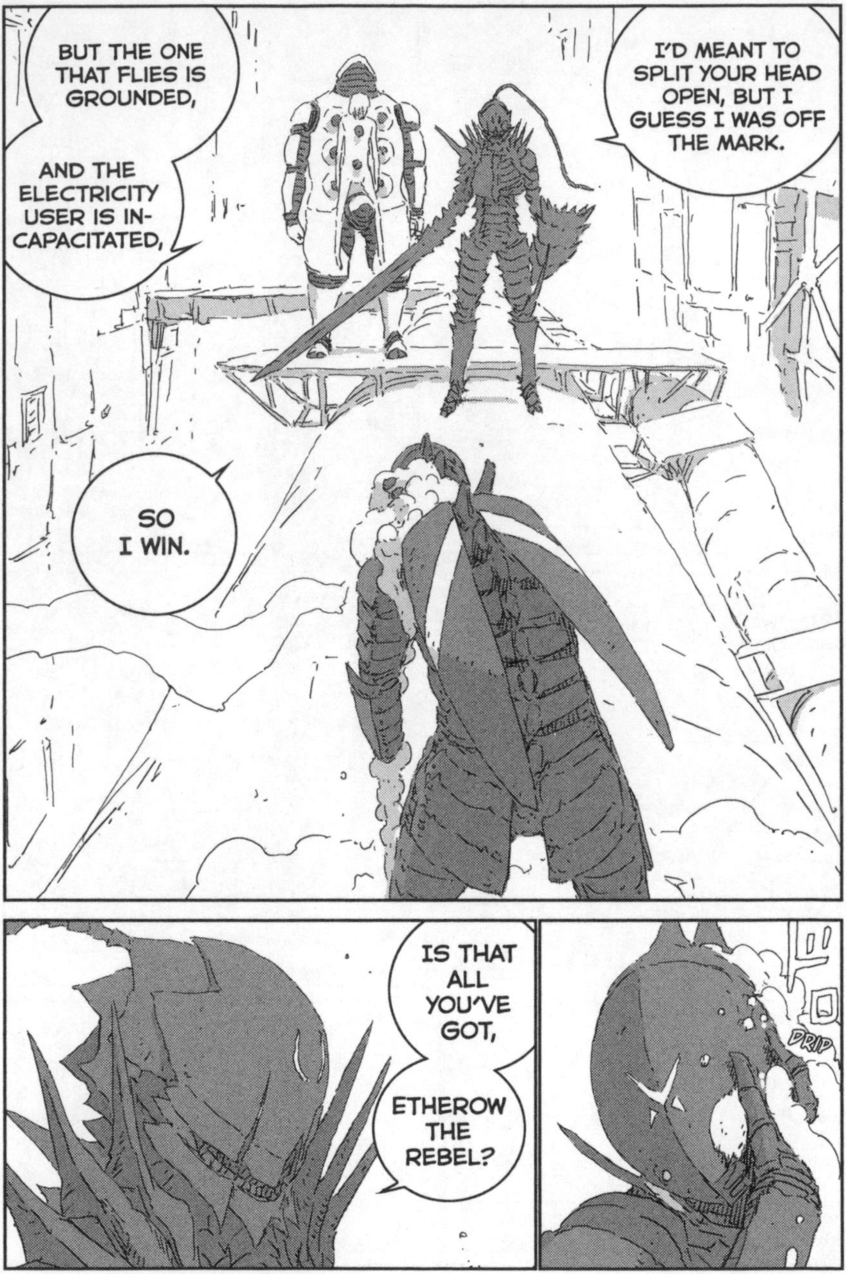
I'D MEANT TO SPLIT YOUR HEAD OPEN, BUT I GUESS I WAS OFF THE MARK.
BUT THE ONE THAT FLIES IS GROUNDED,
AND THE ELECTRICITY USER IS IN-CAPACITATED,
SO I WIN.
DRIP
IS THAT ALL YOU'VE GOT,
ETHEROW THE REBEL?

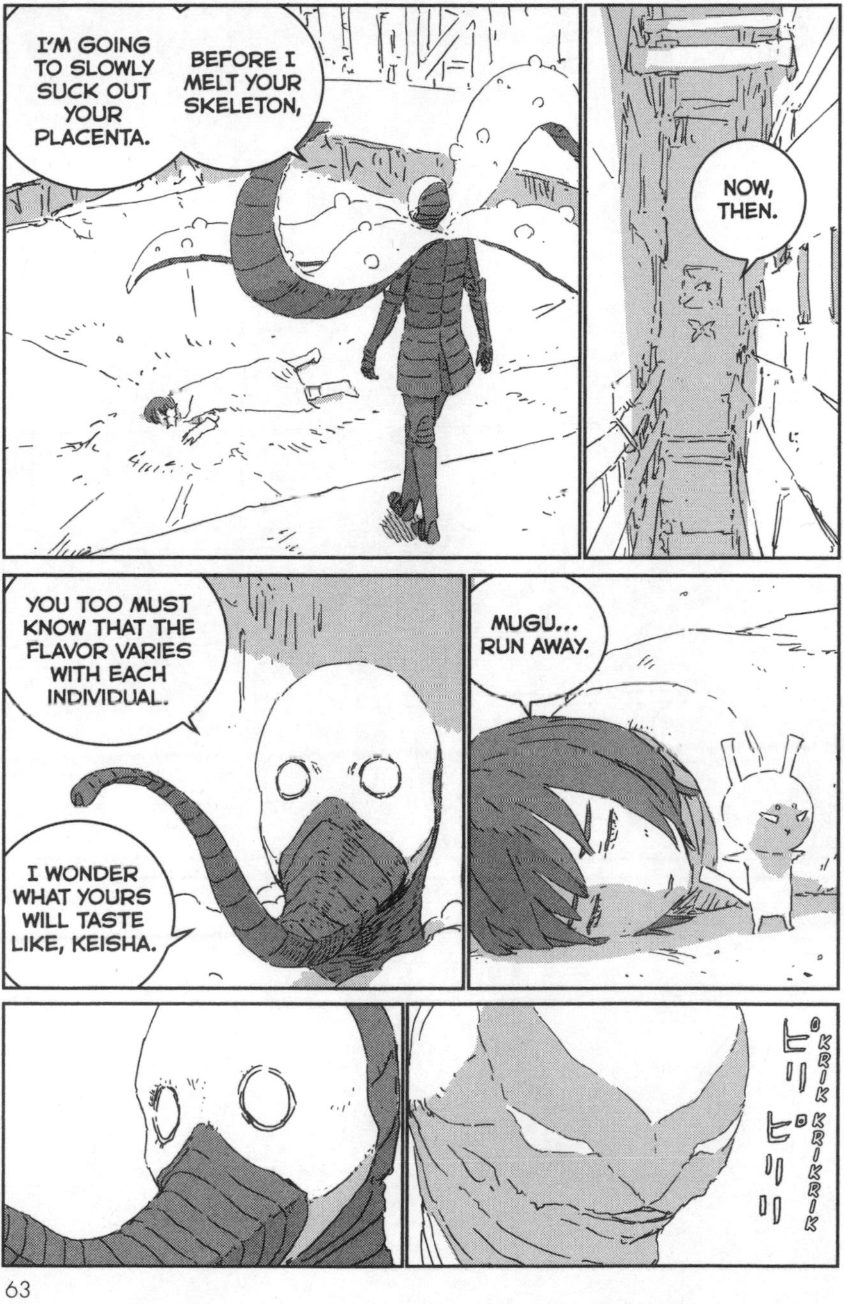
NOW, THEN.
BEFORE I MELT YOUR SKELETON,
I'M GOING TO SLOWLY SUCK OUT YOUR PLACENTA.
MUGU... RUN AWAY.
YOU TOO MUST KNOW THAT THE FLAVOR VARIES WITH EACH INDIVIDUAL.
I WONDER WHAT YOURS WILL TASTE LIKE, KEISHA.
ヒリ ヒリリ
KRIK KRIKKRIK

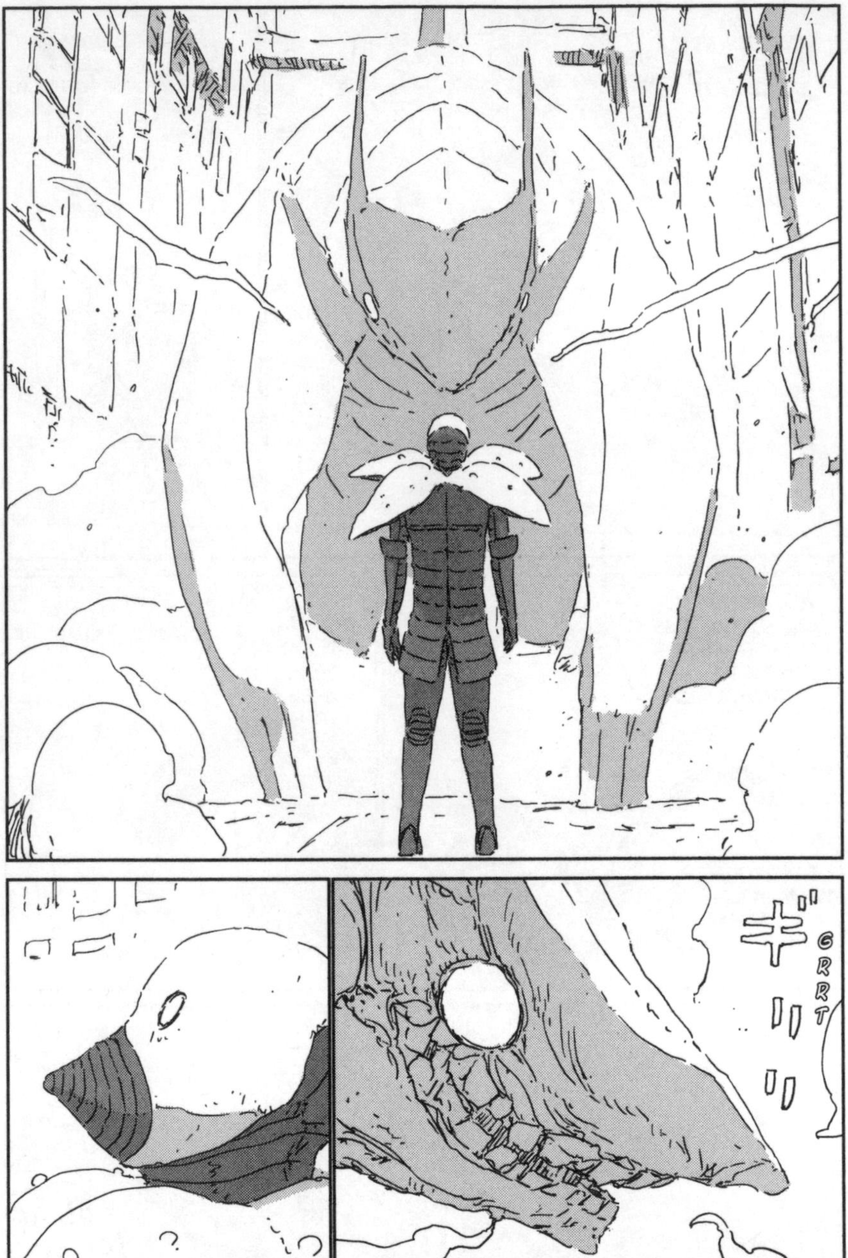
ギリリ
GRRT

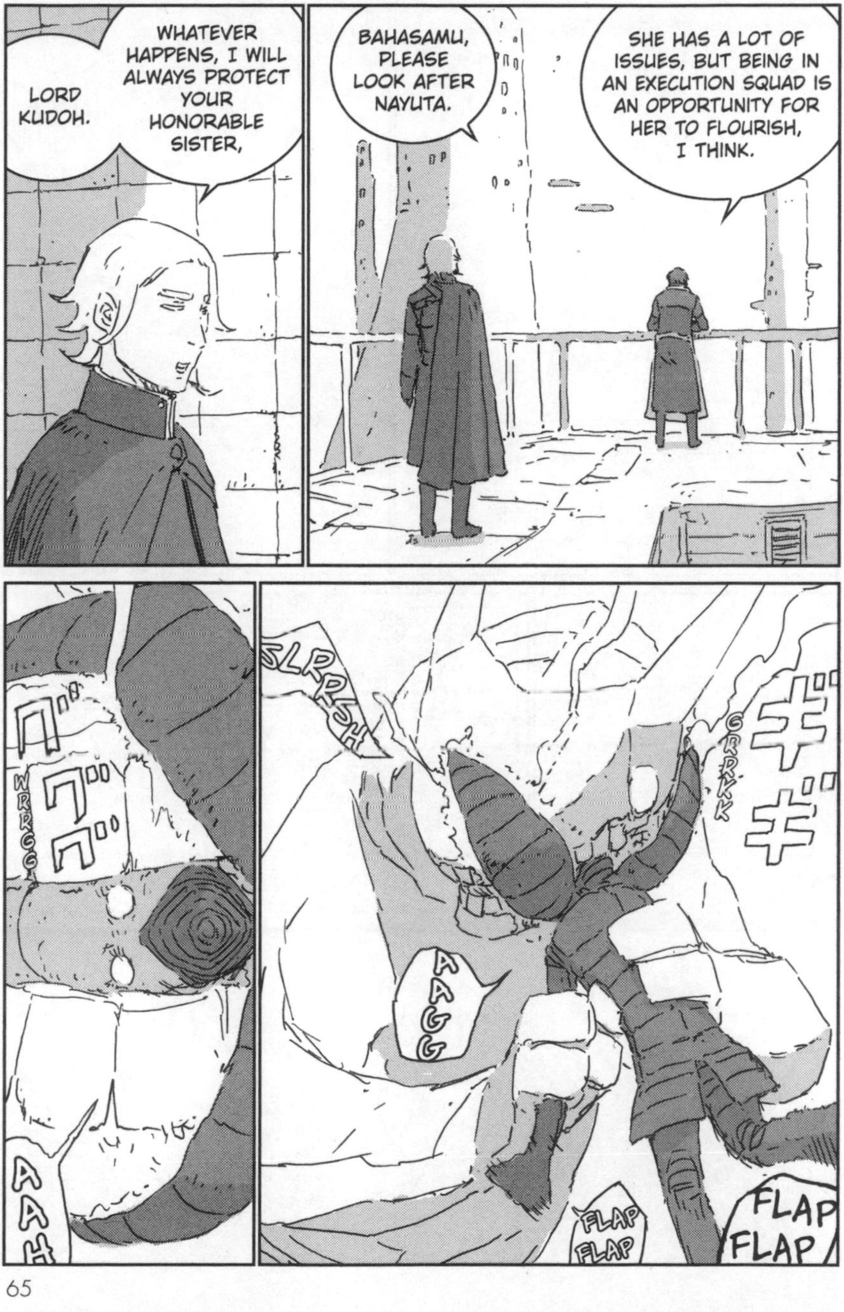
SHE HAS A LOT OF ISSUES, BUT BEING IN AN EXECUTION SQUAD IS AN OPPORTUNITY FOR HER TO FLOURISH, I THINK.
BAHASAMU, PLEASE LOOK AFTER NAYUTA.
WHATEVER HAPPENS, I WILL ALWAYS PROTECT YOUR HONORABLE SISTER,
LORD KUDOH.
GRRKK
ギギ
SLRRSH
AAGG
FLAP FLAP
FLAP FLAP
WRRGG
AAH

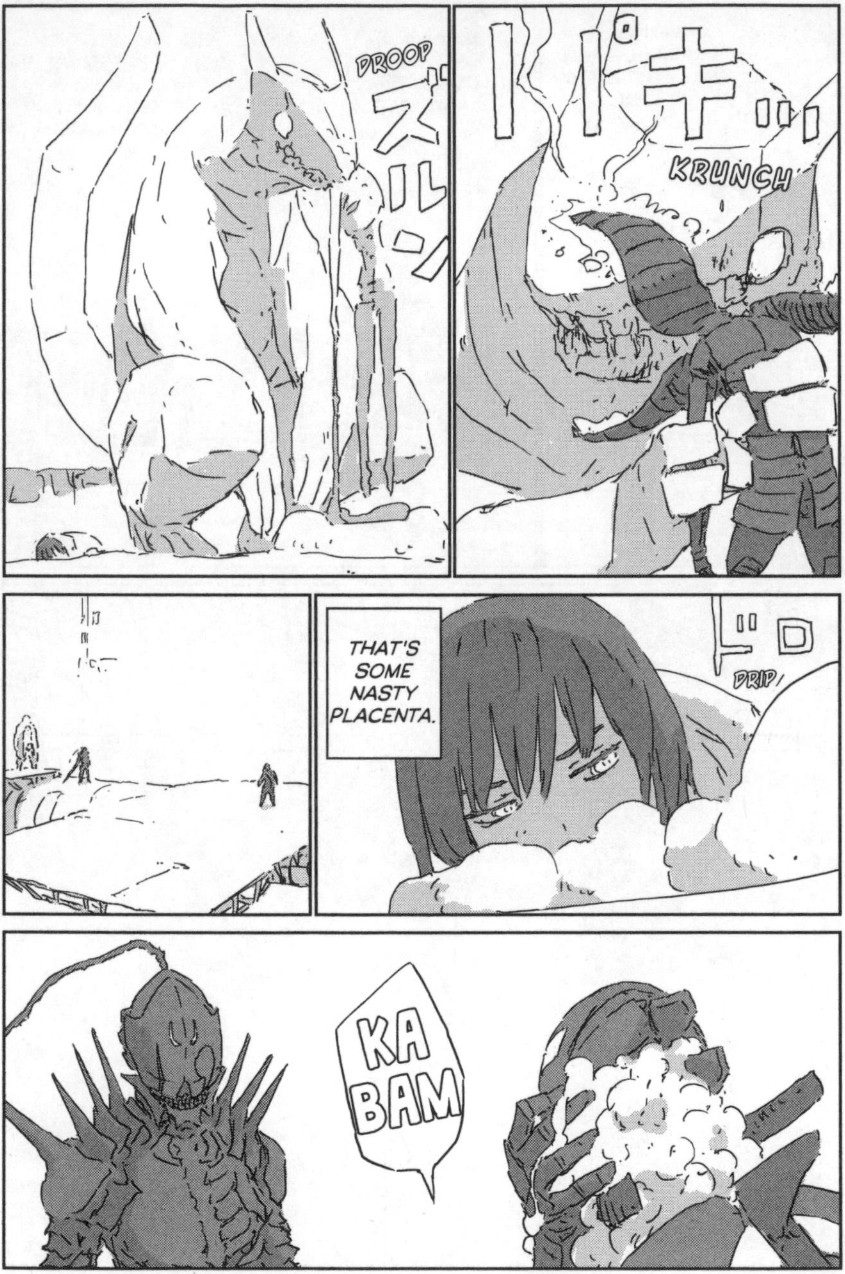
パキッ
KRUNCH
DROOP
ズルッ
ドロ
DRIP
THAT'S SOME NASTY PLACENTA.
KA BAM

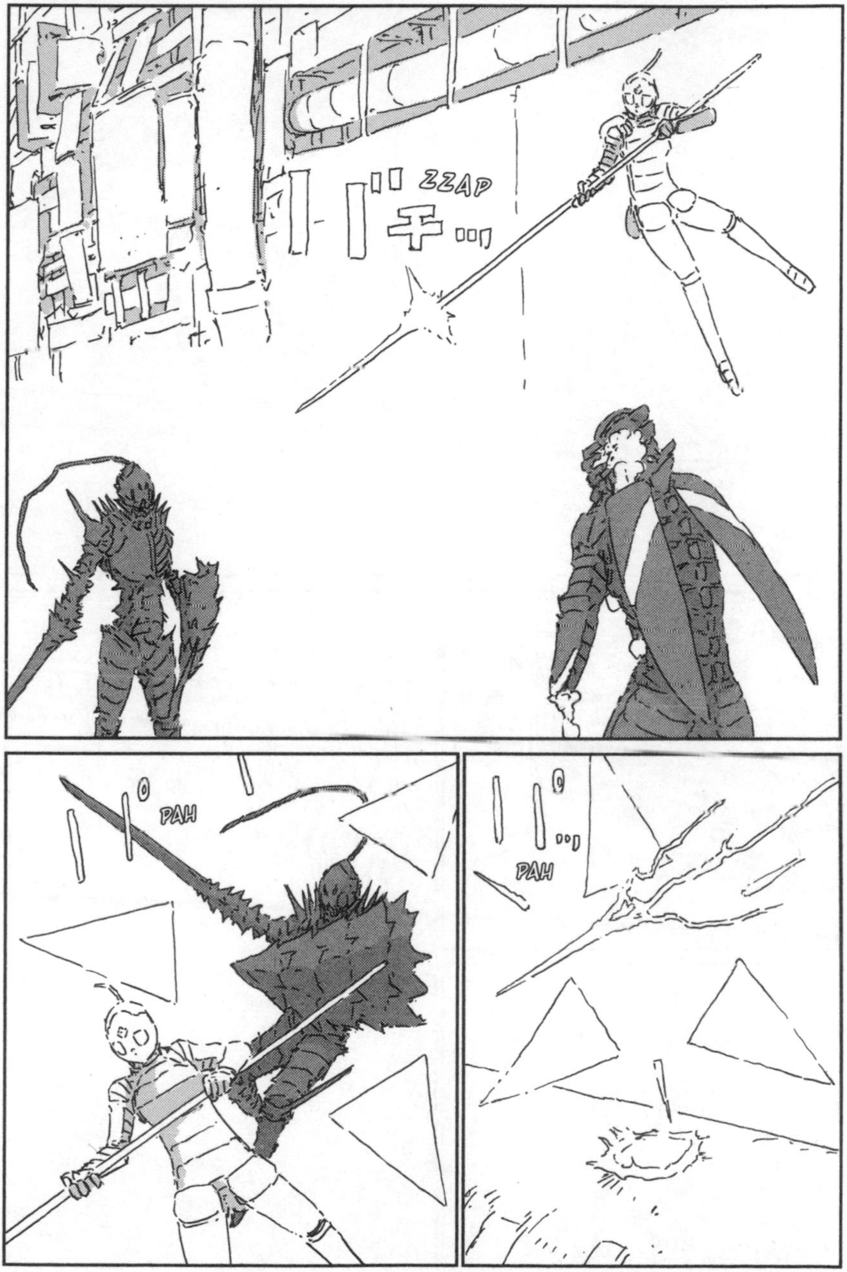
ZZAP
PAH
PAH

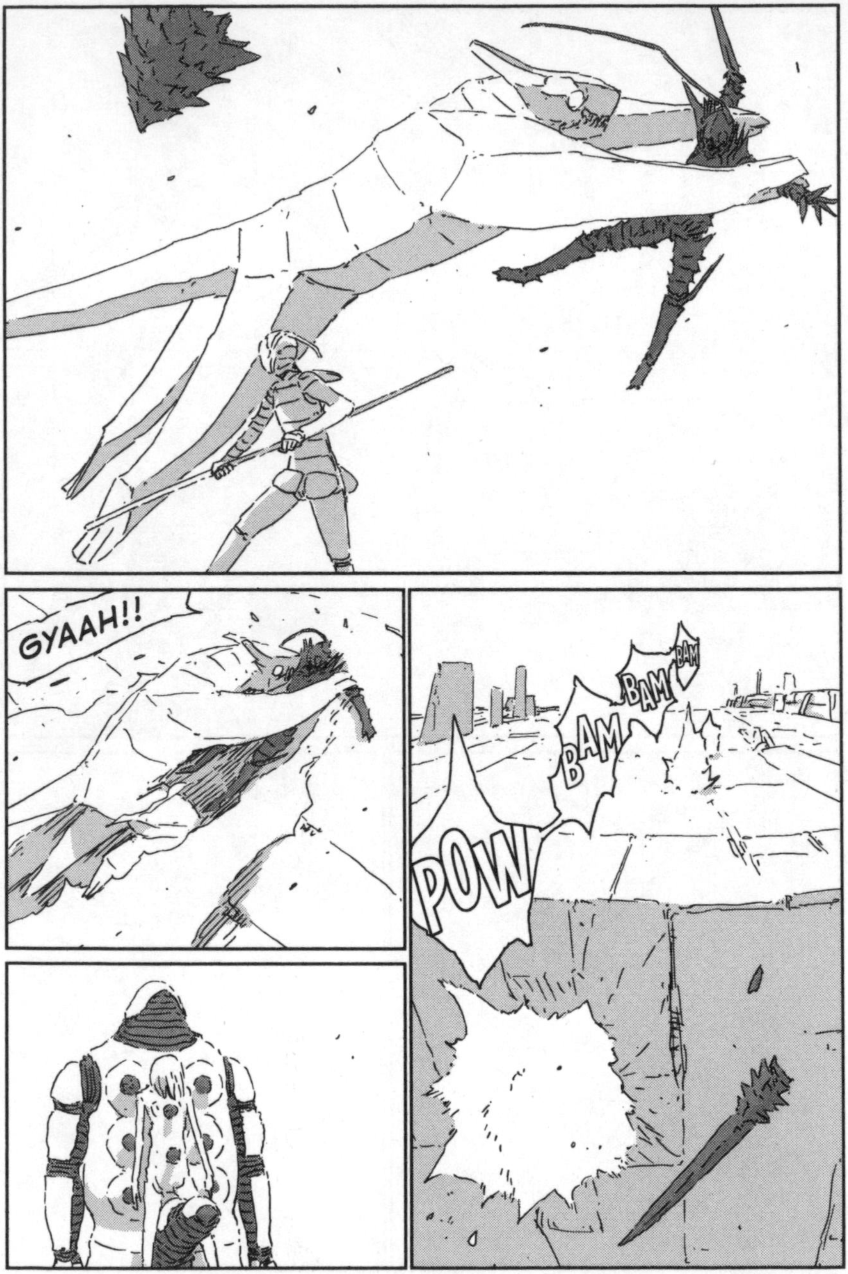
BAM
BAM
BAM
BAM
POW
GYAAH!!

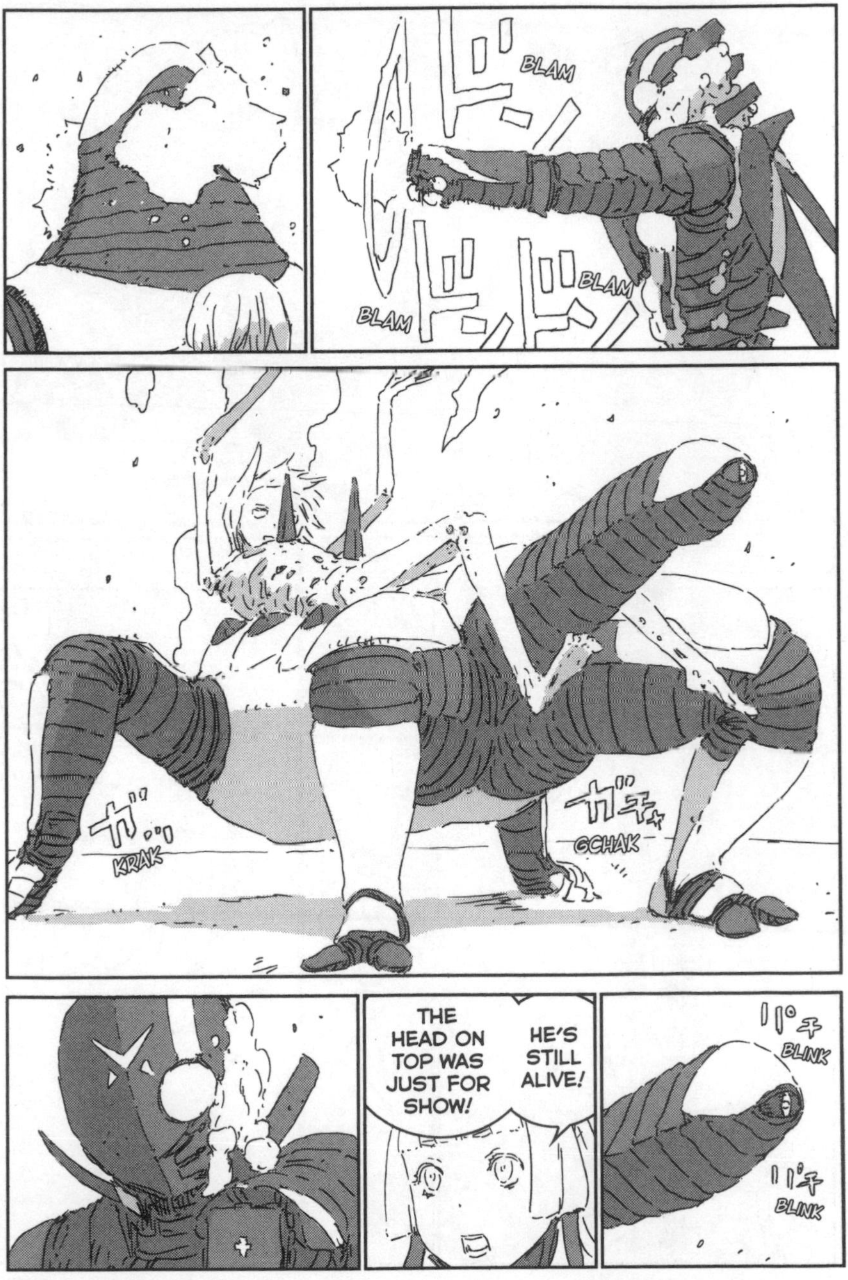
BLAM
BLAM
BLAM
GCHAK
KRAK
BLINK
BLINK
HE'S STILL ALIVE!
THE HEAD ON TOP WAS JUST FOR SHOW!

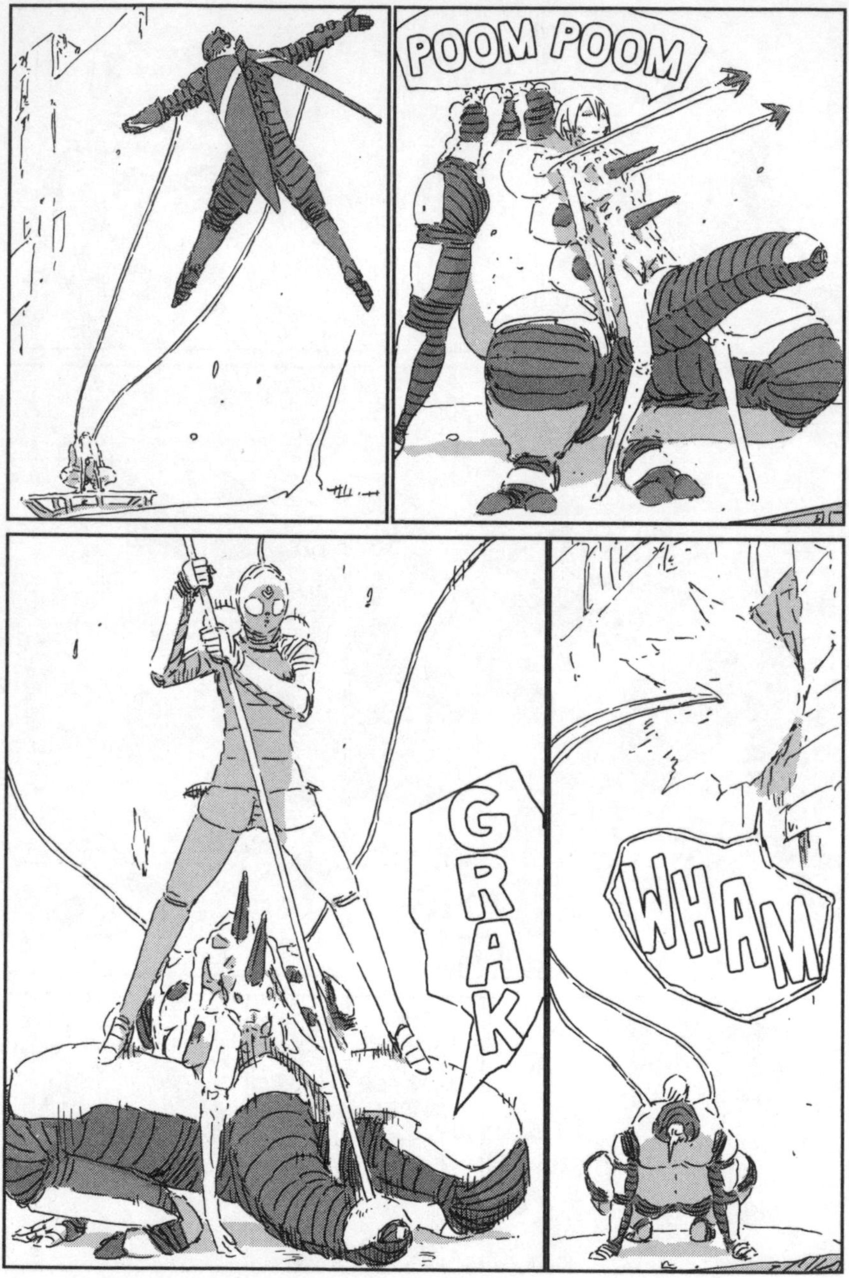
POOM POOM
WHAM
GRAK

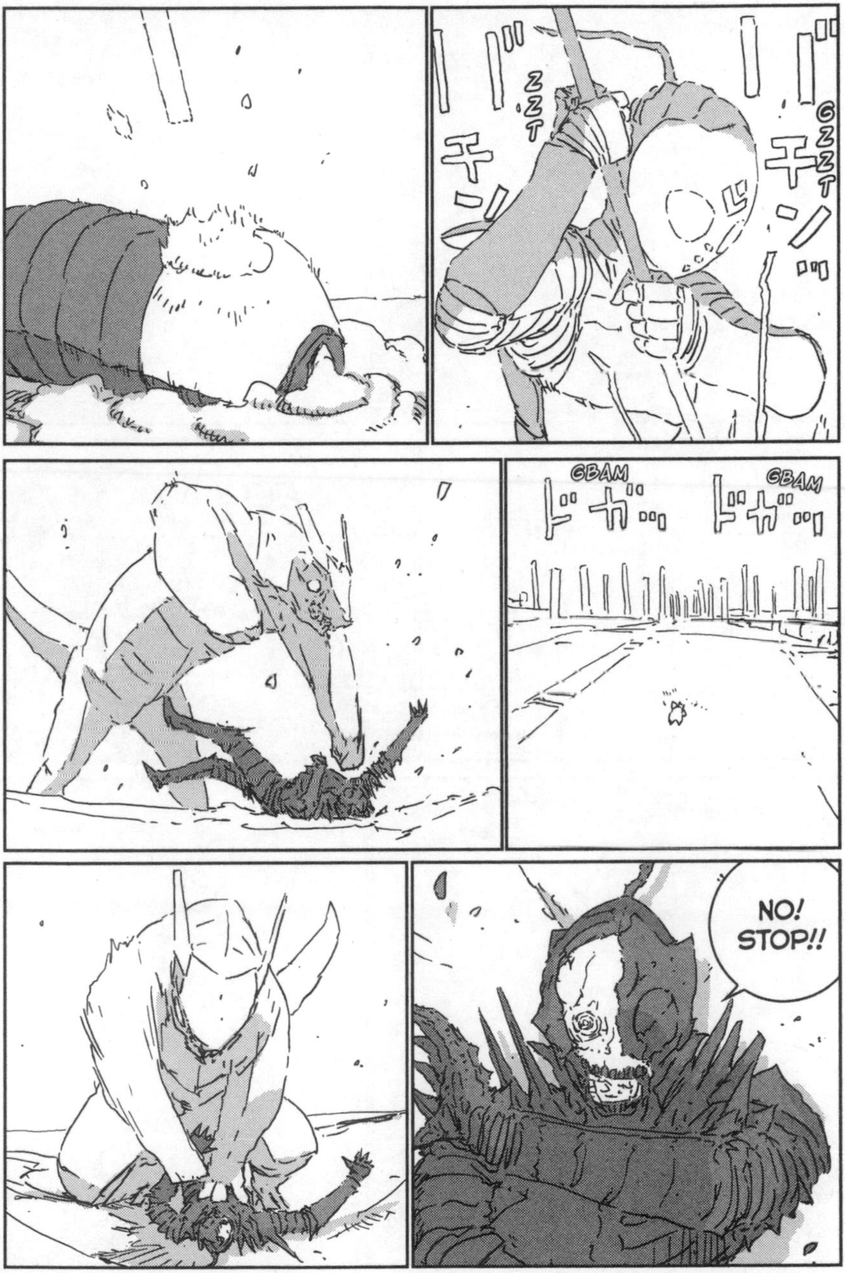
GZZZT
ZZZT
GBAM
ドガッ
GBAM
ドガッ
NO! STOP!!

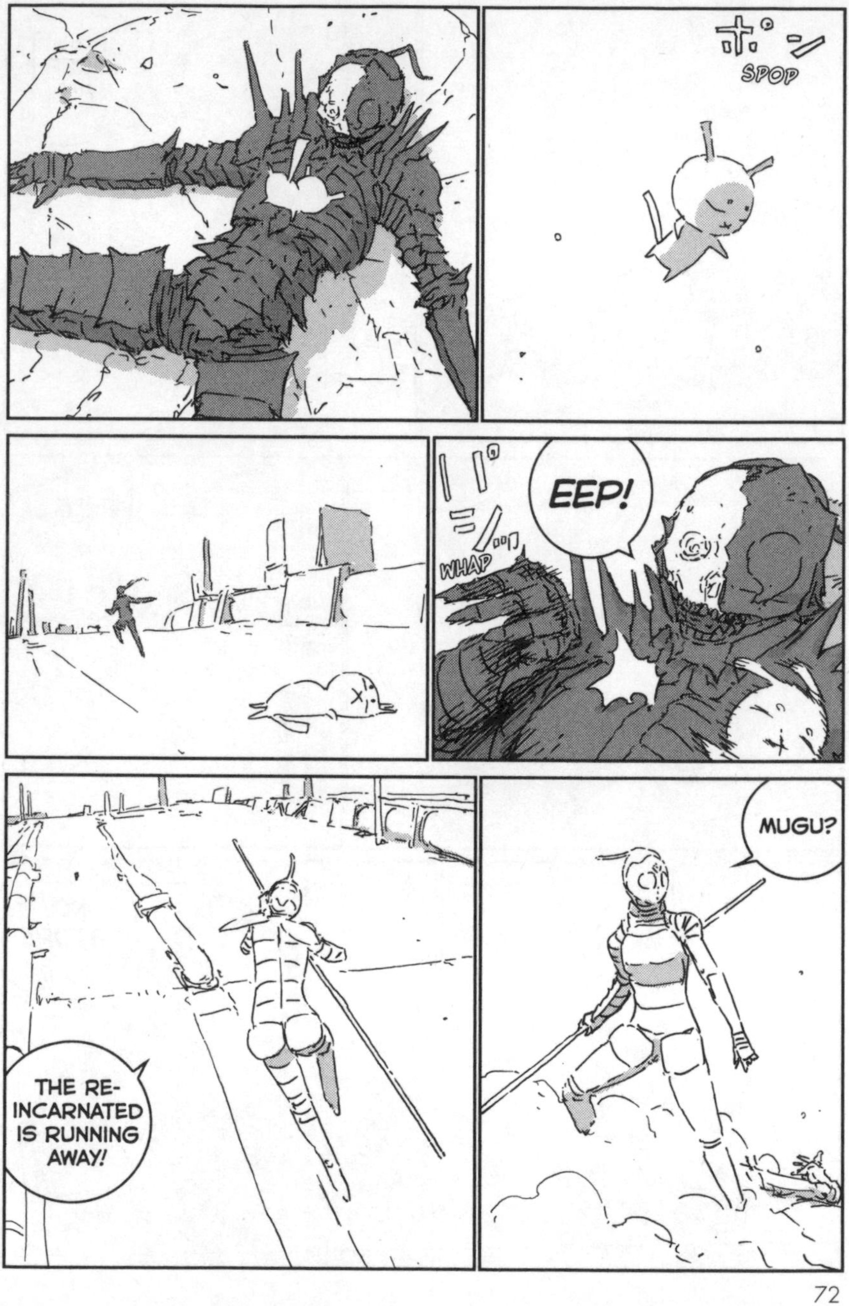
ポン
SPOP
WHAP
EEP!
MUGU?
THE RE-INCARNATED IS RUNNING AWAY!

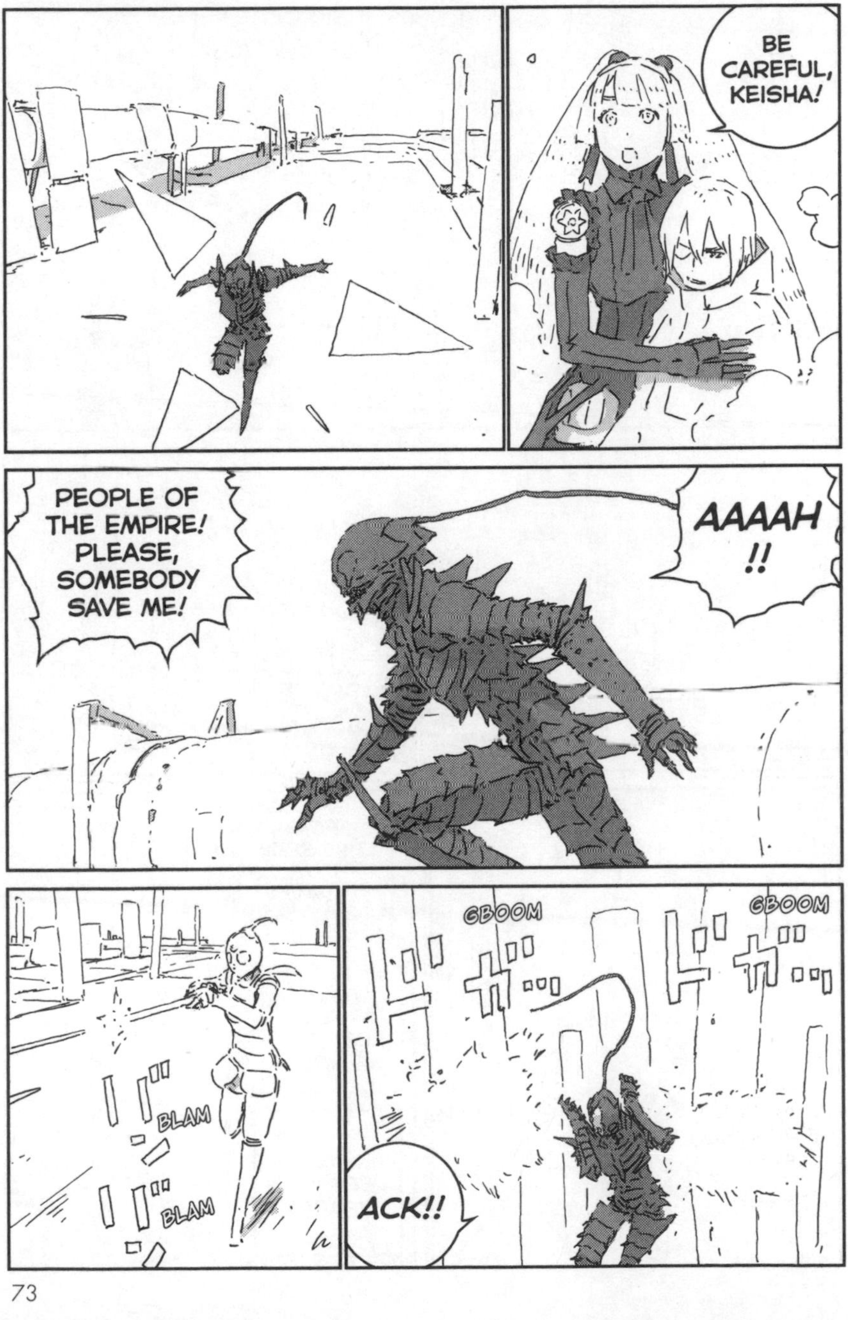
BE CAREFUL, KEISHA!
AAAAH!!
PEOPLE OF THE EMPIRE! PLEASE, SOMEBODY SAVE ME!
GBOOM
GBOOM
ACK!!
BLAM
BLAM

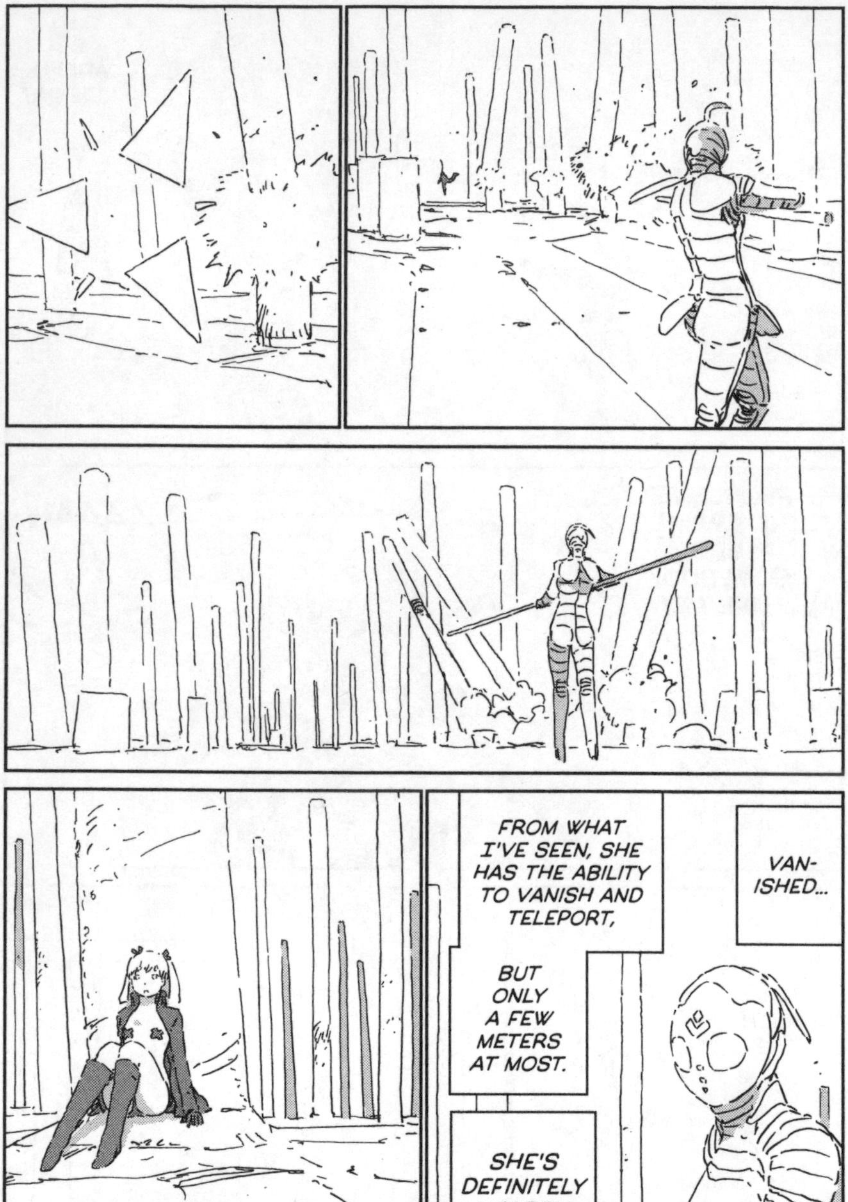
VAN-
ISHED...
FROM WHAT I'VE SEEN, SHE HAS THE ABILITY TO VANISH AND TELEPORT,
BUT ONLY A FEW METERS AT MOST.
SHE'S DEFINITELY NEARBY.

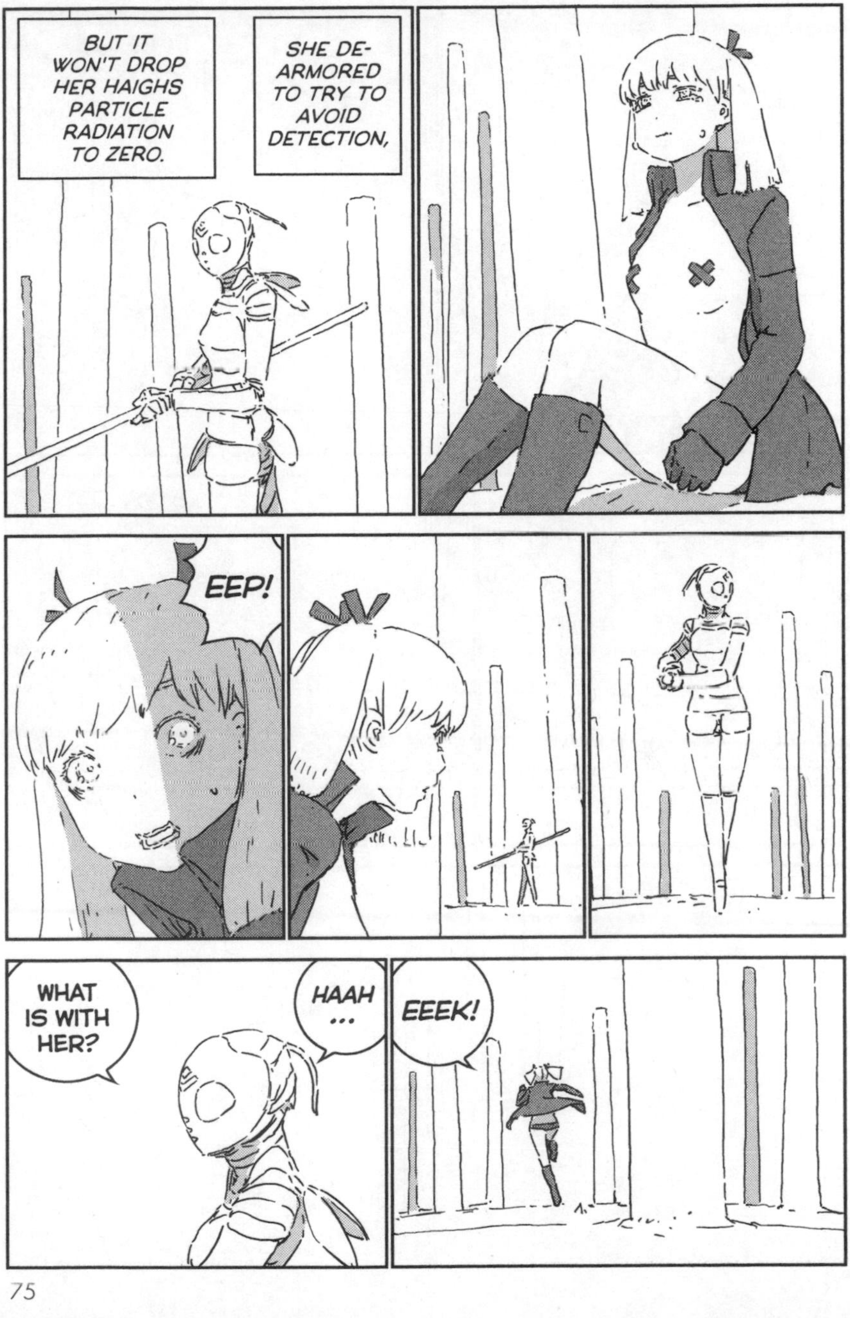
SHE DE-ARMORED TO TRY TO AVOID DETECTION,
BUT IT WON'T DROP HER HAIGHS PARTICLE RADIATION TO ZERO.
EEP!
EEEK!
HAAH ...
WHAT IS WITH HER?

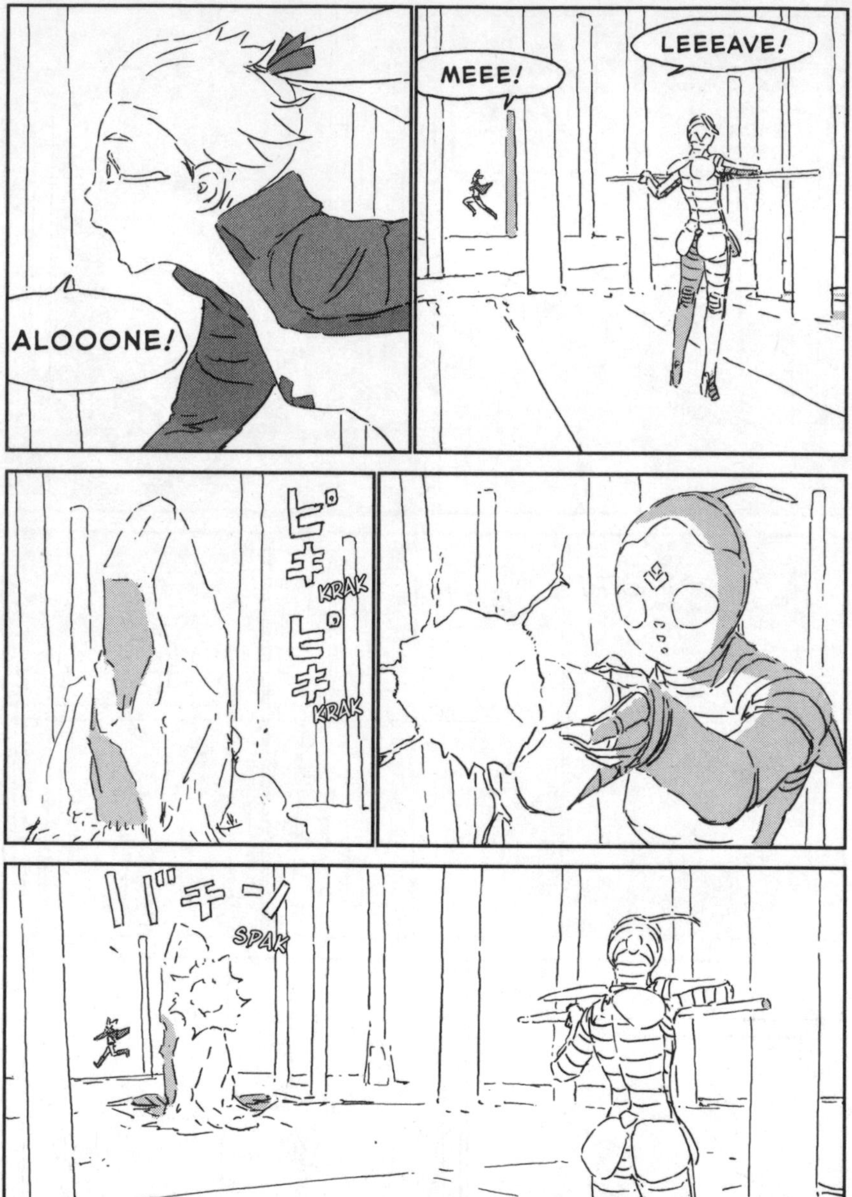
LEEEAVE!
MEEE!
ALOOONE!
ピキ
KRAK
ピキ
KRAK
バチーン
SPAK

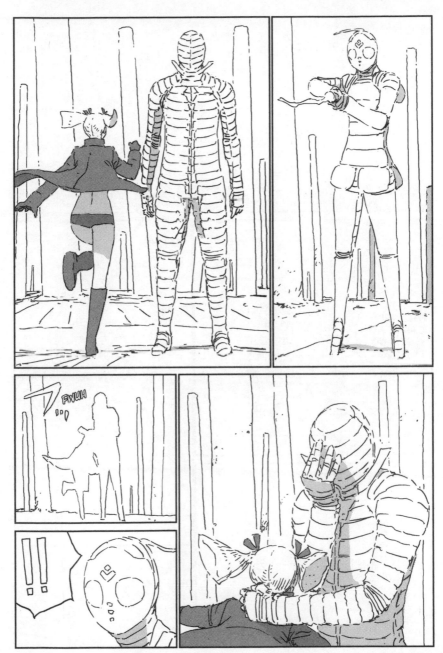

FWUH

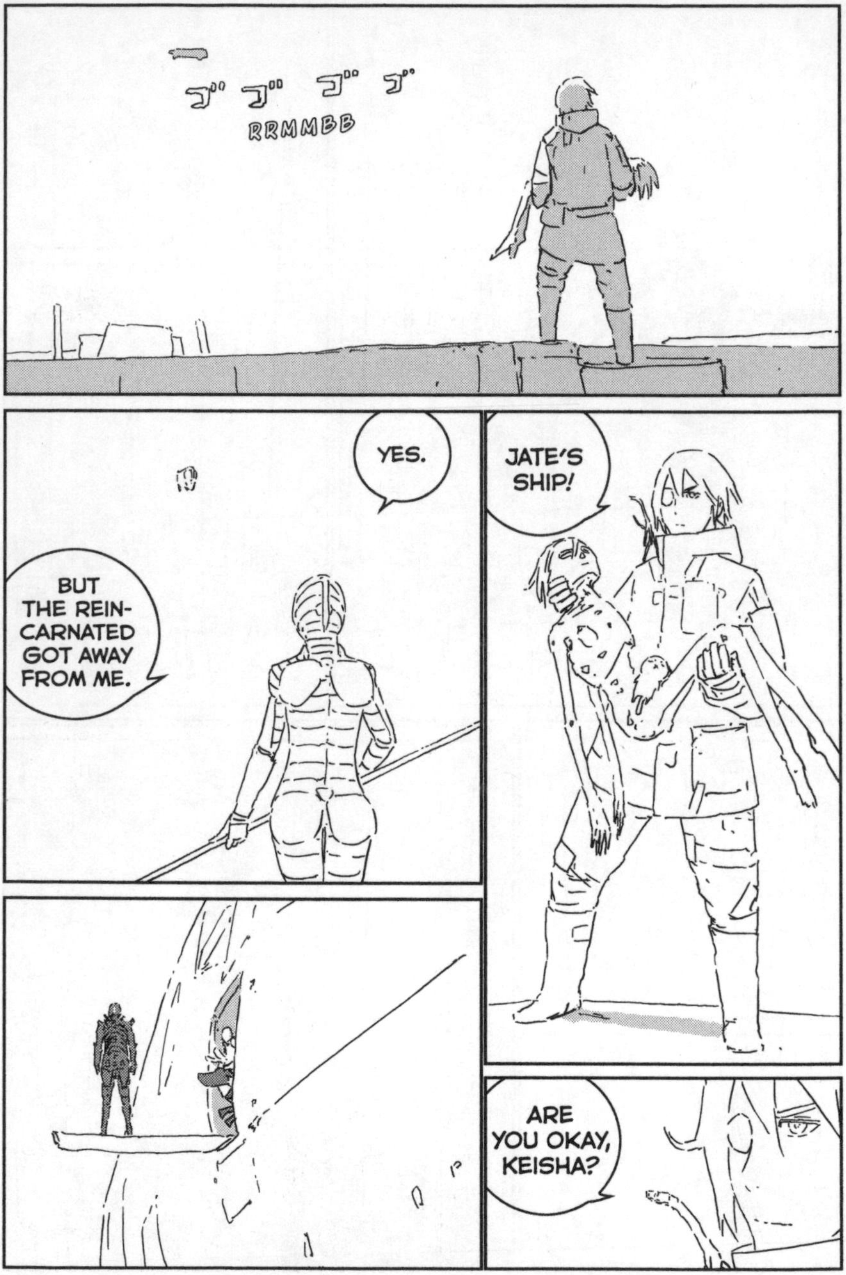
ゴゴゴゴ
RRMMBB
JATE'S SHIP!
YES.
BUT THE REIN-CARNATED GOT AWAY FROM ME.
ARE YOU OKAY, KEISHA?

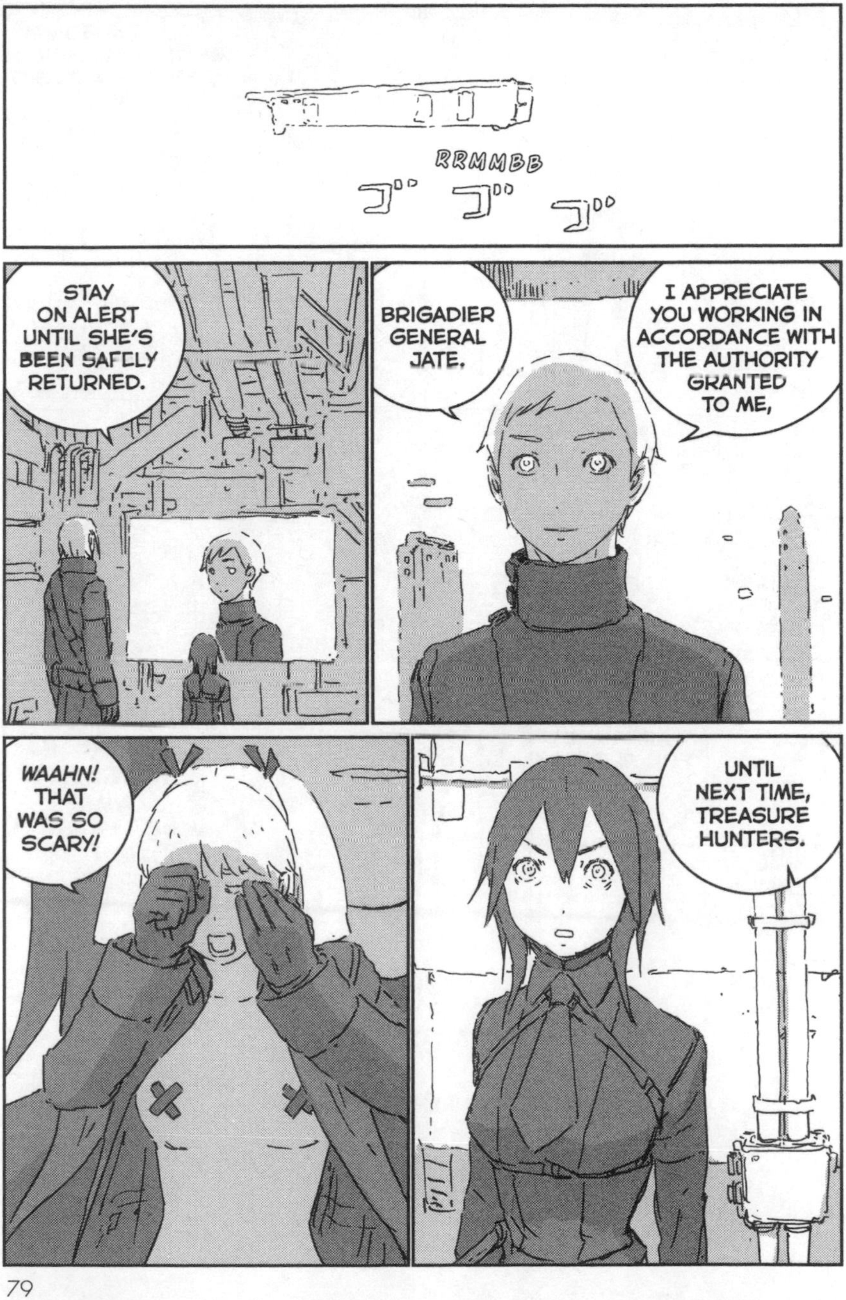
RRMMBB
ゴゴゴ
I APPRECIATE YOU WORKING IN ACCORDANCE WITH THE AUTHORITY GRANTED TO ME,
BRIGADIER GENERAL JATE.
STAY ON ALERT UNTIL SHE'S BEEN SAFELY RETURNED.
UNTIL NEXT TIME, TREASURE HUNTERS.
WAAHN! THAT WAS SO SCARY!

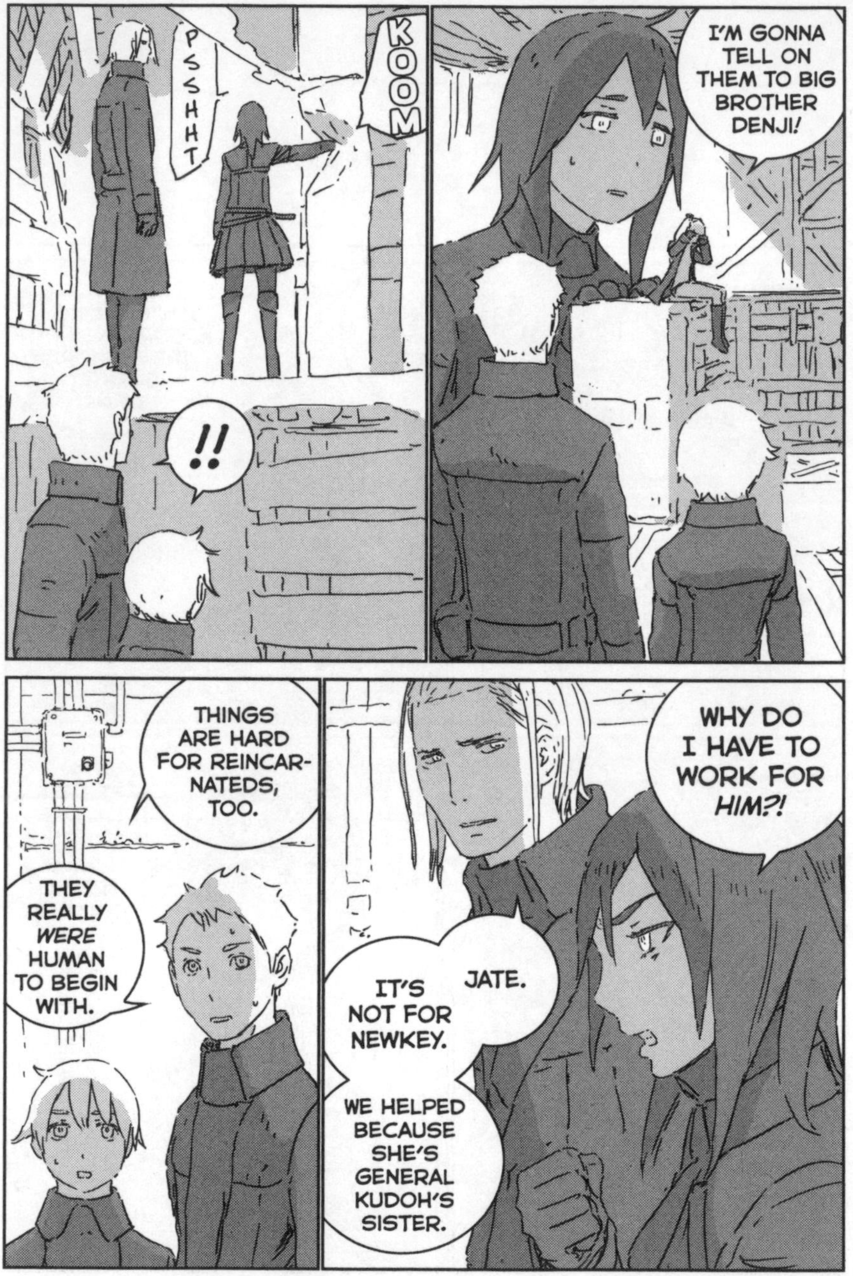
I'M GONNA TELL ON THEM TO BIG BROTHER DENJI!
KOOM
PSSHHT
!!
WHY DO I HAVE TO WORK FOR *HIM?!*
JATE. IT'S NOT FOR NEWKEY.
WE HELPED BECAUSE SHE'S GENERAL KUDOH'S SISTER.
THINGS ARE HARD FOR REINCAR-NATEDS, TOO.
THEY REALLY *WERE* HUMAN TO BEGIN WITH.

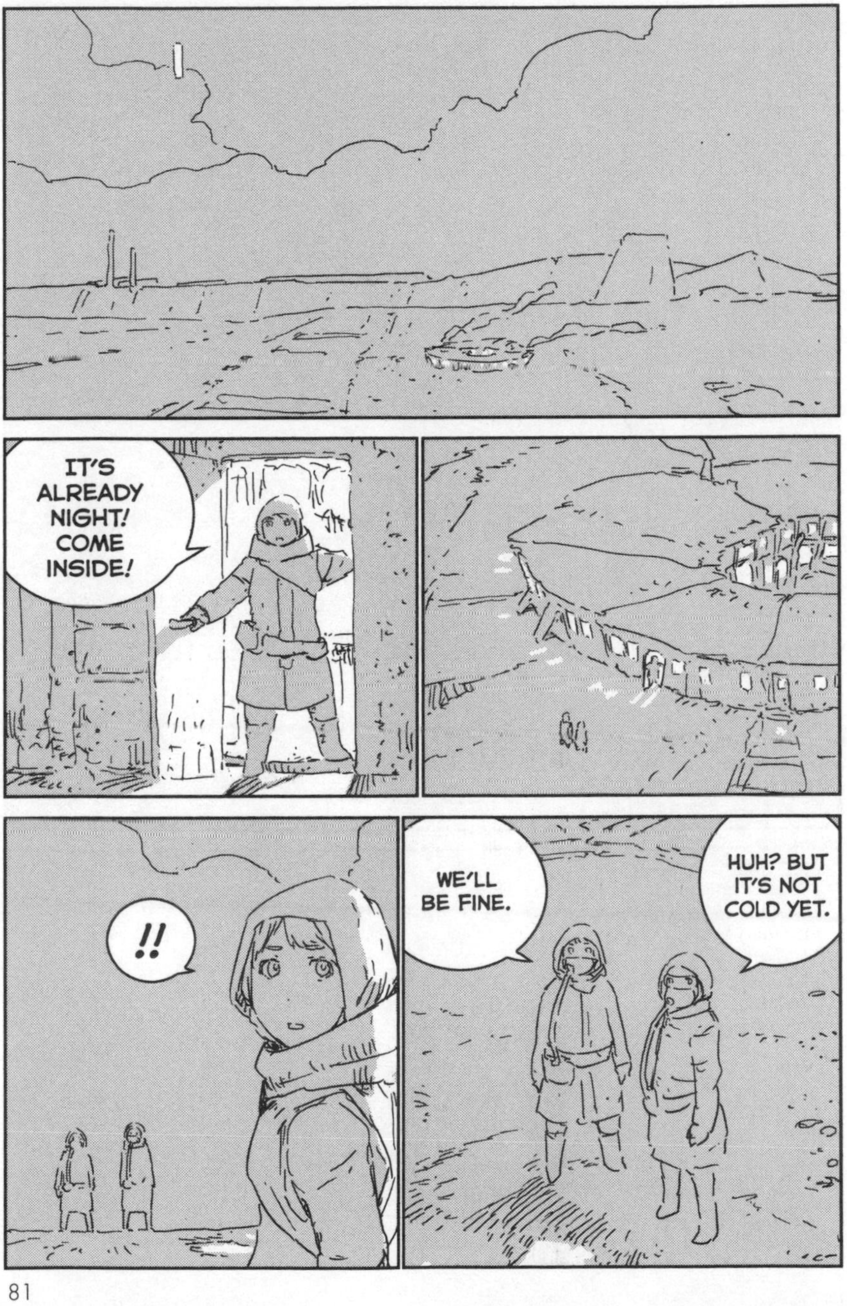
IT'S ALREADY NIGHT! COME INSIDE!
HUH? BUT IT'S NOT COLD YET.
WE'LL BE FINE.
!!

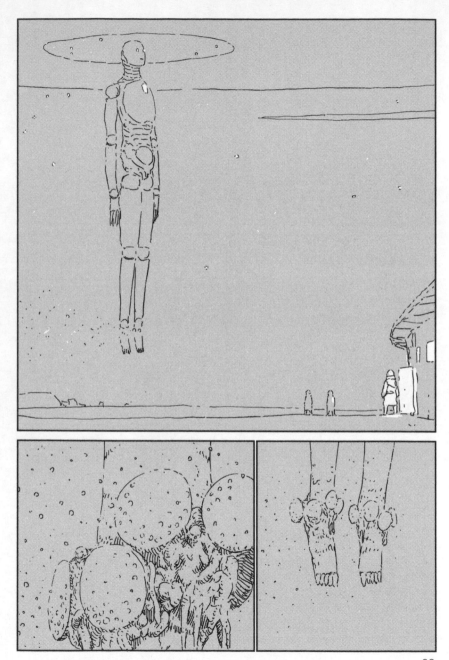

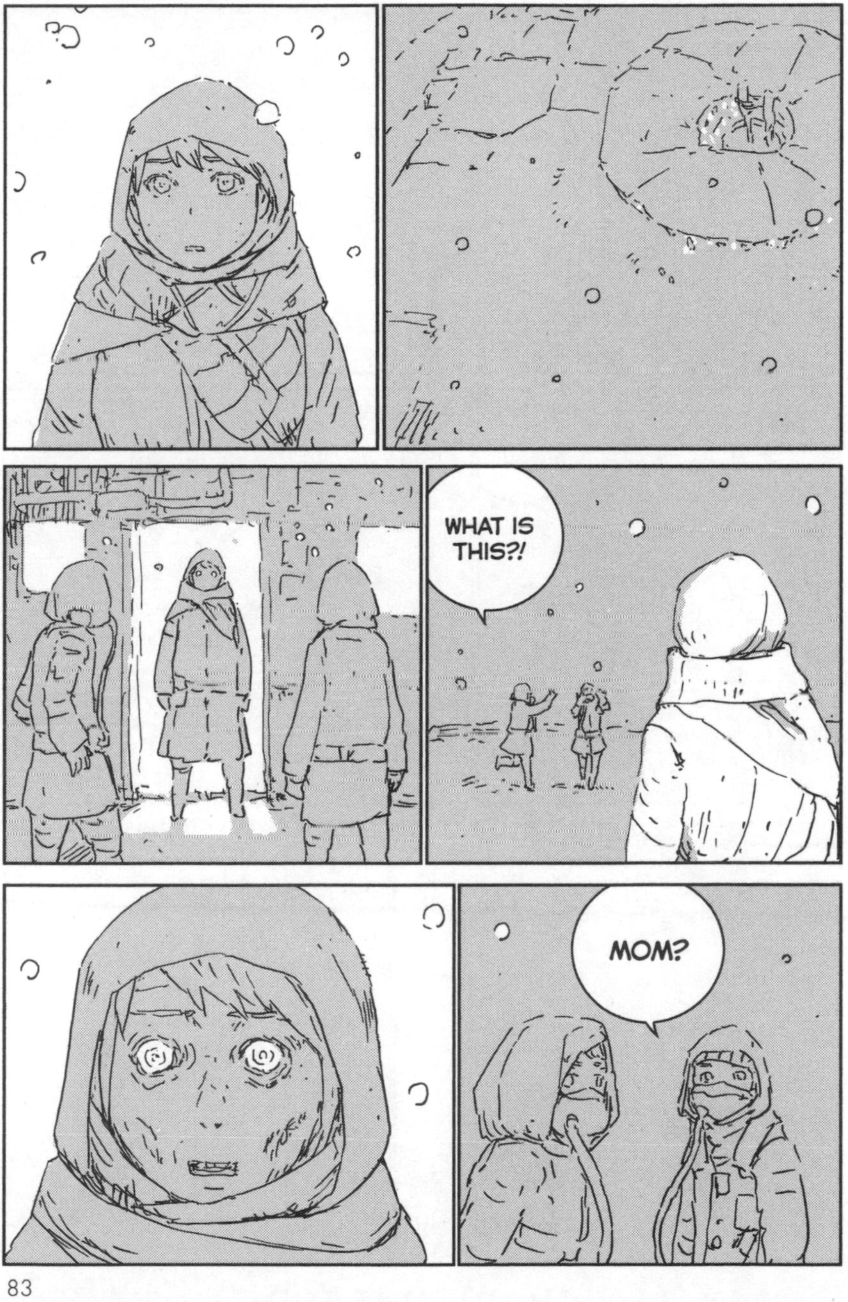
WHAT IS THIS?!
MOM?

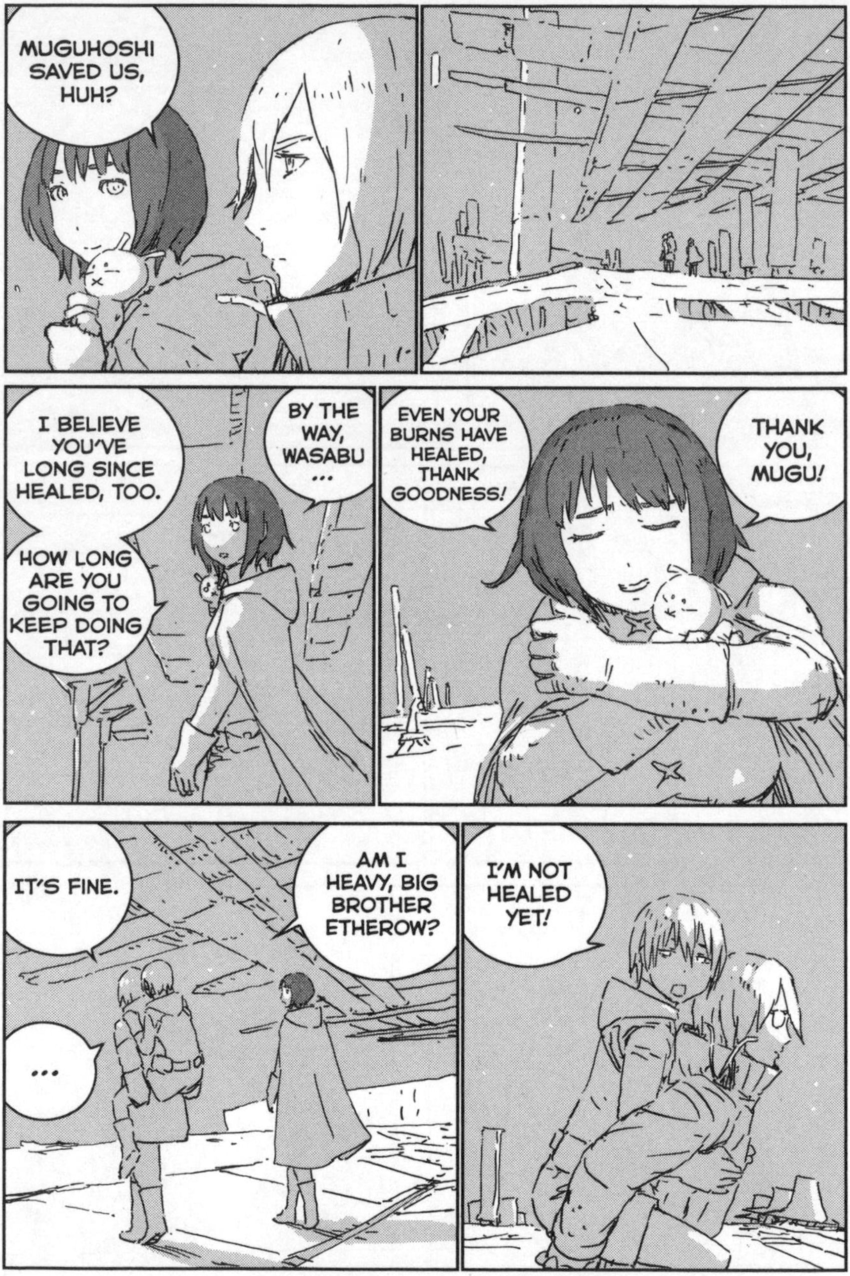
MUGUHOSHI SAVED US, HUH?
THANK YOU, MUGU!
EVEN YOUR BURNS HAVE HEALED, THANK GOODNESS!
BY THE WAY, WASABU ...
I BELIEVE YOU'VE LONG SINCE HEALED, TOO.
HOW LONG ARE YOU GOING TO KEEP DOING THAT?
I'M NOT HEALED YET!
AM I HEAVY, BIG BROTHER ETHEROW?
IT'S FINE.
...

CHAPTER 45 END

APOSIMZ

CHAPTER 46

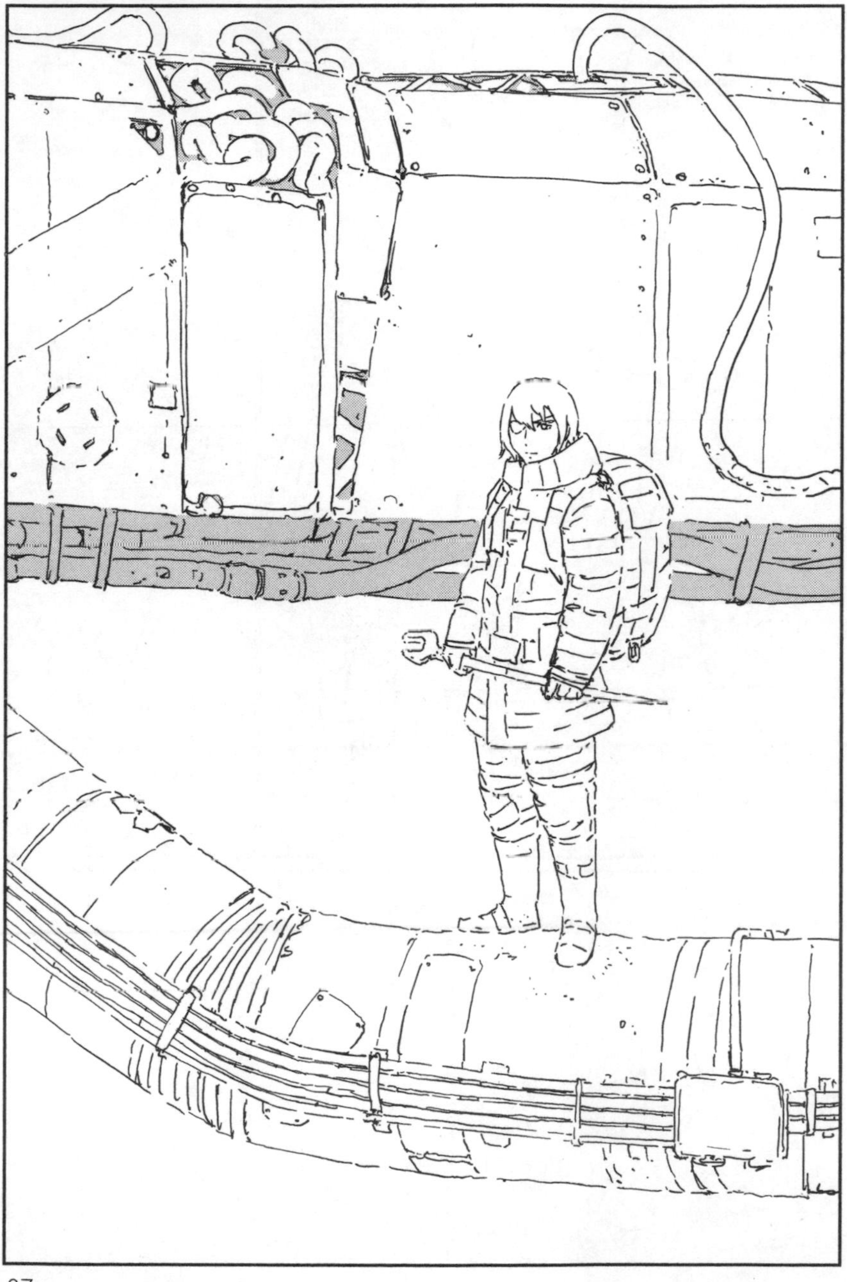

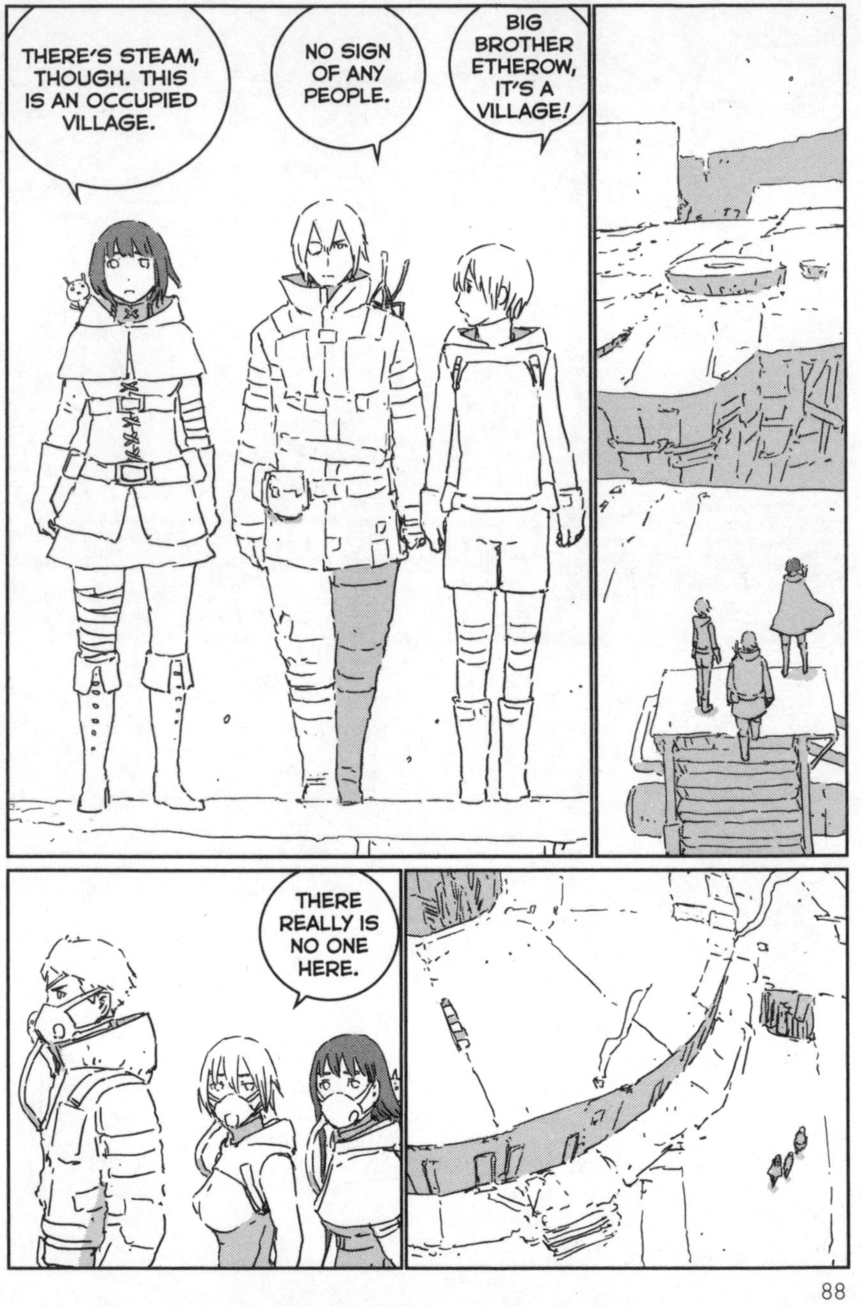
BIG BROTHER ETHEROW, IT'S A VILLAGE!
NO SIGN OF ANY PEOPLE.
THERE'S STEAM, THOUGH. THIS IS AN OCCUPIED VILLAGE.
THERE REALLY IS NO ONE HERE.

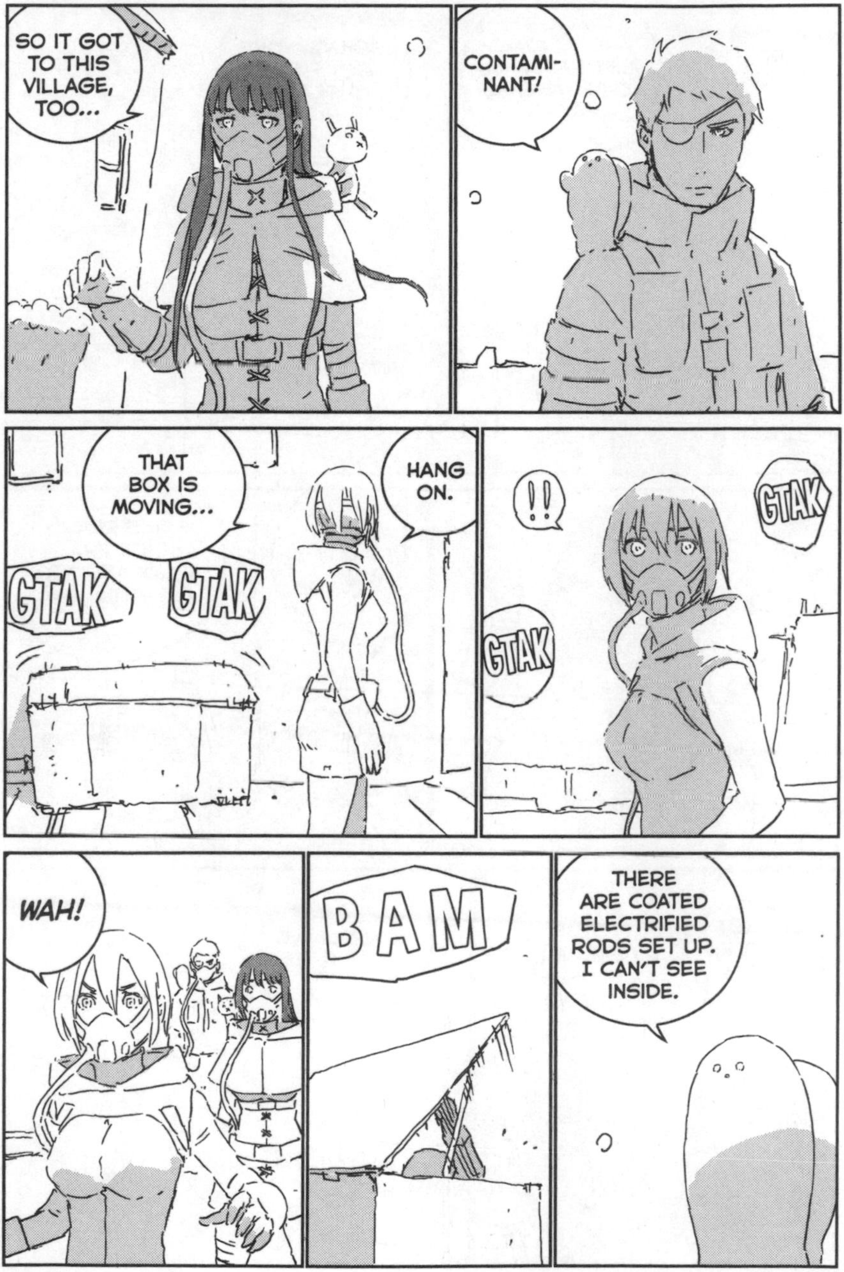
CONTAMI-NANT!
SO IT GOT TO THIS VILLAGE, TOO...
GTAK
!!
GTAK
HANG ON.
THAT BOX IS MOVING...
GTAK
GTAK
THERE ARE COATED ELECTRIFIED RODS SET UP. I CAN'T SEE INSIDE.
BAM
WAH!

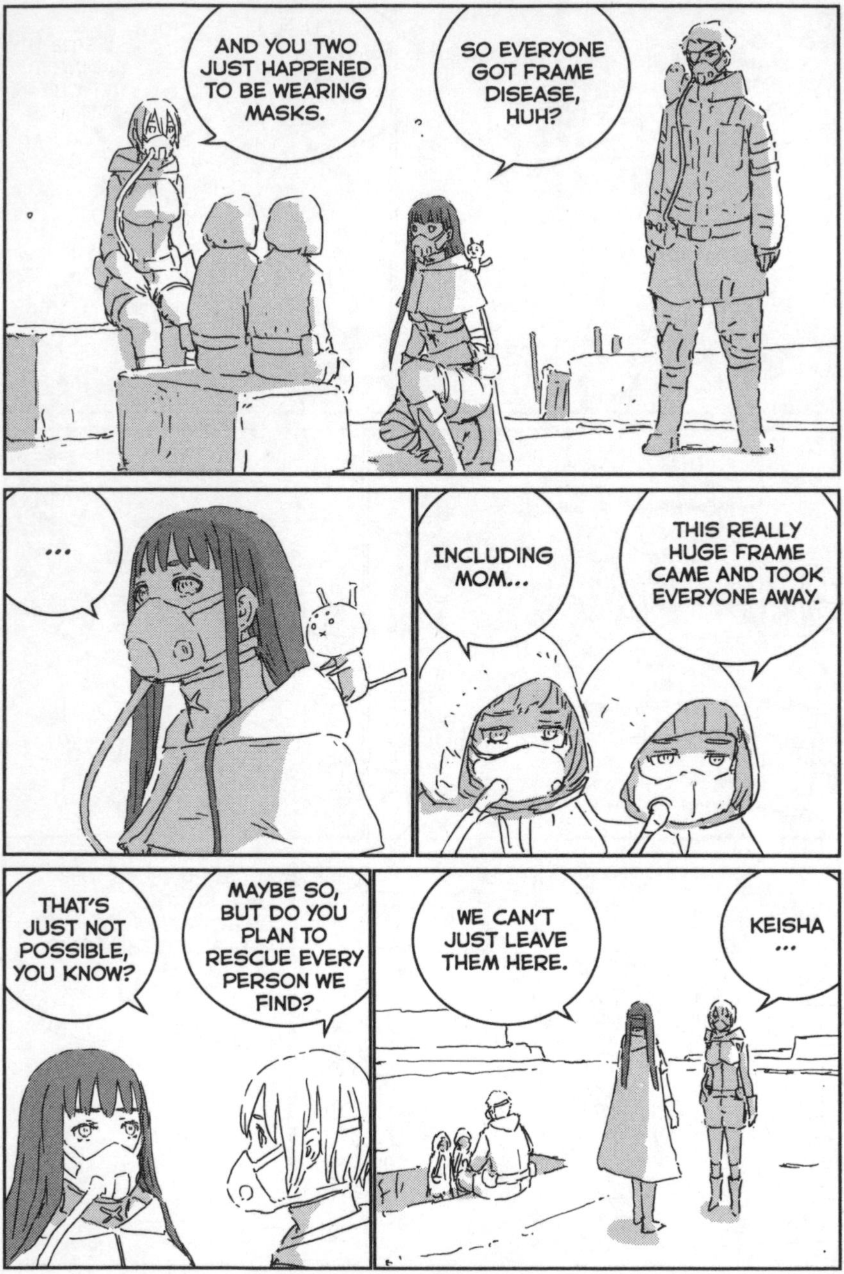
SO EVERYONE GOT FRAME DISEASE, HUH?
AND YOU TWO JUST HAPPENED TO BE WEARING MASKS.
THIS REALLY HUGE FRAME CAME AND TOOK EVERYONE AWAY.
INCLUDING MOM...
...
KEISHA ...
WE CAN'T JUST LEAVE THEM HERE.
MAYBE SO, BUT DO YOU PLAN TO RESCUE EVERY PERSON WE FIND?
THAT'S JUST NOT POSSIBLE, YOU KNOW?

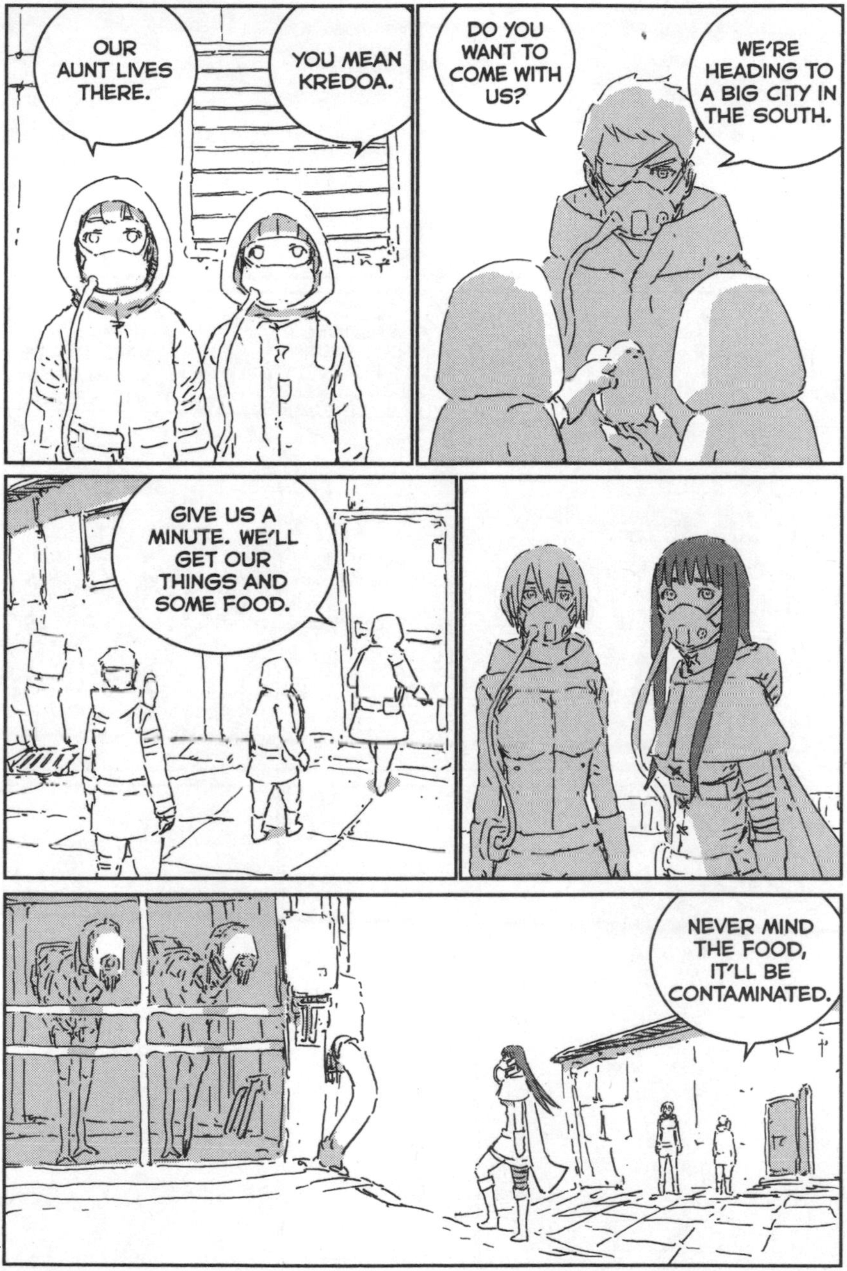
WE'RE HEADING TO A BIG CITY IN THE SOUTH.
DO YOU WANT TO COME WITH US?
YOU MEAN KREDOA.
OUR AUNT LIVES THERE.
GIVE US A MINUTE. WE'LL GET OUR THINGS AND SOME FOOD.
NEVER MIND THE FOOD, IT'LL BE CONTAMINATED.

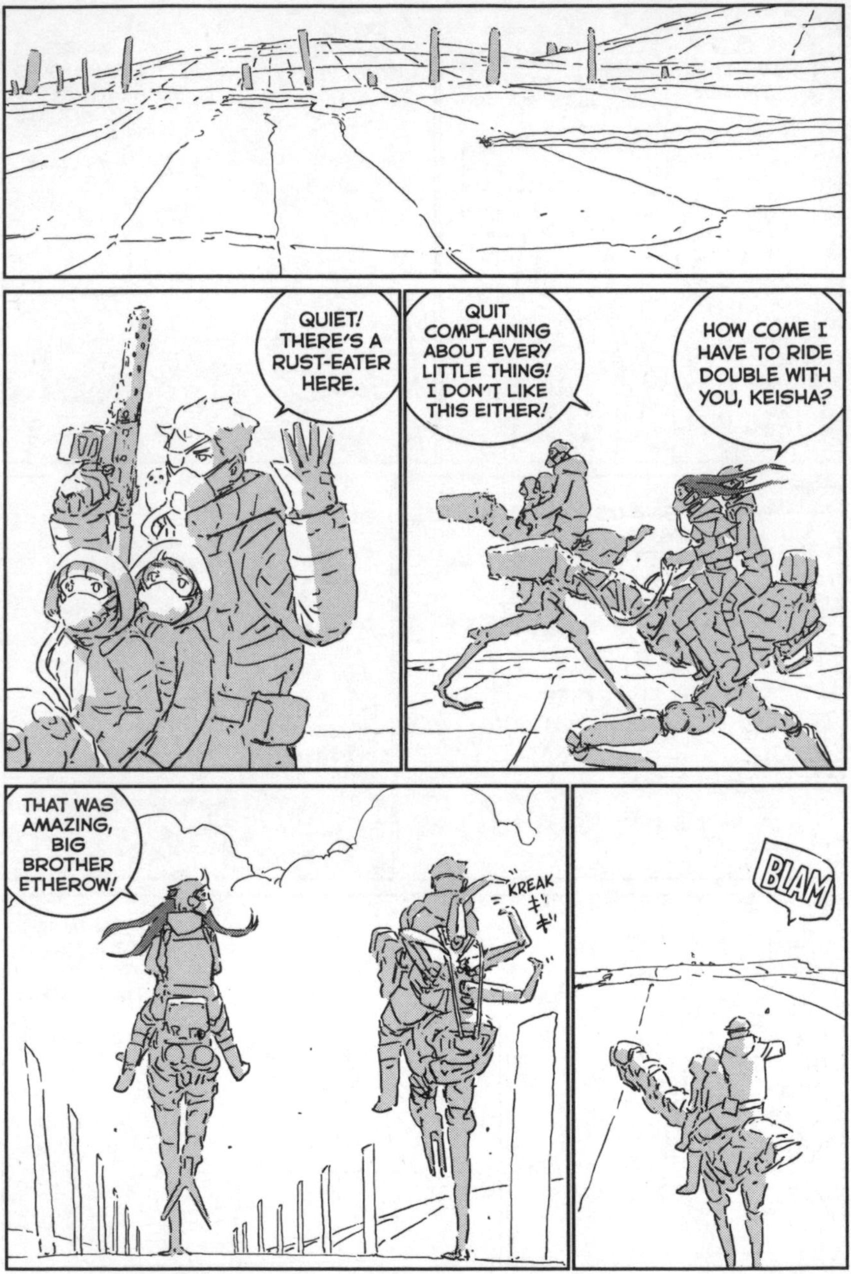
HOW COME I HAVE TO RIDE DOUBLE WITH YOU, KEISHA?
QUIT COMPLAINING ABOUT EVERY LITTLE THING! I DON'T LIKE THIS EITHER!
QUIET! THERE'S A RUST-EATER HERE.
BLAM
THAT WAS AMAZING, BIG BROTHER ETHEROW!
KREAK

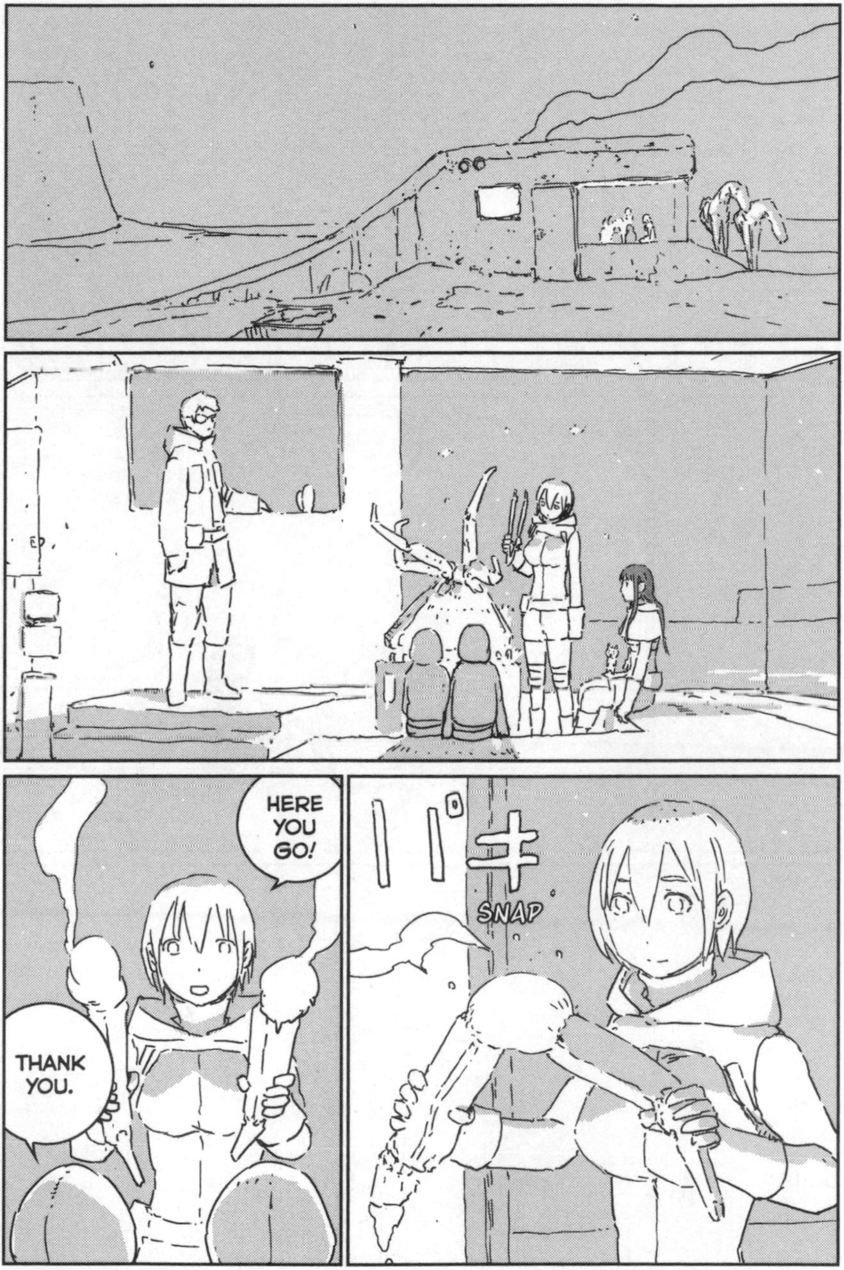
パキ
SNAP
HERE YOU GO!
THANK YOU.

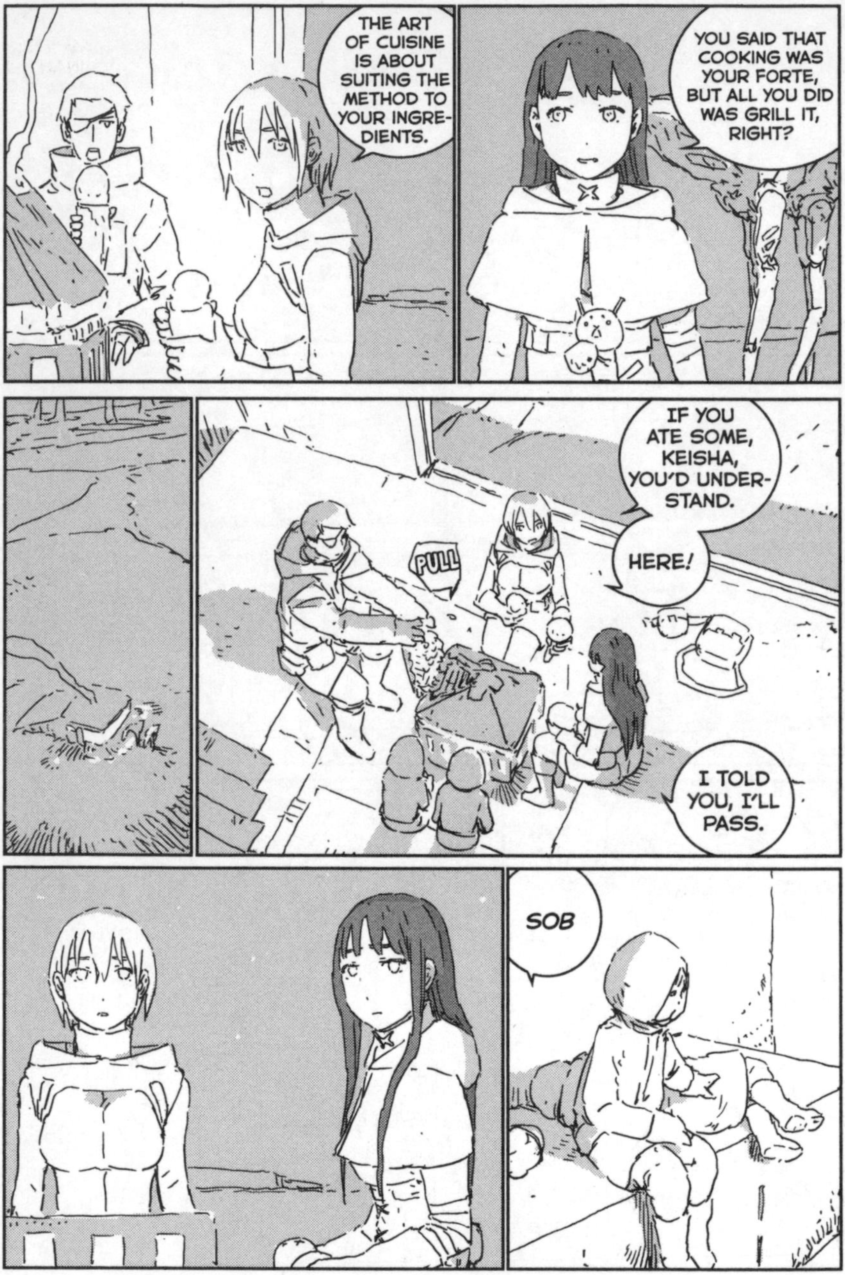
YOU SAID THAT COOKING WAS YOUR FORTE, BUT ALL YOU DID WAS GRILL IT, RIGHT?
THE ART OF CUISINE IS ABOUT SUITING THE METHOD TO YOUR INGREDIENTS.
IF YOU ATE SOME, KEISHA, YOU'D UNDERSTAND.
HERE!
PULL
I TOLD YOU, I'LL PASS.
SOB

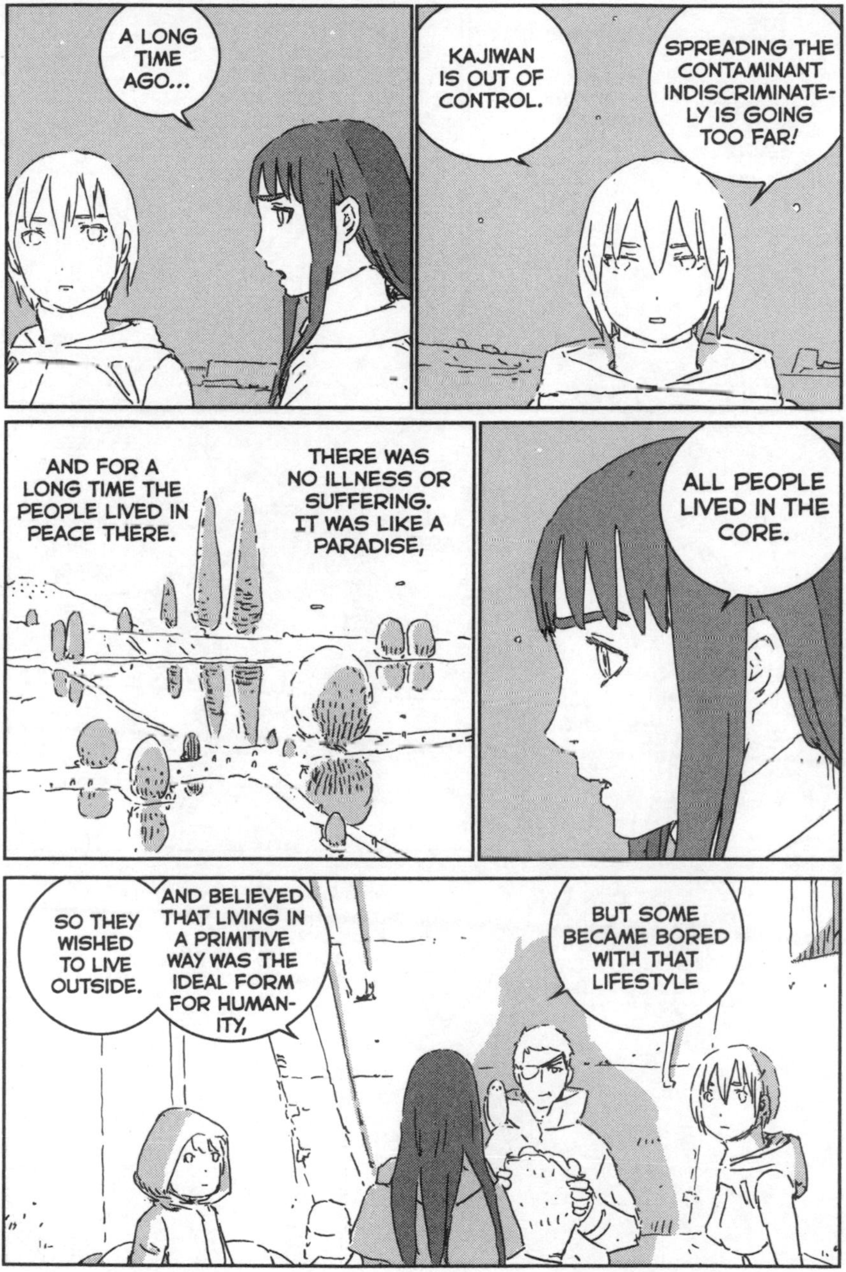
SPREADING THE CONTAMINANT INDISCRIMINATE-LY IS GOING TOO FAR!
KAJIWAN IS OUT OF CONTROL.
A LONG TIME AGO...
ALL PEOPLE LIVED IN THE CORE.
THERE WAS NO ILLNESS OR SUFFERING. IT WAS LIKE A PARADISE,
AND FOR A LONG TIME THE PEOPLE LIVED IN PEACE THERE.
BUT SOME BECAME BORED WITH THAT LIFESTYLE
AND BELIEVED THAT LIVING IN A PRIMITIVE WAY WAS THE IDEAL FORM FOR HUMAN-ITY,
SO THEY WISHED TO LIVE OUTSIDE.

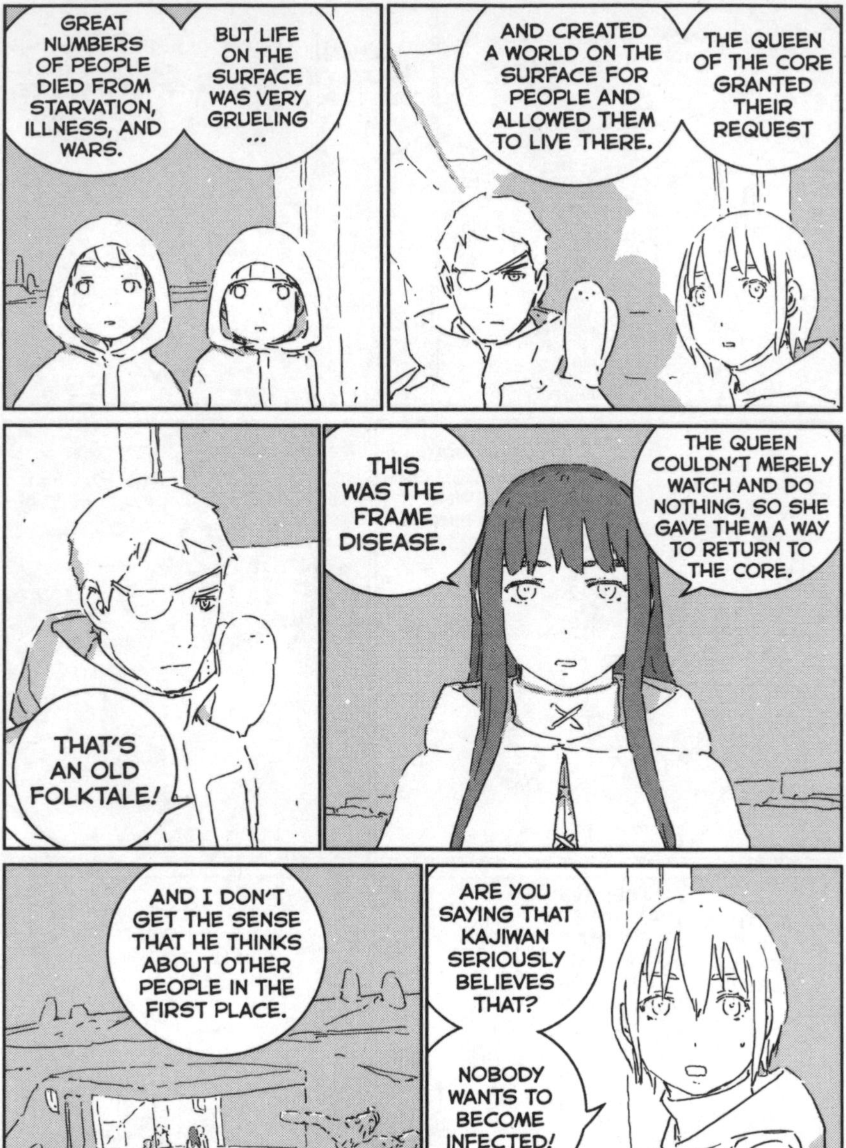
THE QUEEN OF THE CORE GRANTED THEIR REQUEST
AND CREATED A WORLD ON THE SURFACE FOR PEOPLE AND ALLOWED THEM TO LIVE THERE.
BUT LIFE ON THE SURFACE WAS VERY GRUELING ...
GREAT NUMBERS OF PEOPLE DIED FROM STARVATION, ILLNESS, AND WARS.
THE QUEEN COULDN'T MERELY WATCH AND DO NOTHING, SO SHE GAVE THEM A WAY TO RETURN TO THE CORE.
THIS WAS THE FRAME DISEASE.
THAT'S AN OLD FOLKTALE!
ARE YOU SAYING THAT KAJIWAN SERIOUSLY BELIEVES THAT?
NOBODY WANTS TO BECOME INFECTED!
AND I DON'T GET THE SENSE THAT HE THINKS ABOUT OTHER PEOPLE IN THE FIRST PLACE.

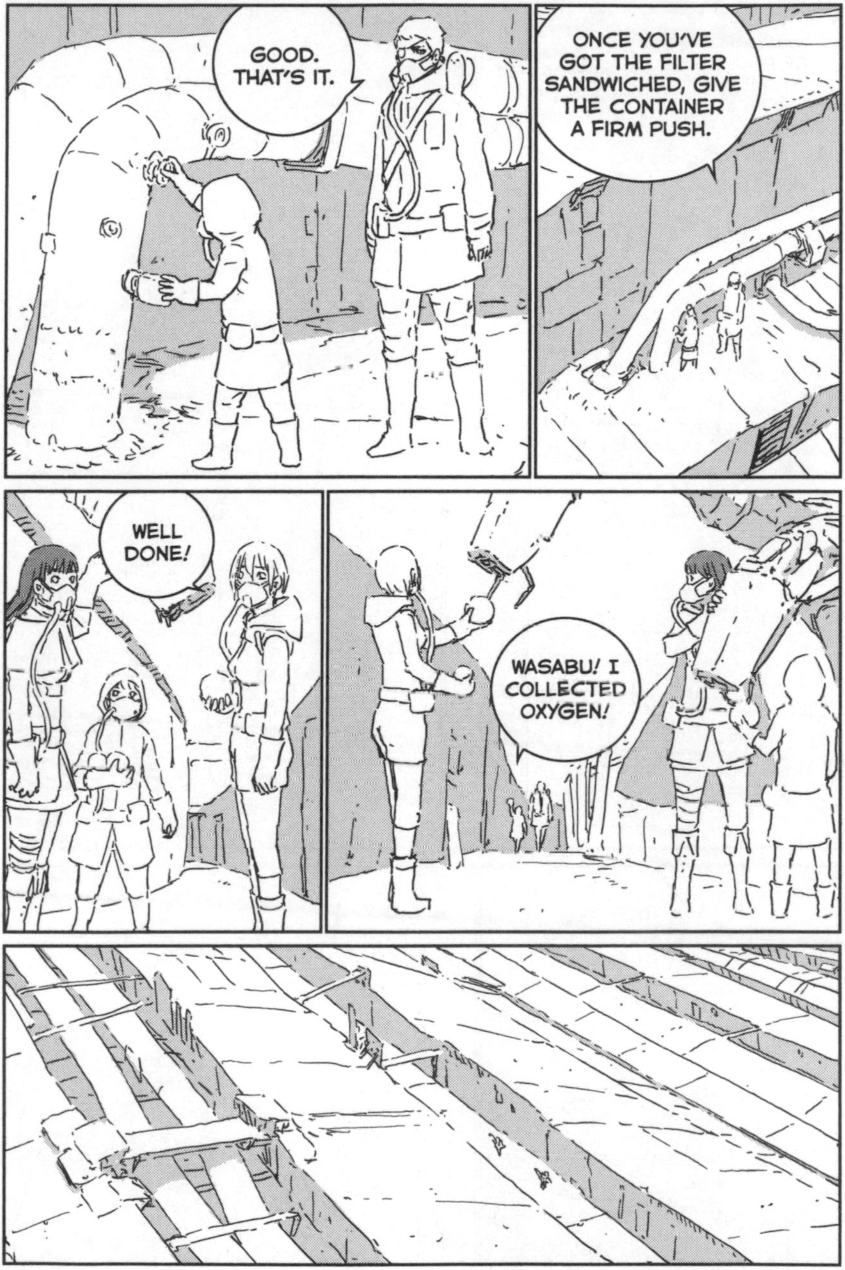
ONCE YOU'VE GOT THE FILTER SANDWICHED, GIVE THE CONTAINER A FIRM PUSH.
GOOD. THAT'S IT.
WASABU! I COLLECTED OXYGEN!
WELL DONE!

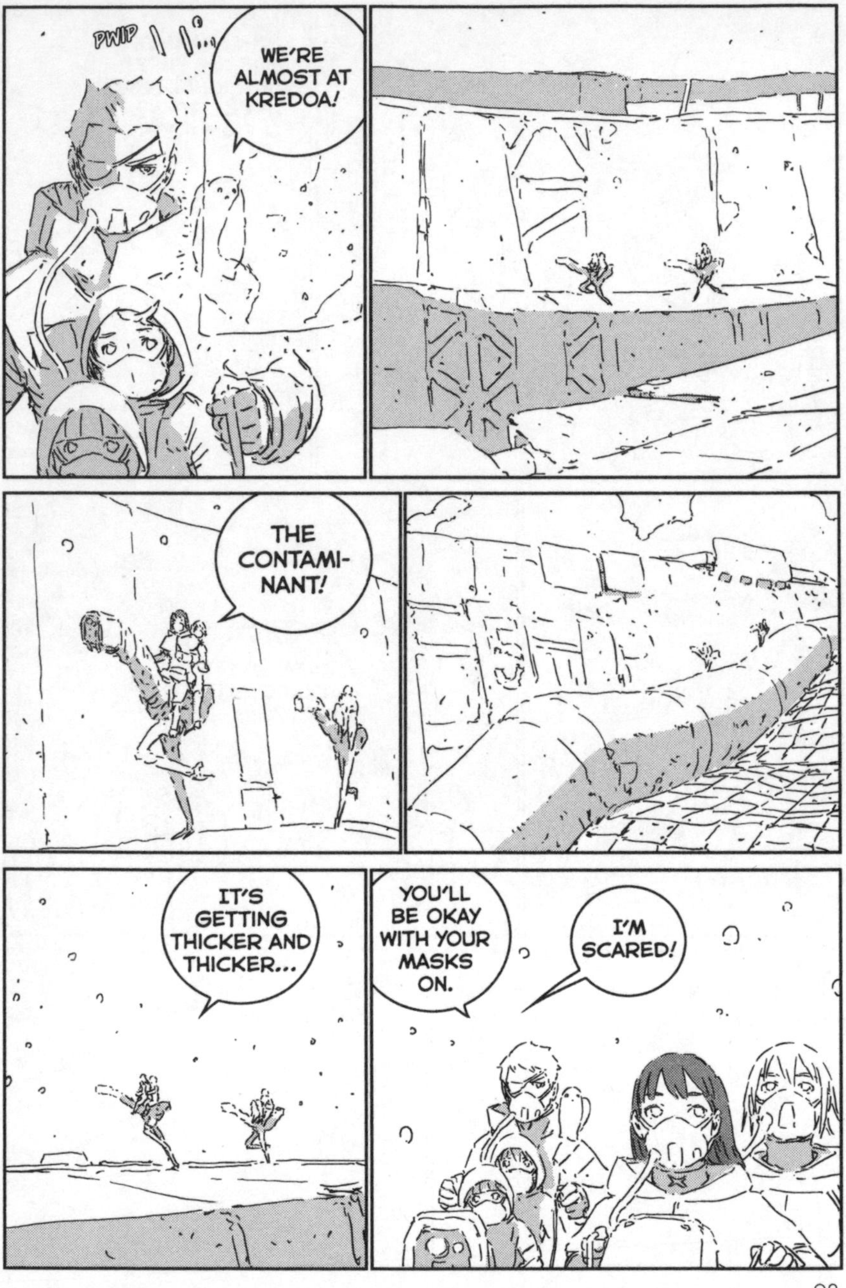
PWIP
WE'RE ALMOST AT KREDOA!
THE CONTAMI-NANT!
I'M SCARED!
YOU'LL BE OKAY WITH YOUR MASKS ON.
IT'S GETTING THICKER AND THICKER...

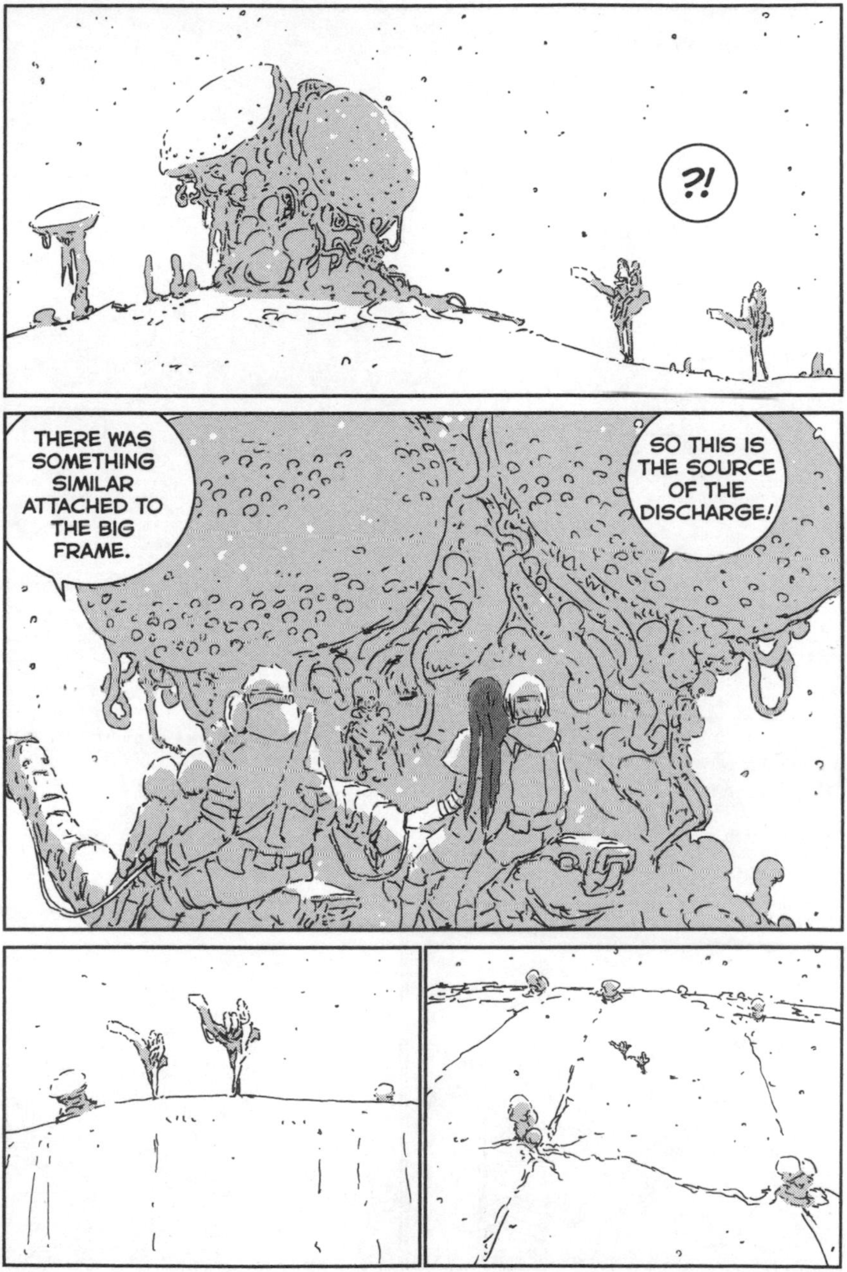
?!
SO THIS IS THE SOURCE OF THE DISCHARGE!
THERE WAS SOMETHING SIMILAR ATTACHED TO THE BIG FRAME.

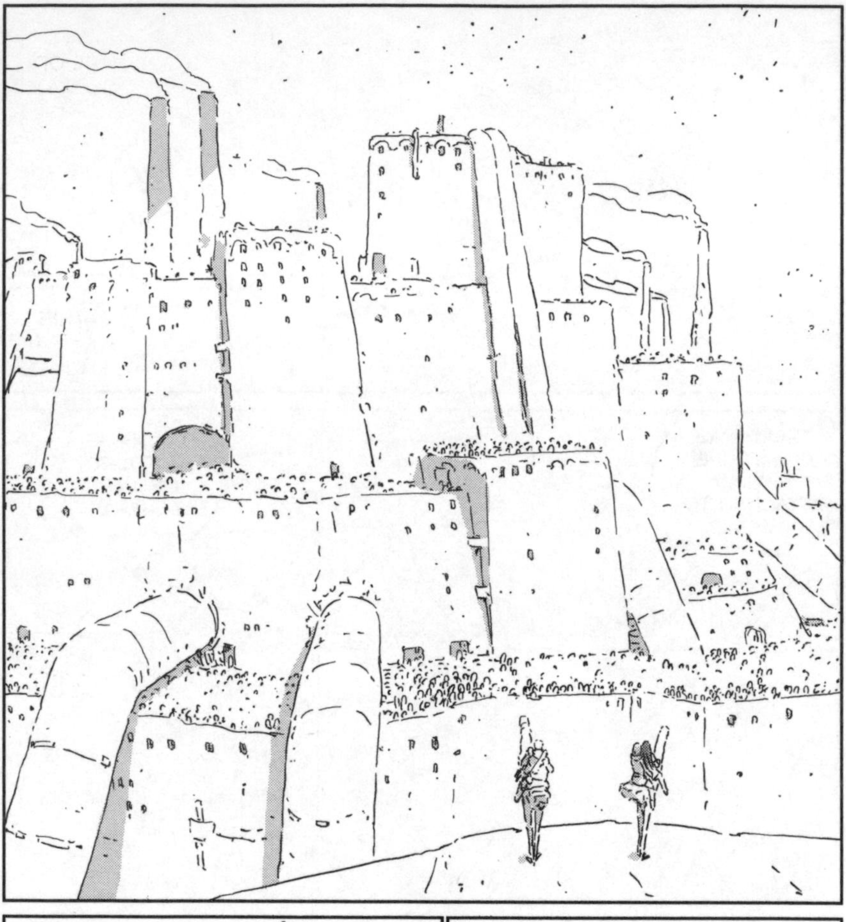

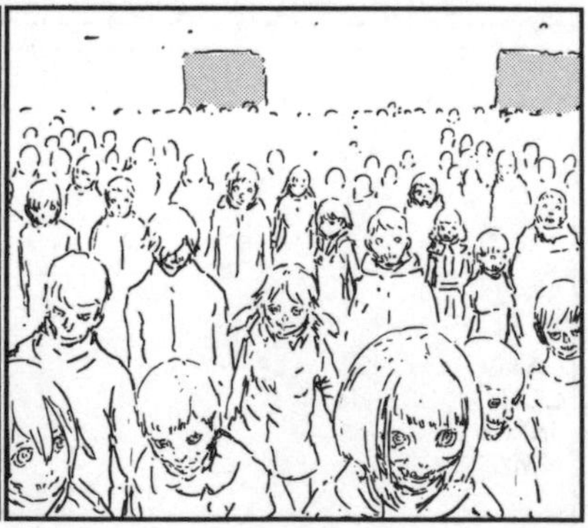

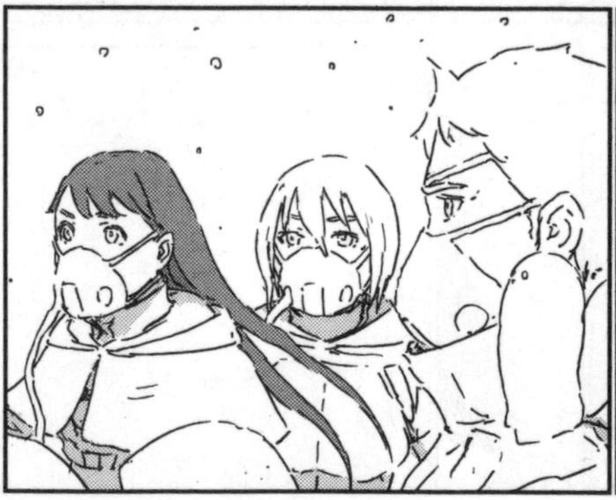

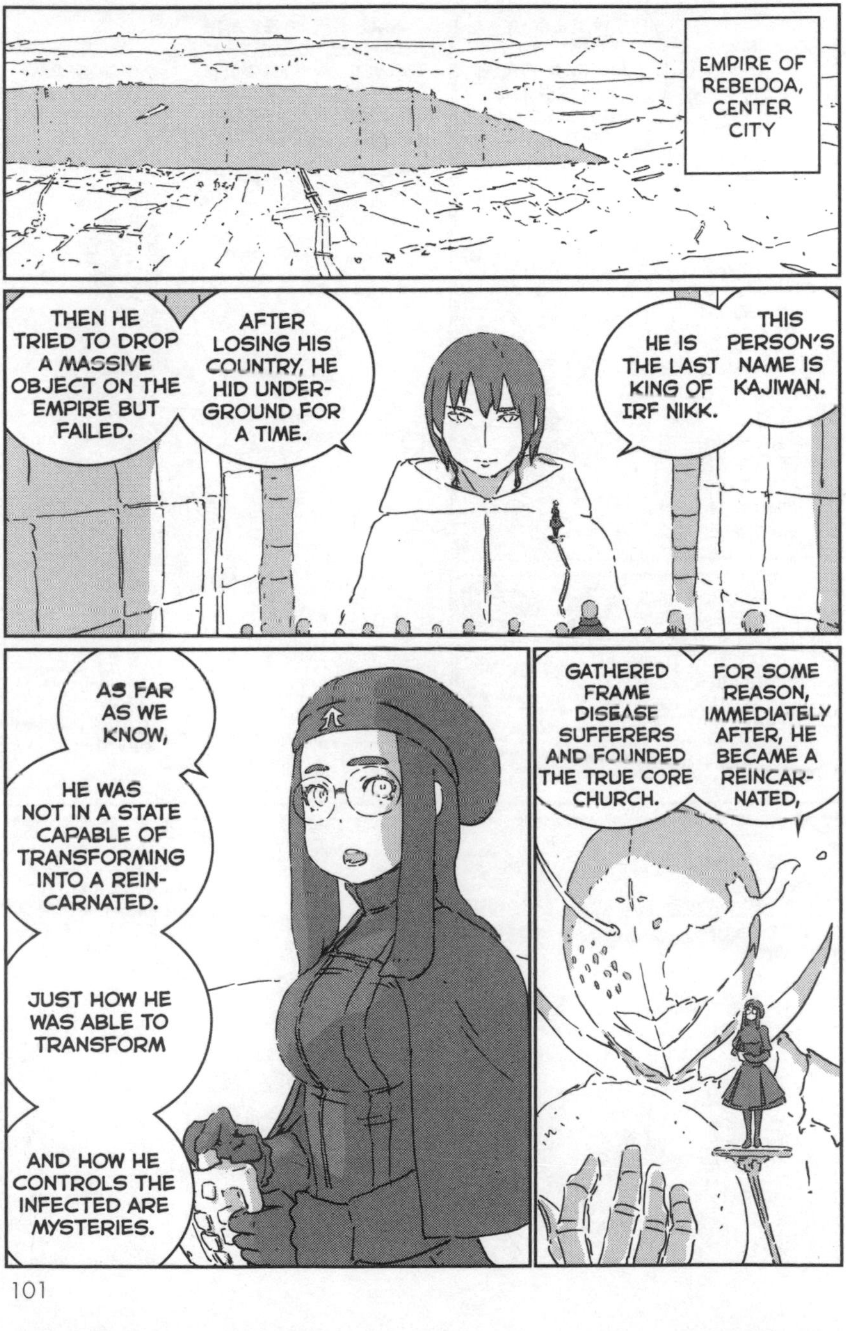
EMPIRE OF REBEDOA, CENTER CITY
THIS PERSON'S NAME IS KAJIWAN.
HE IS THE LAST KING OF IRF NIKK.
AFTER LOSING HIS COUNTRY, HE HID UNDER-GROUND FOR A TIME.
THEN HE TRIED TO DROP A MASSIVE OBJECT ON THE EMPIRE BUT FAILED.
FOR SOME REASON, IMMEDIATELY AFTER, HE BECAME A REINCAR-NATED,
GATHERED FRAME DISEASE SUFFERERS AND FOUNDED THE TRUE CORE CHURCH.
AS FAR AS WE KNOW,
HE WAS NOT IN A STATE CAPABLE OF TRANSFORMING INTO A REIN-CARNATED.
JUST HOW HE WAS ABLE TO TRANSFORM
AND HOW HE CONTROLS THE INFECTED ARE MYSTERIES.

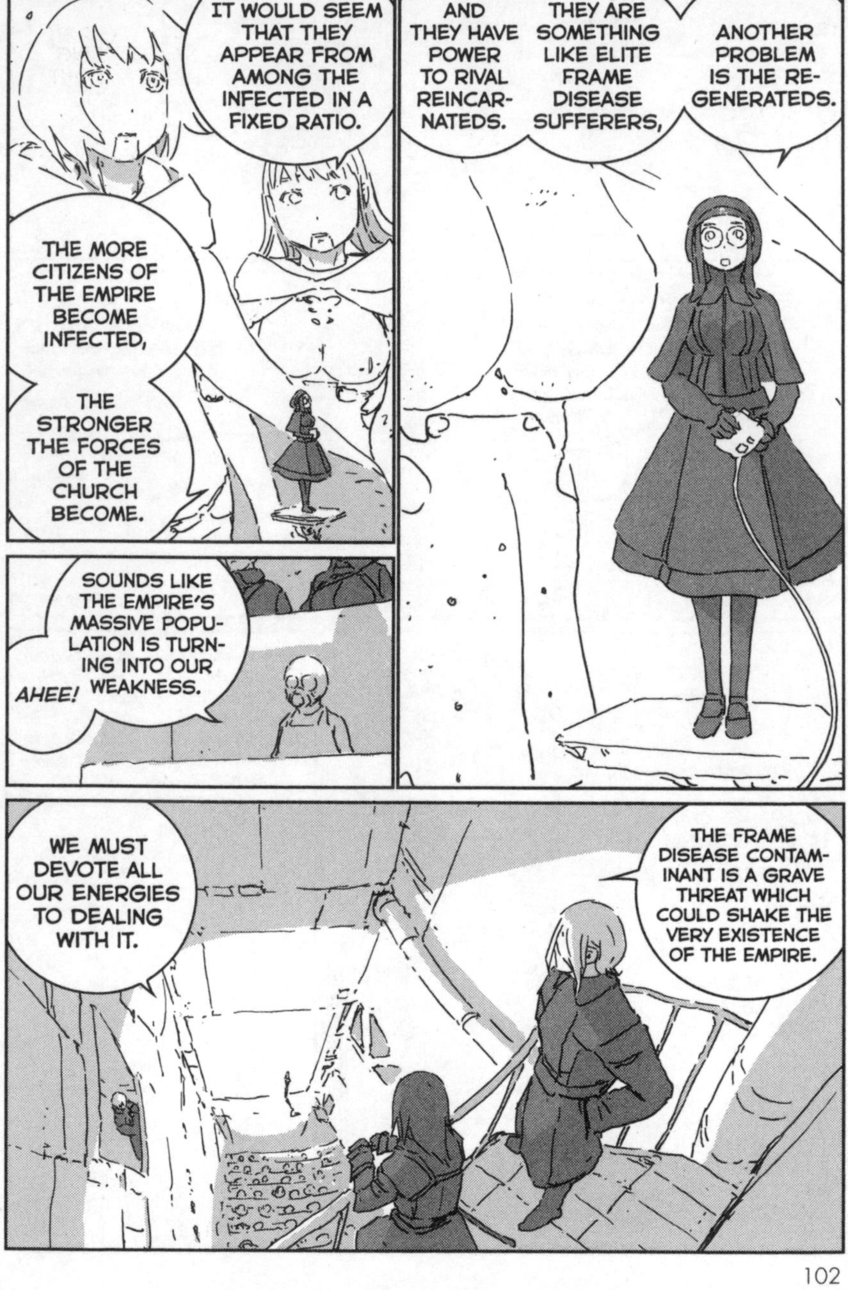
ANOTHER PROBLEM IS THE RE-GENERATEDS.
THEY ARE SOMETHING LIKE ELITE FRAME DISEASE SUFFERERS,
AND THEY HAVE POWER TO RIVAL REINCAR-NATEDS.
IT WOULD SEEM THAT THEY APPEAR FROM AMONG THE INFECTED IN A FIXED RATIO.
THE MORE CITIZENS OF THE EMPIRE BECOME INFECTED,
THE STRONGER THE FORCES OF THE CHURCH BECOME.
SOUNDS LIKE THE EMPIRE'S MASSIVE POPU-LATION IS TURN-ING INTO OUR WEAKNESS.
AHEE!
THE FRAME DISEASE CONTAM-INANT IS A GRAVE THREAT WHICH COULD SHAKE THE VERY EXISTENCE OF THE EMPIRE.
WE MUST DEVOTE ALL OUR ENERGIES TO DEALING WITH IT.

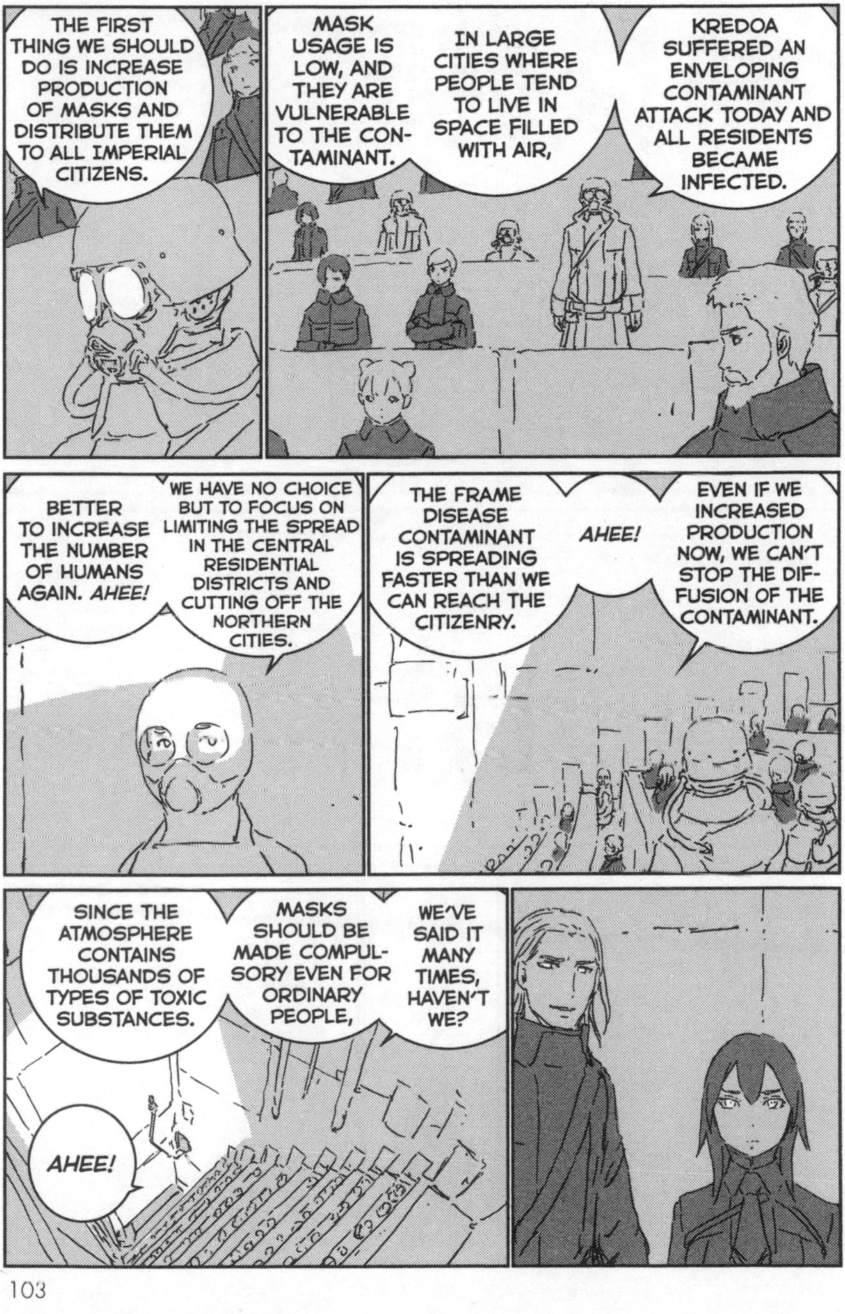
KREDOA SUFFERED AN ENVELOPING CONTAMINANT ATTACK TODAY AND ALL RESIDENTS BECAME INFECTED.
IN LARGE CITIES WHERE PEOPLE TEND TO LIVE IN SPACE FILLED WITH AIR,
MASK USAGE IS LOW, AND THEY ARE VULNERABLE TO THE CON-TAMINANT.
THE FIRST THING WE SHOULD DO IS INCREASE PRODUCTION OF MASKS AND DISTRIBUTE THEM TO ALL IMPERIAL CITIZENS.
EVEN IF WE INCREASED PRODUCTION NOW, WE CAN'T STOP THE DIF-FUSION OF THE CONTAMINANT.
AHEE!
THE FRAME DISEASE CONTAMINANT IS SPREADING FASTER THAN WE CAN REACH THE CITIZENRY.
WE HAVE NO CHOICE BUT TO FOCUS ON LIMITING THE SPREAD IN THE CENTRAL RESIDENTIAL DISTRICTS AND CUTTING OFF THE NORTHERN CITIES.
BETTER TO INCREASE THE NUMBER OF HUMANS AGAIN. AHEE!
WE'VE SAID IT MANY TIMES, HAVEN'T WE?
MASKS SHOULD BE MADE COMPUL-SORY EVEN FOR ORDINARY PEOPLE,
SINCE THE ATMOSPHERE CONTAINS THOUSANDS OF TYPES OF TOXIC SUBSTANCES.
AHEE!

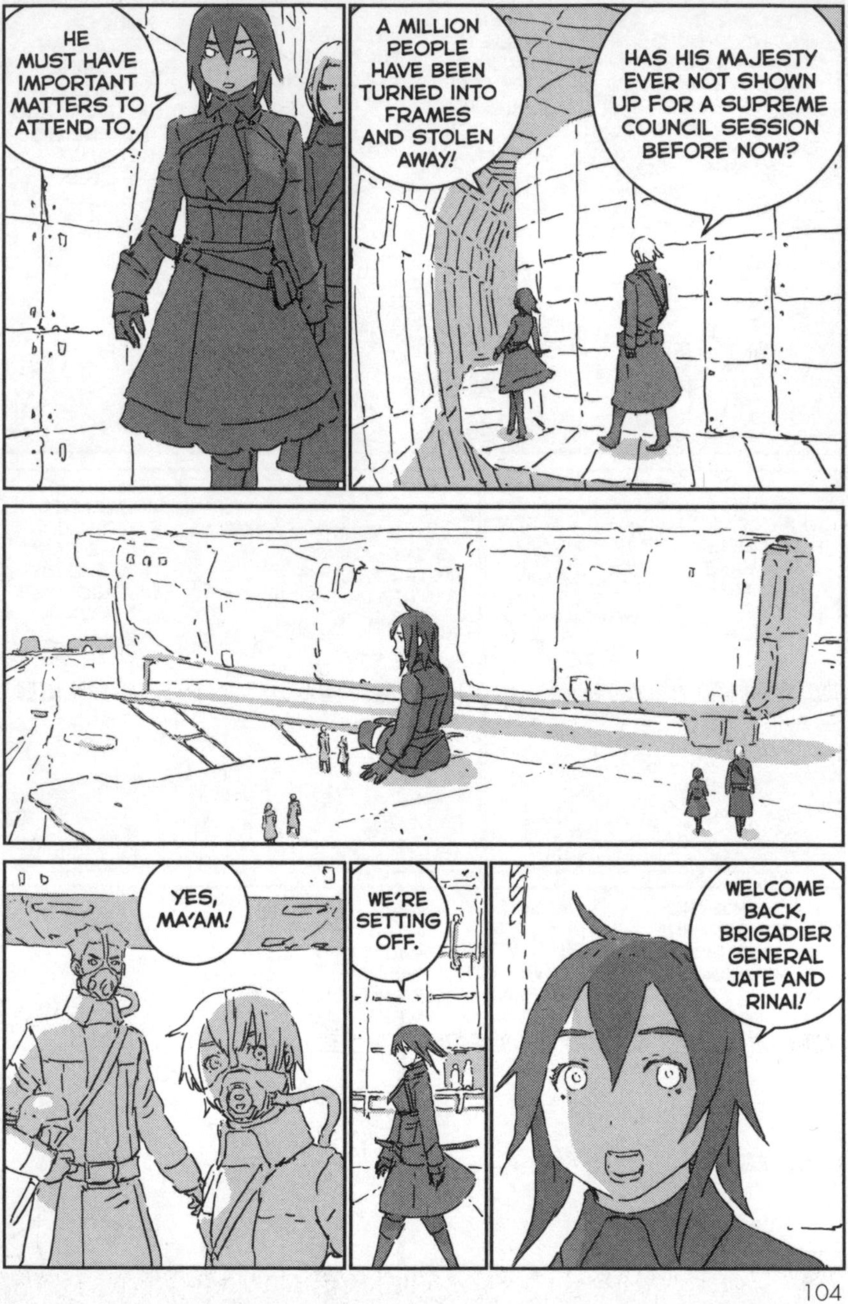
HAS HIS MAJESTY EVER NOT SHOWN UP FOR A SUPREME COUNCIL SESSION BEFORE NOW?
A MILLION PEOPLE HAVE BEEN TURNED INTO FRAMES AND STOLEN AWAY!
HE MUST HAVE IMPORTANT MATTERS TO ATTEND TO.
WELCOME BACK, BRIGADIER GENERAL JATE AND RINAI!
WE'RE SETTING OFF.
YES, MA'AM!

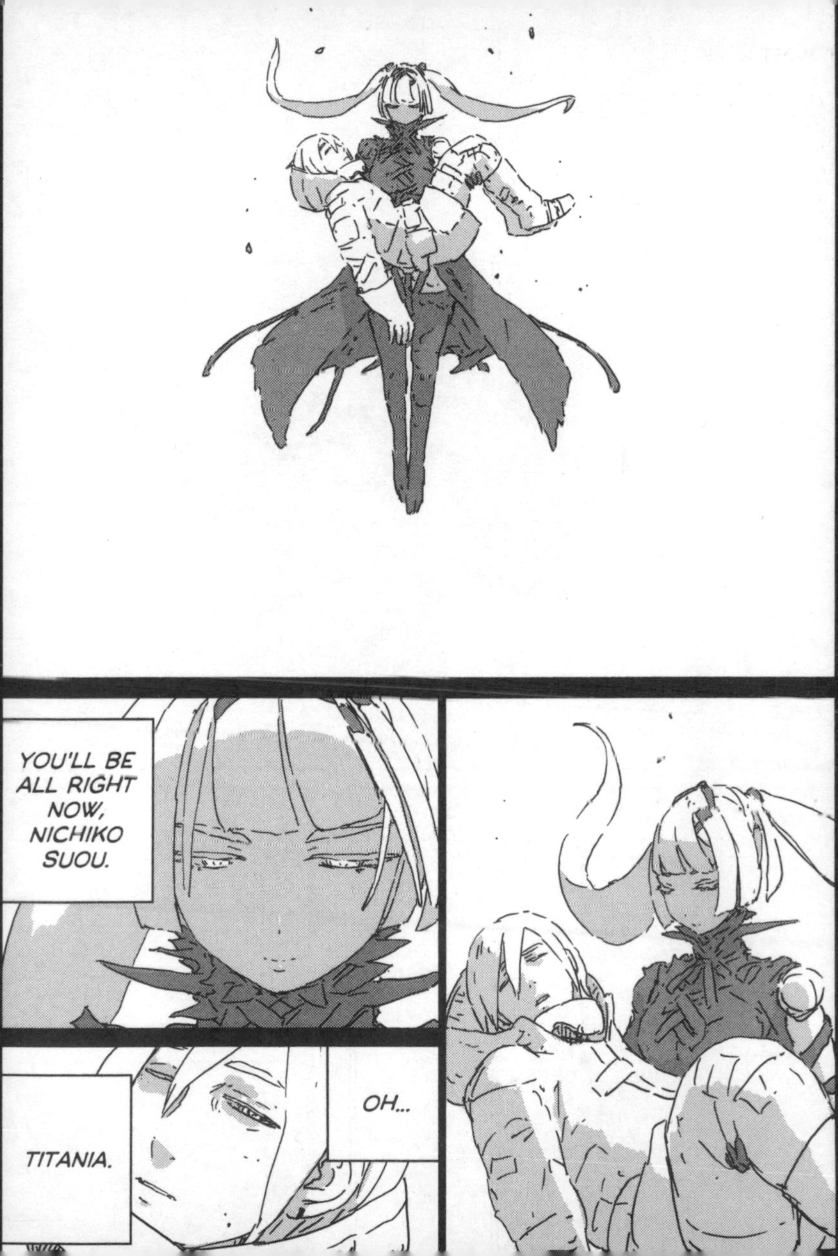
YOU'LL BE ALL RIGHT NOW, NICHIKO SUOU.
OH...
TITANIA.

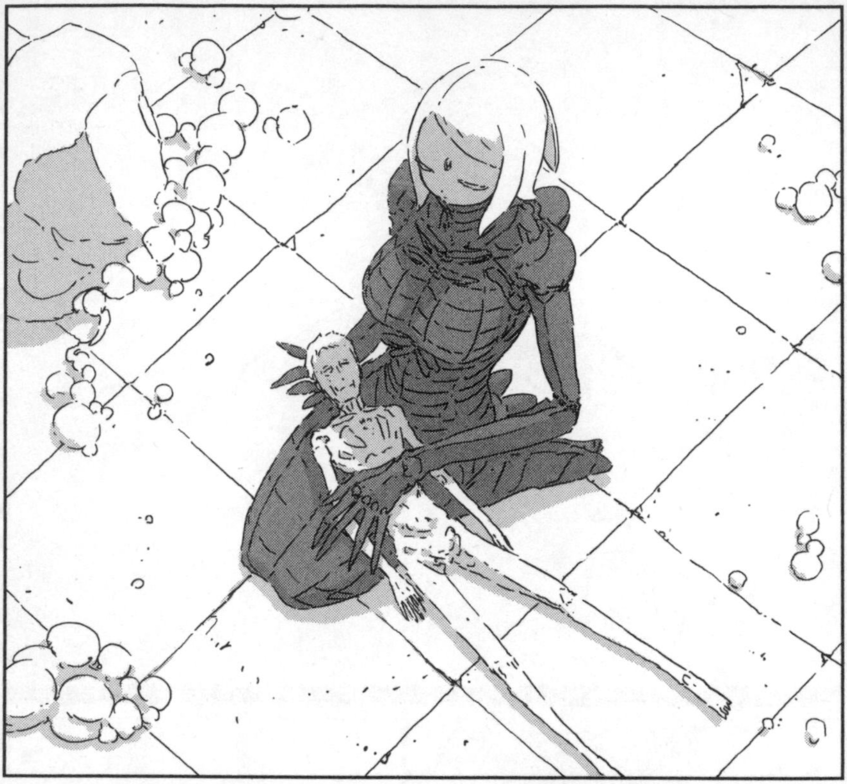

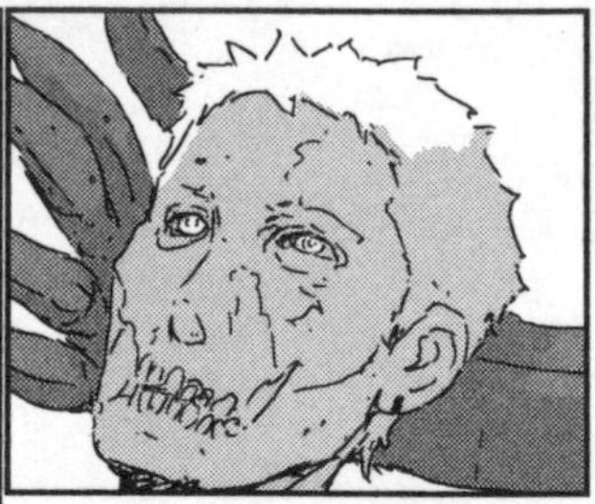

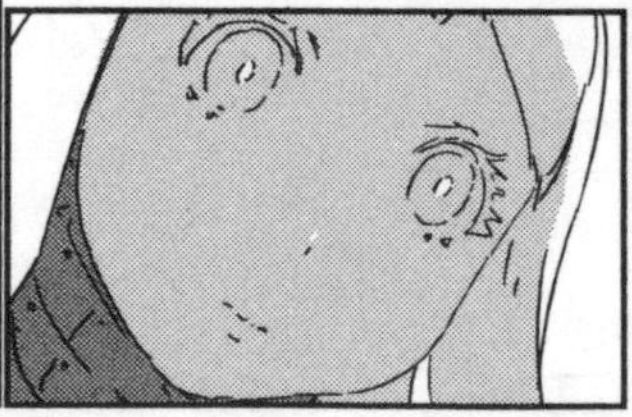

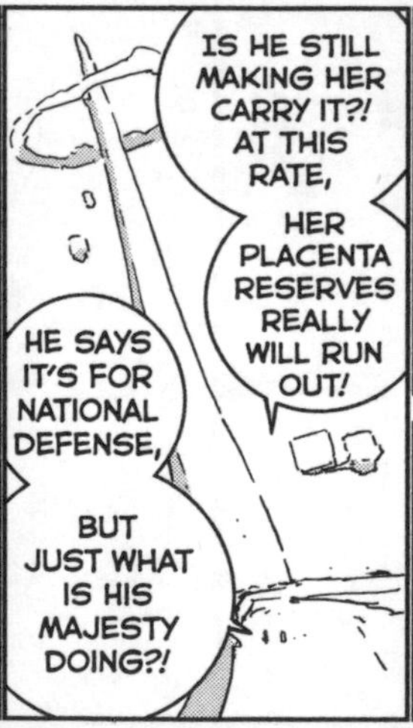
IS HE STILL MAKING HER CARRY IT?! AT THIS RATE,
HER PLACENTA RESERVES REALLY WILL RUN OUT!
HE SAYS IT'S FOR NATIONAL DEFENSE,
BUT JUST WHAT IS HIS MAJESTY DOING?!

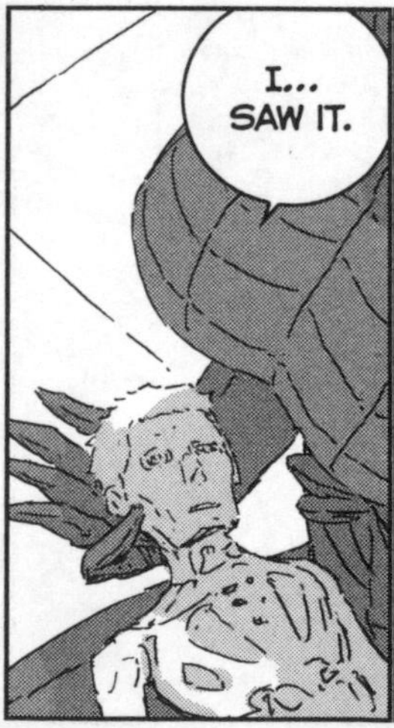
I... SAW IT.

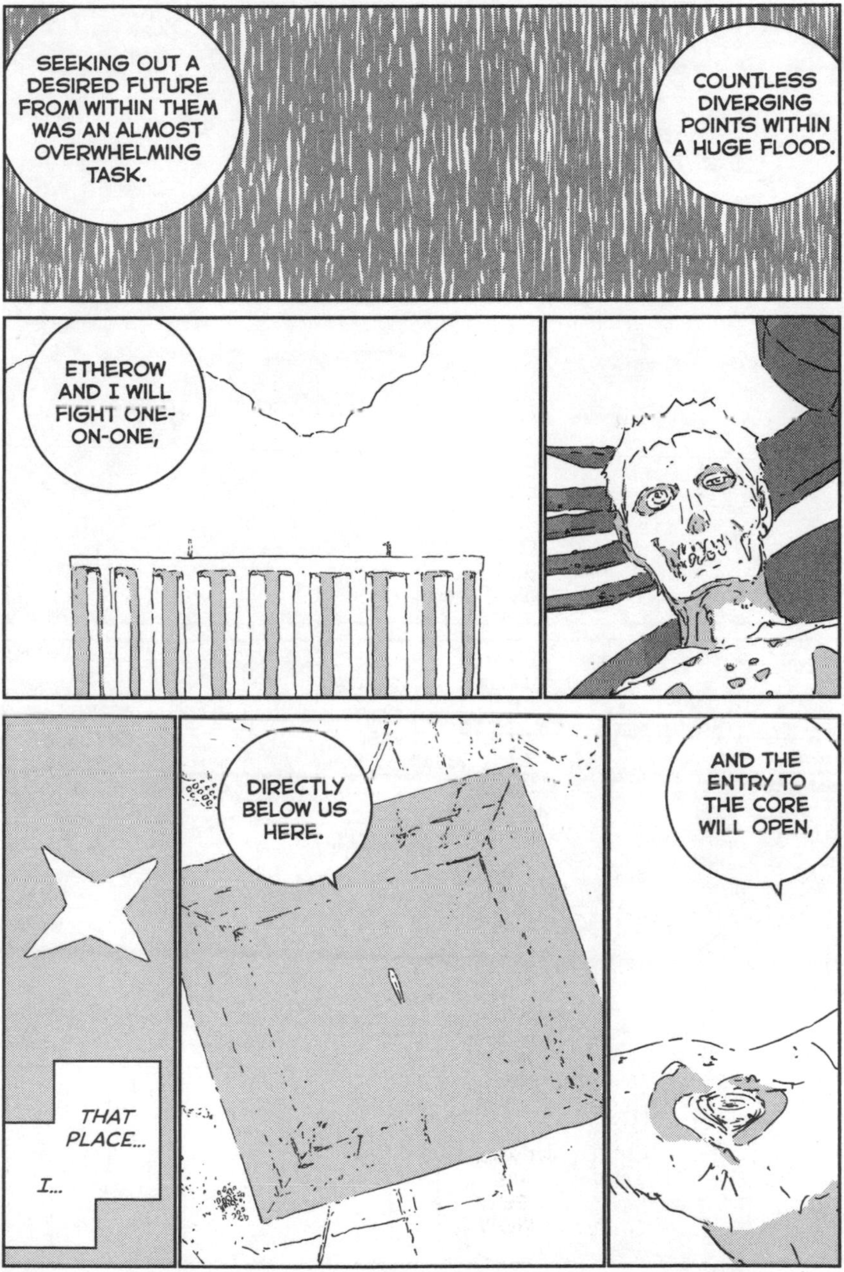
COUNTLESS DIVERGING POINTS WITHIN A HUGE FLOOD.
SEEKING OUT A DESIRED FUTURE FROM WITHIN THEM WAS AN ALMOST OVERWHELMING TASK.
ETHEROW AND I WILL FIGHT ONE-ON-ONE,
AND THE ENTRY TO THE CORE WILL OPEN,
DIRECTLY BELOW US HERE.
THAT PLACE...
I...

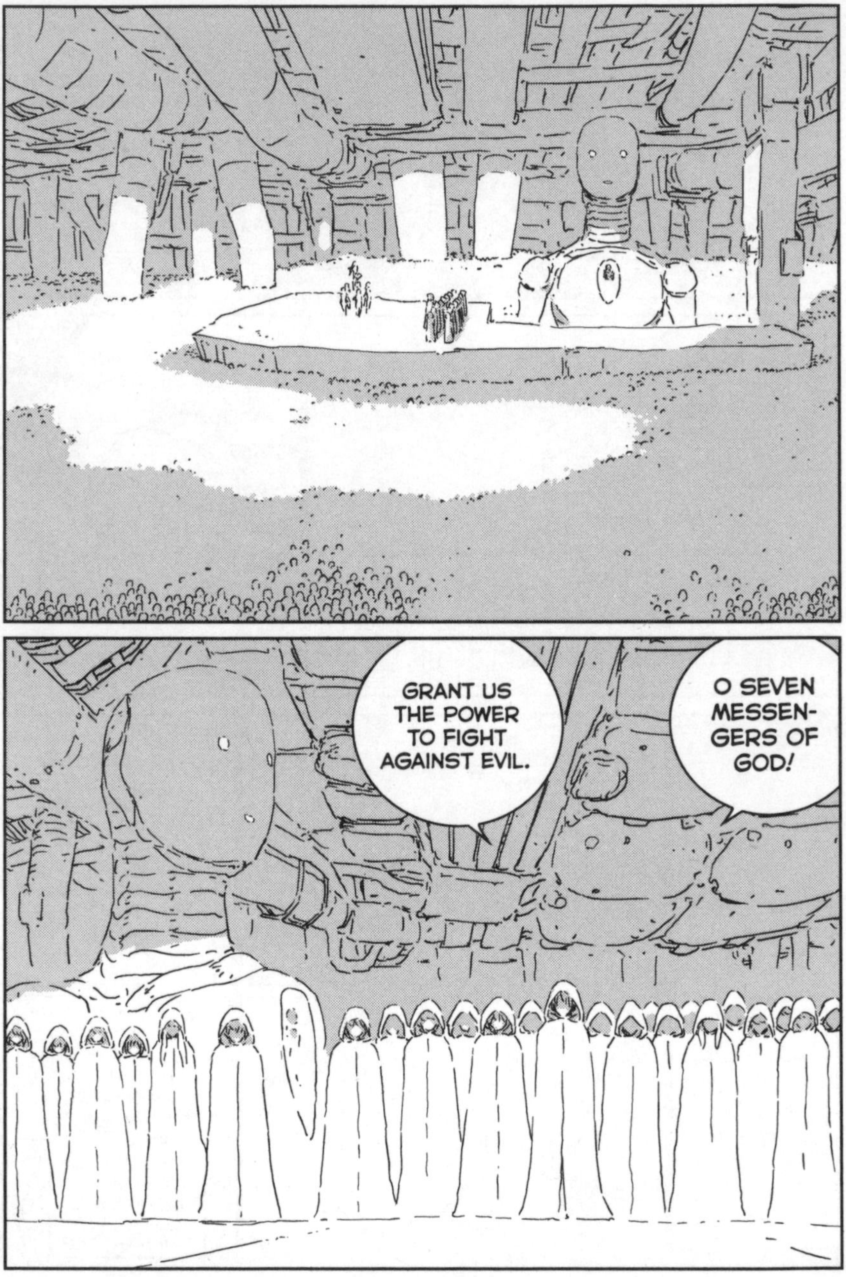
O SEVEN MESSEN-GERS OF GOD!
GRANT US THE POWER TO FIGHT AGAINST EVIL.

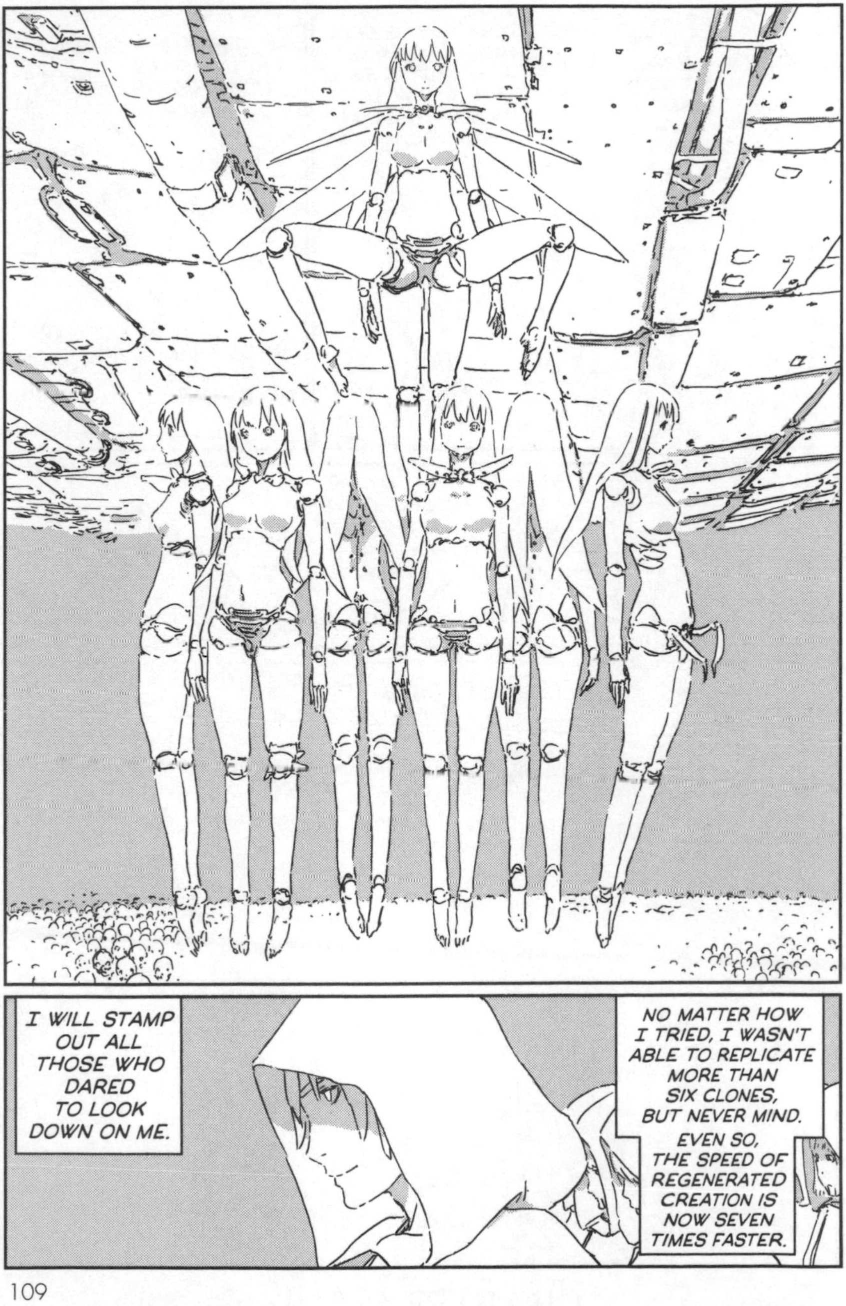
NO MATTER HOW I TRIED, I WASN'T ABLE TO REPLICATE MORE THAN SIX CLONES, BUT NEVER MIND.
EVEN SO, THE SPEED OF REGENERATED CREATION IS NOW SEVEN TIMES FASTER.
I WILL STAMP OUT ALL THOSE WHO DARED TO LOOK DOWN ON ME.

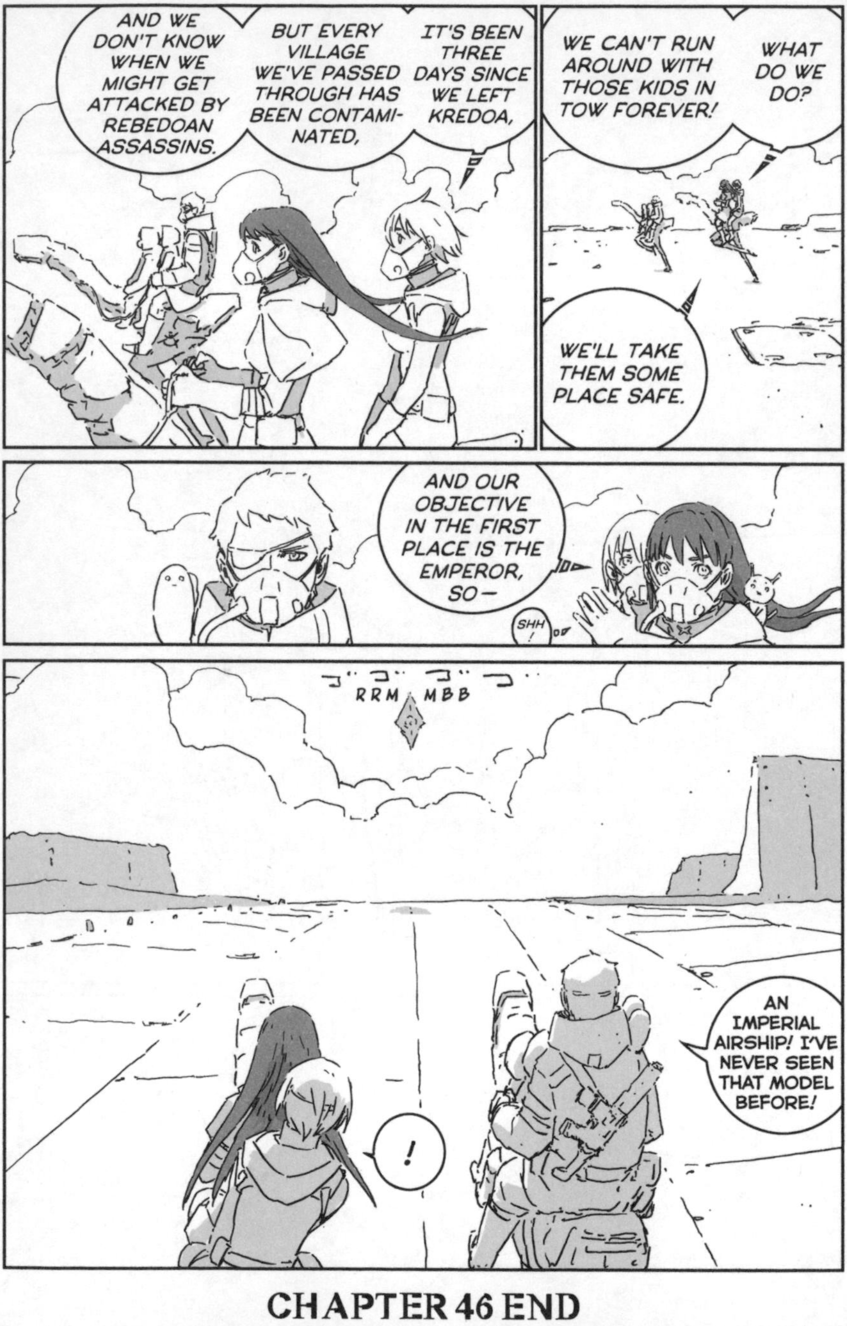
WHAT DO WE DO?
WE CAN'T RUN AROUND WITH THOSE KIDS IN TOW FOREVER!
WE'LL TAKE THEM SOME PLACE SAFE.
IT'S BEEN THREE DAYS SINCE WE LEFT KREDOA,
BUT EVERY VILLAGE WE'VE PASSED THROUGH HAS BEEN CONTAMI-NATED,
AND WE DON'T KNOW WHEN WE MIGHT GET ATTACKED BY REBEDOAN ASSASSINS.
AND OUR OBJECTIVE IN THE FIRST PLACE IS THE EMPEROR, SO—
SHH!
RRM MBB
AN IMPERIAL AIRSHIP! I'VE NEVER SEEN THAT MODEL BEFORE!
!

CHAPTER 46 END

APOSIMZ

CHAPTER 47

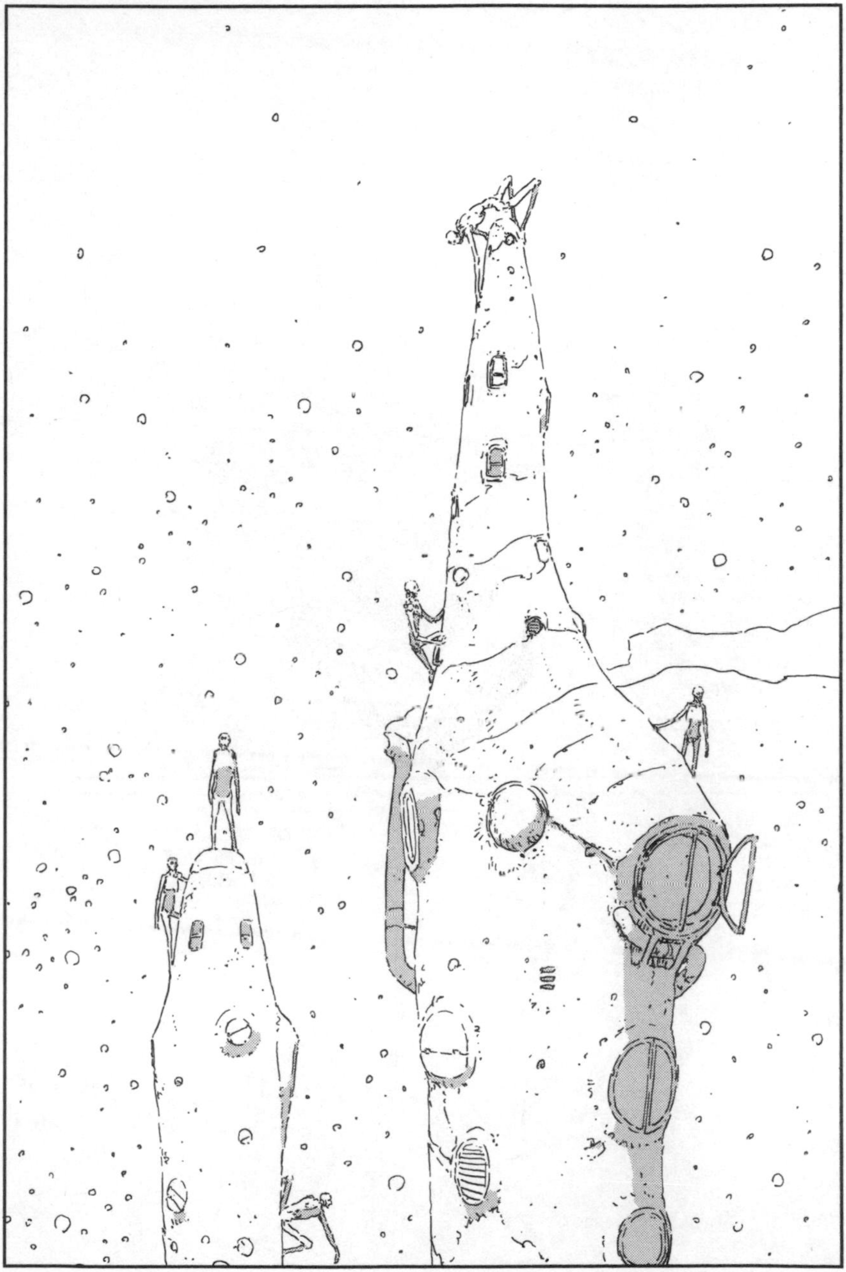

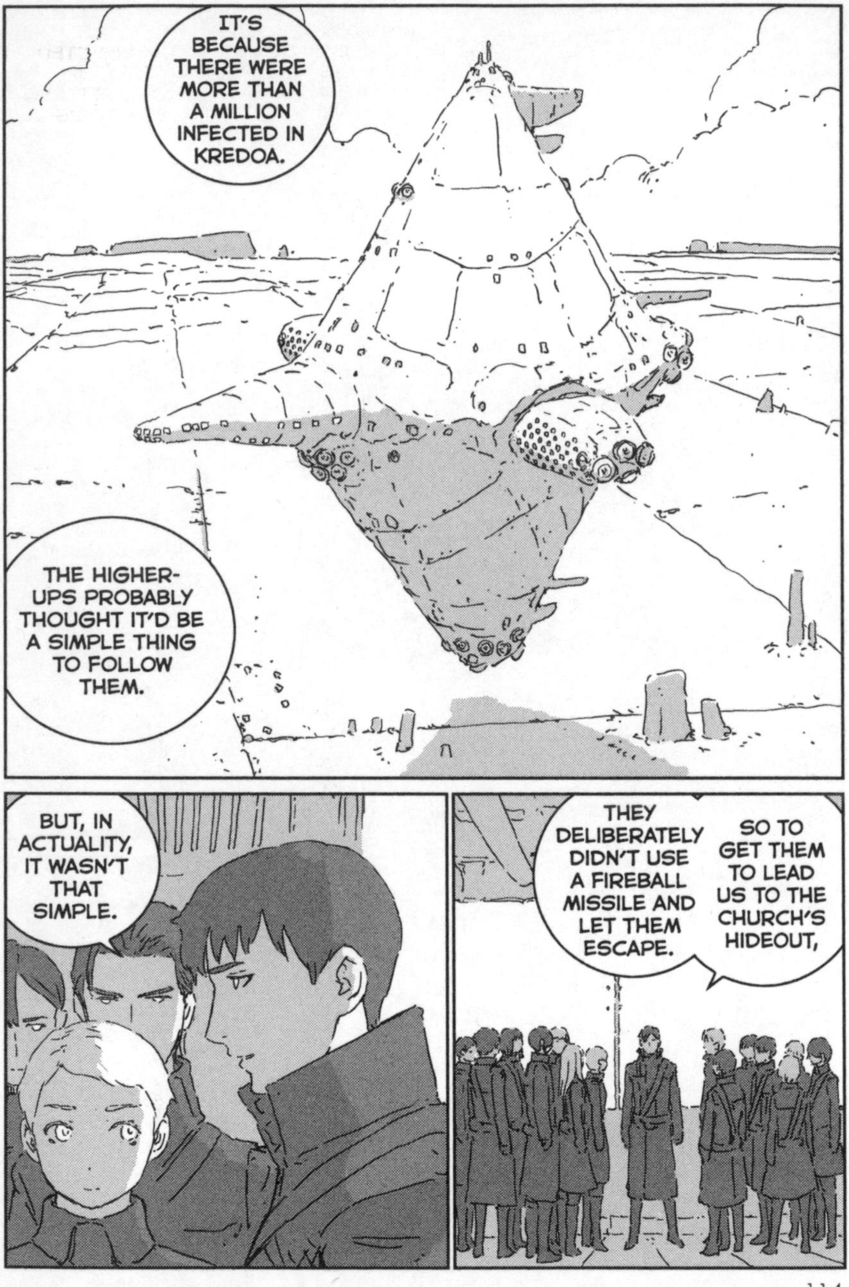
IT'S BECAUSE THERE WERE MORE THAN A MILLION INFECTED IN KREDOA.
THE HIGHER-UPS PROBABLY THOUGHT IT'D BE A SIMPLE THING TO FOLLOW THEM.
SO TO GET THEM TO LEAD US TO THE CHURCH'S HIDEOUT,
THEY DELIBERATELY DIDN'T USE A FIREBALL MISSILE AND LET THEM ESCAPE.
BUT, IN ACTUALITY, IT WASN'T THAT SIMPLE.

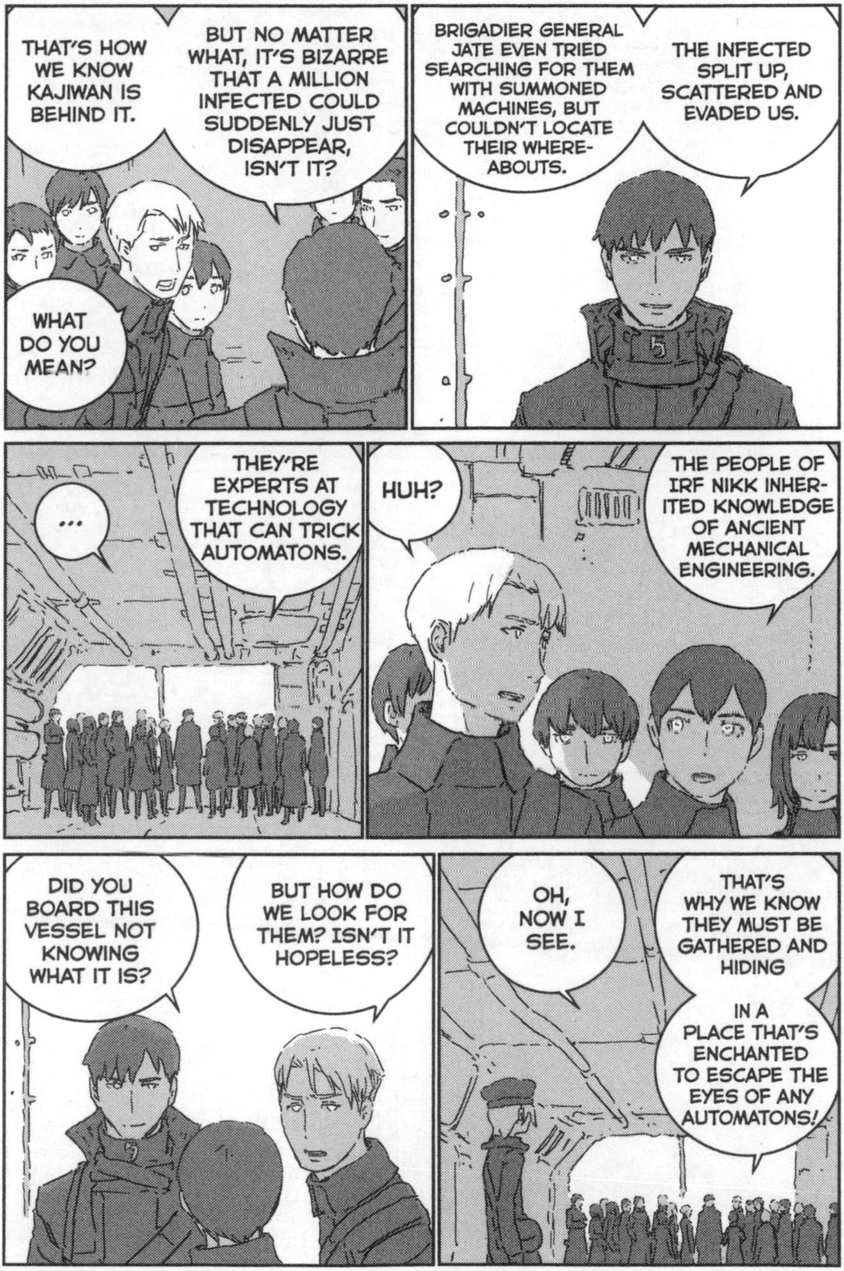
THE INFECTED SPLIT UP, SCATTERED AND EVADED US.
BRIGADIER GENERAL JATE EVEN TRIED SEARCHING FOR THEM WITH SUMMONED MACHINES, BUT COULDN'T LOCATE THEIR WHERE-ABOUTS.
BUT NO MATTER WHAT, IT'S BIZARRE THAT A MILLION INFECTED COULD SUDDENLY JUST DISAPPEAR, ISN'T IT?
THAT'S HOW WE KNOW KAJIWAN IS BEHIND IT.
WHAT DO YOU MEAN?
THE PEOPLE OF IRF NIKK INHER-ITED KNOWLEDGE OF ANCIENT MECHANICAL ENGINEERING.
HUH?
THEY'RE EXPERTS AT TECHNOLOGY THAT CAN TRICK AUTOMATONS.
...
THAT'S WHY WE KNOW THEY MUST BE GATHERED AND HIDING
OH, NOW I SEE.
IN A PLACE THAT'S ENCHANTED TO ESCAPE THE EYES OF ANY AUTOMATONS!
BUT HOW DO WE LOOK FOR THEM? ISN'T IT HOPELESS?
DID YOU BOARD THIS VESSEL NOT KNOWING WHAT IT IS?

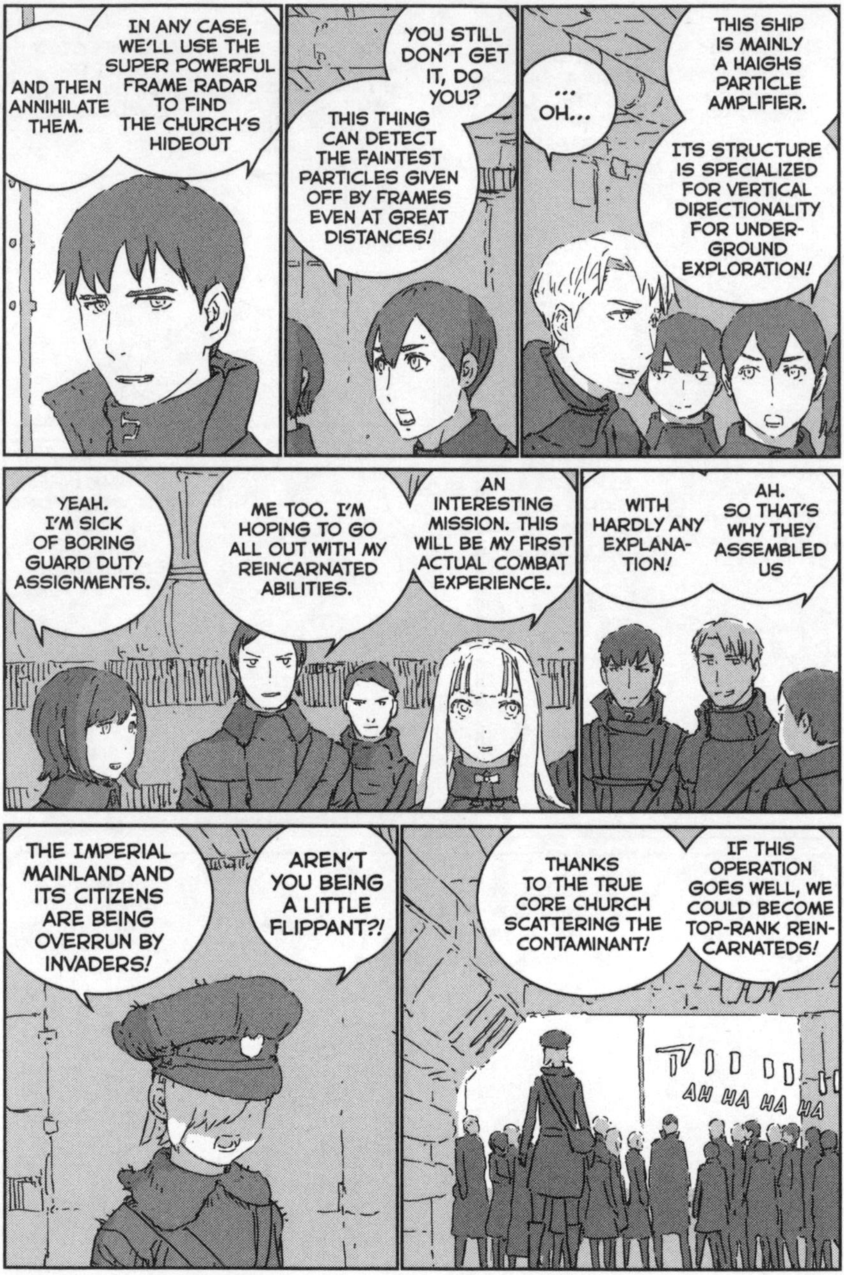
THIS SHIP IS MAINLY A HAIGHS PARTICLE AMPLIFIER.
... OH...
ITS STRUCTURE IS SPECIALIZED FOR VERTICAL DIRECTIONALITY FOR UNDER-GROUND EXPLORATION!
YOU STILL DON'T GET IT, DO YOU?
THIS THING CAN DETECT THE FAINTEST PARTICLES GIVEN OFF BY FRAMES EVEN AT GREAT DISTANCES!
IN ANY CASE, WE'LL USE THE SUPER POWERFUL FRAME RADAR TO FIND THE CHURCH'S HIDEOUT
AND THEN ANNIHILATE THEM.
AH. SO THAT'S WHY THEY ASSEMBLED US
WITH HARDLY ANY EXPLANA-TION!
AN INTERESTING MISSION. THIS WILL BE MY FIRST ACTUAL COMBAT EXPERIENCE.
ME TOO. I'M HOPING TO GO ALL OUT WITH MY REINCARNATED ABILITIES.
YEAH. I'M SICK OF BORING GUARD DUTY ASSIGNMENTS.
IF THIS OPERATION GOES WELL, WE COULD BECOME TOP-RANK REIN-CARNATEDS!
THANKS TO THE TRUE CORE CHURCH SCATTERING THE CONTAMINANT!
AH HA HA HA
AREN'T YOU BEING A LITTLE FLIPPANT?!
THE IMPERIAL MAINLAND AND ITS CITIZENS ARE BEING OVERRUN BY INVADERS!

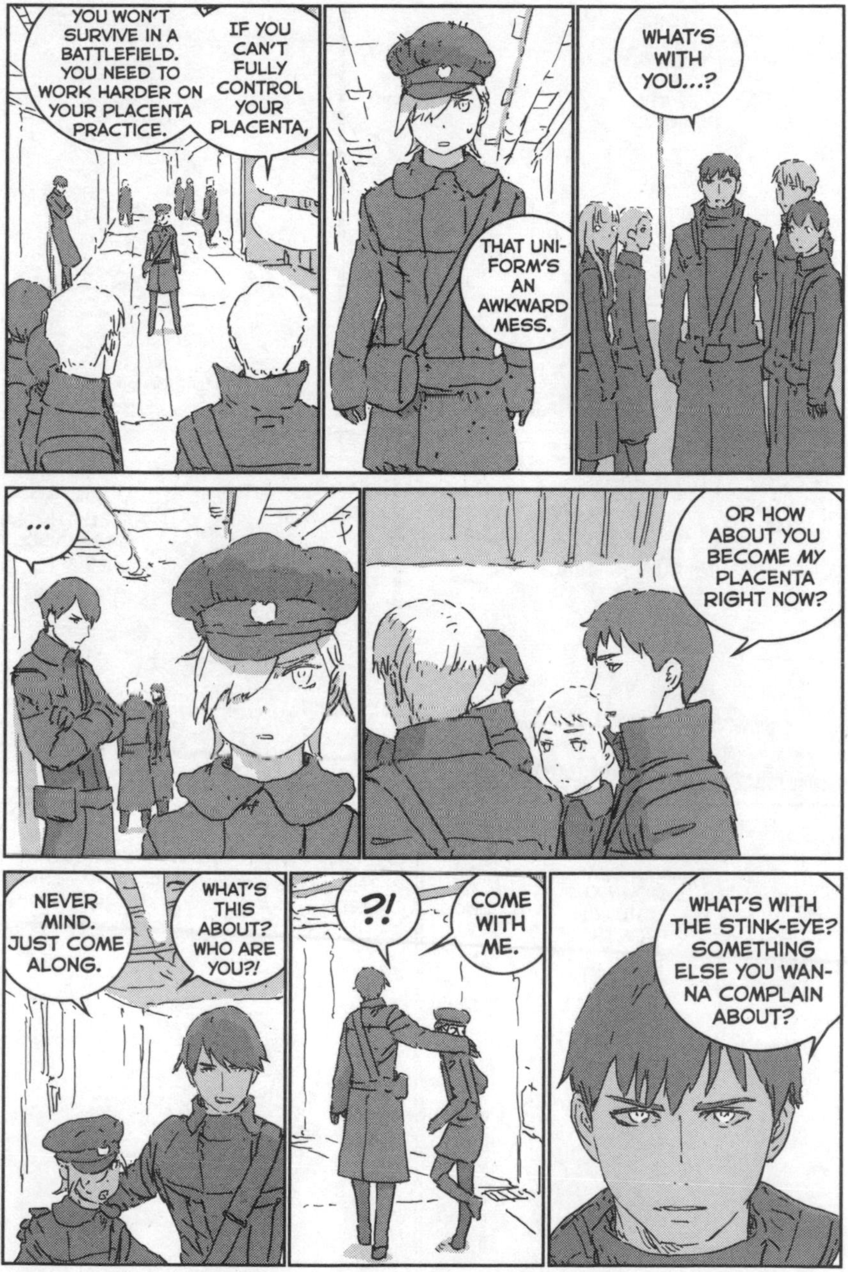
WHAT'S WITH YOU...?
THAT UNIFORM'S AN AWKWARD MESS.
IF YOU CAN'T FULLY CONTROL YOUR PLACENTA,
YOU WON'T SURVIVE IN A BATTLEFIELD. YOU NEED TO WORK HARDER ON YOUR PLACENTA PRACTICE.
OR HOW ABOUT YOU BECOME *MY* PLACENTA RIGHT NOW?
...
WHAT'S WITH THE STINK-EYE? SOMETHING ELSE YOU WANNA COMPLAIN ABOUT?
COME WITH ME.
?!
WHAT'S THIS ABOUT? WHO ARE YOU?!
NEVER MIND. JUST COME ALONG.

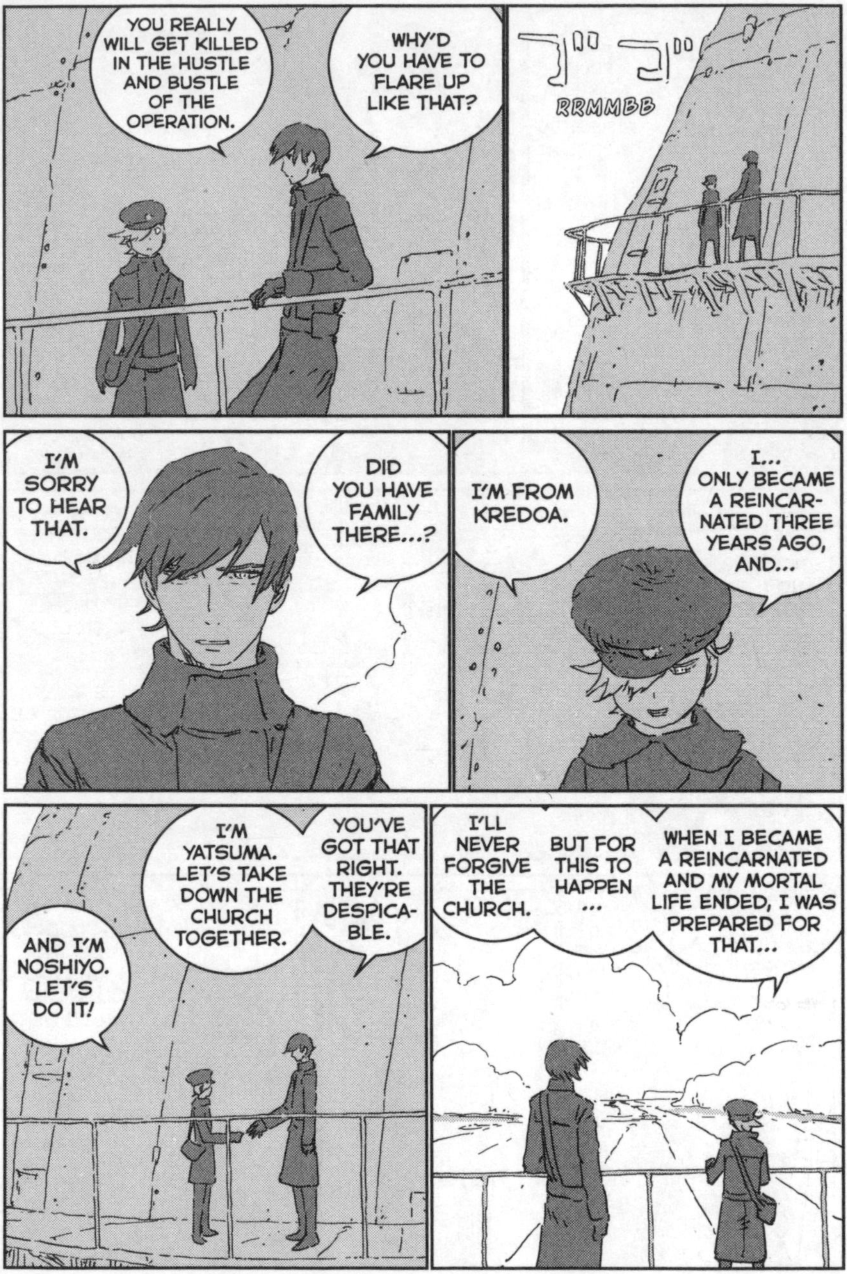
RRMMBB
WHY'D YOU HAVE TO FLARE UP LIKE THAT?
YOU REALLY WILL GET KILLED IN THE HUSTLE AND BUSTLE OF THE OPERATION.
I... ONLY BECAME A REINCARNATED THREE YEARS AGO, AND...
I'M FROM KREDOA.
DID YOU HAVE FAMILY THERE...?
I'M SORRY TO HEAR THAT.
WHEN I BECAME A REINCARNATED AND MY MORTAL LIFE ENDED, I WAS PREPARED FOR THAT...
BUT FOR THIS TO HAPPEN ...
I'LL NEVER FORGIVE THE CHURCH.
YOU'VE GOT THAT RIGHT. THEY'RE DESPICABLE.
I'M YATSUMA. LET'S TAKE DOWN THE CHURCH TOGETHER.
AND I'M NOSHIYO. LET'S DO IT!

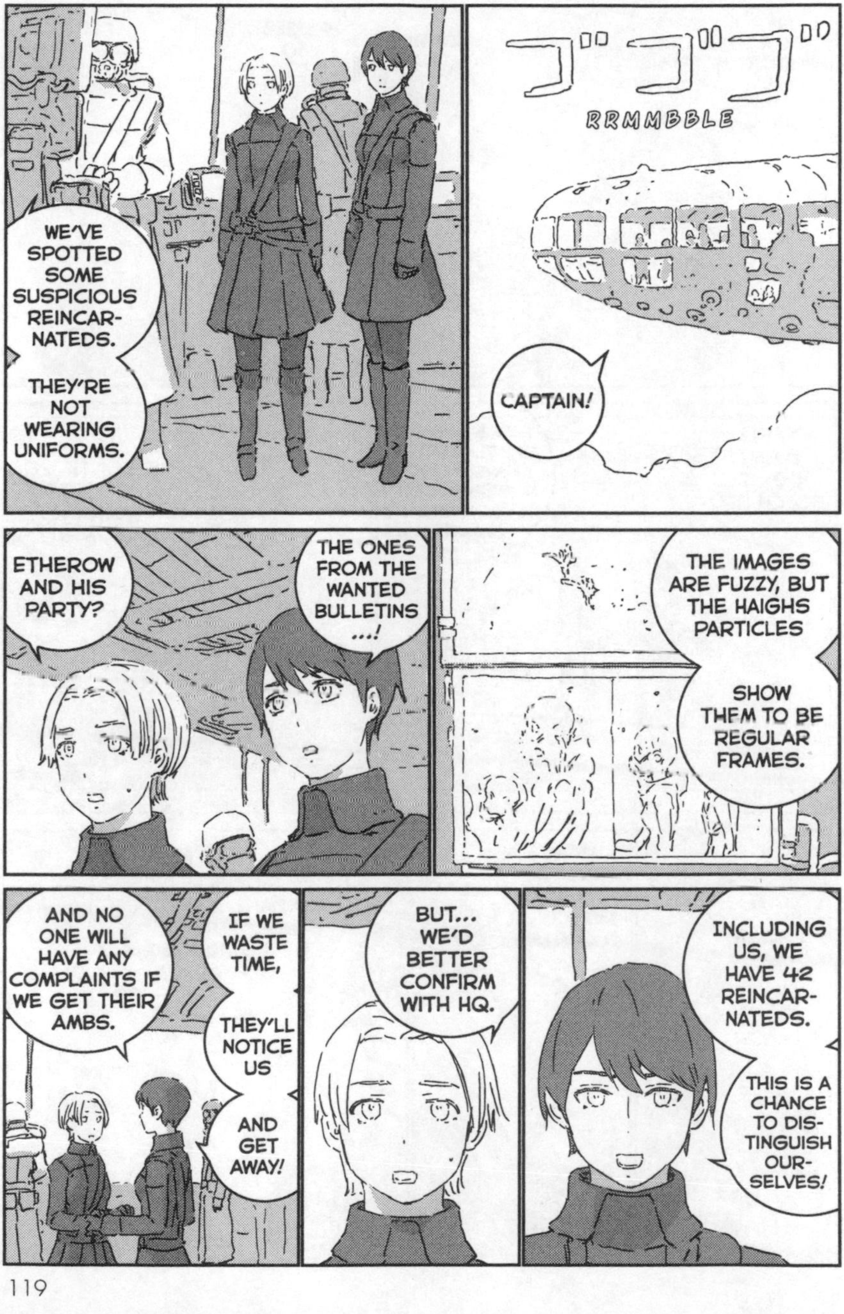
ゴゴゴ
RRMMBBLE
CAPTAIN!
WE'VE SPOTTED SOME SUSPICIOUS REINCAR-NATEDS.
THEY'RE NOT WEARING UNIFORMS.
THE IMAGES ARE FUZZY, BUT THE HAIGHS PARTICLES
SHOW THEM TO BE REGULAR FRAMES.
THE ONES FROM THE WANTED BULLETINS ...!
ETHEROW AND HIS PARTY?
INCLUDING US, WE HAVE 42 REINCAR-NATEDS.
THIS IS A CHANCE TO DIS-TINGUISH OUR-SELVES!
BUT... WE'D BETTER CONFIRM WITH HQ.
IF WE WASTE TIME,
THEY'LL NOTICE US
AND GET AWAY!
AND NO ONE WILL HAVE ANY COMPLAINTS IF WE GET THEIR AMBS.

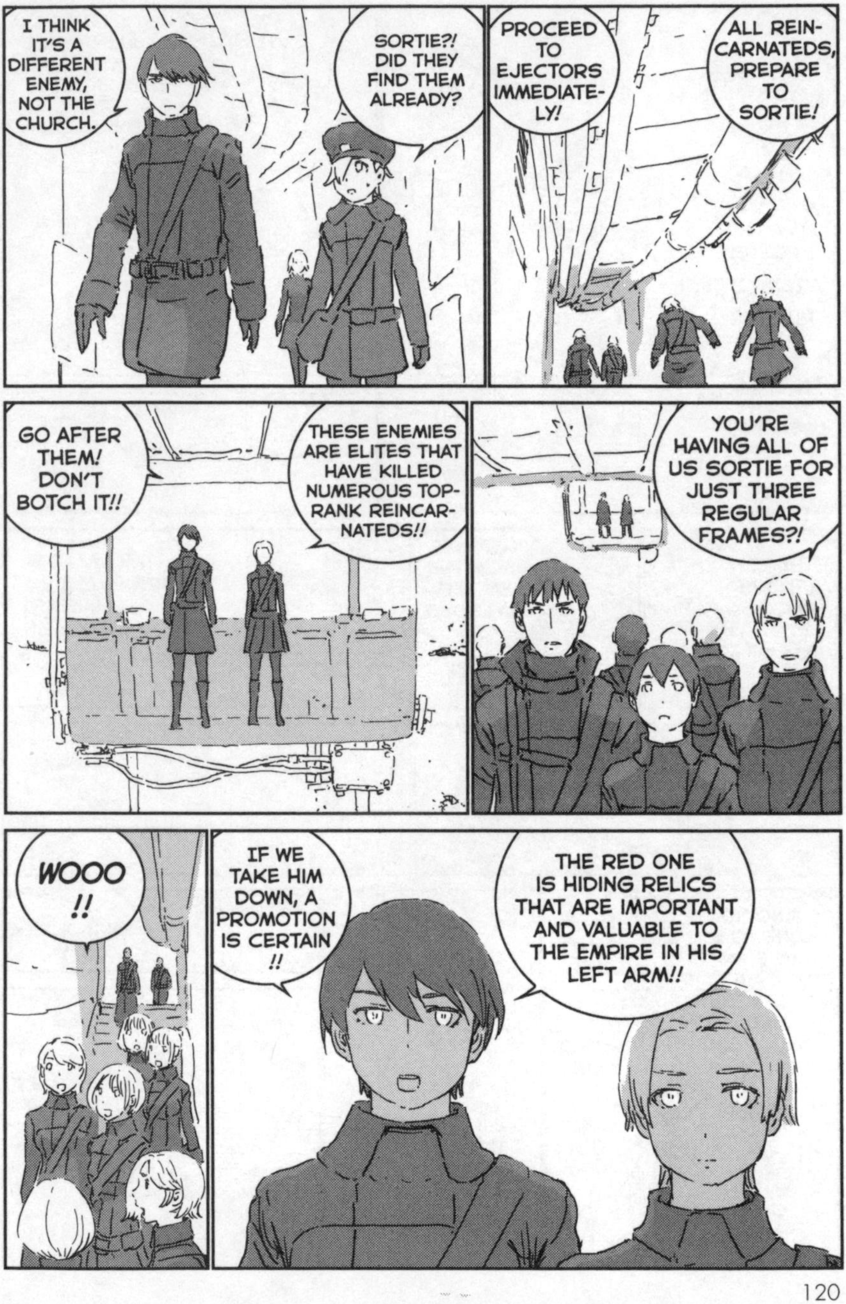
ALL REIN-CARNATEDS, PREPARE TO SORTIE!
PROCEED TO EJECTORS IMMEDIATE-LY!
SORTIE?! DID THEY FIND THEM ALREADY?
I THINK IT'S A DIFFERENT ENEMY, NOT THE CHURCH.
YOU'RE HAVING ALL OF US SORTIE FOR JUST THREE REGULAR FRAMES?!
THESE ENEMIES ARE ELITES THAT HAVE KILLED NUMEROUS TOP-RANK REINCAR-NATEDS!!
GO AFTER THEM! DON'T BOTCH IT!!
THE RED ONE IS HIDING RELICS THAT ARE IMPORTANT AND VALUABLE TO THE EMPIRE IN HIS LEFT ARM!!
IF WE TAKE HIM DOWN, A PROMOTION IS CERTAIN !!
WOOO !!

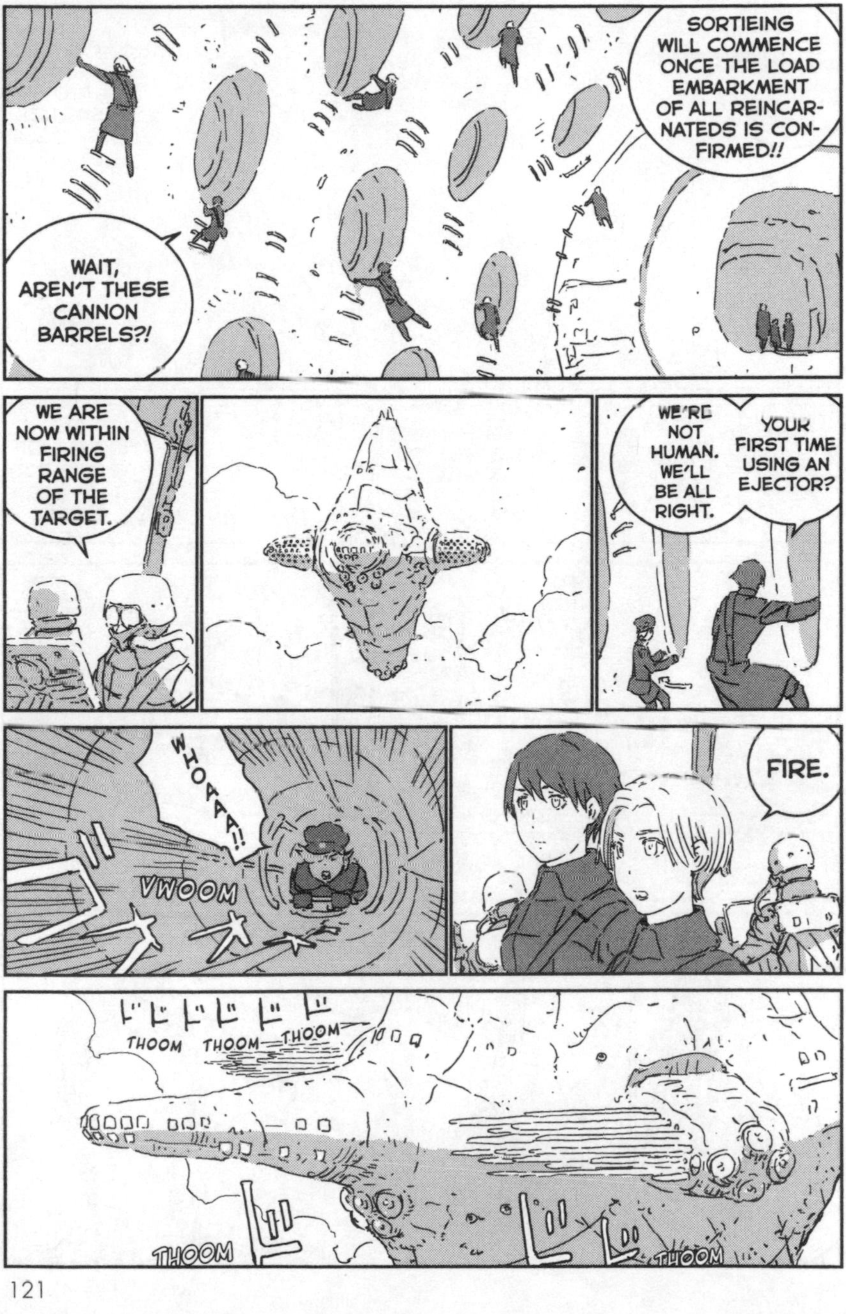
SORTIEING WILL COMMENCE ONCE THE LOAD EMBARKMENT OF ALL REINCARNATEDS IS CONFIRMED!!
WAIT, AREN'T THESE CANNON BARRELS?!
YOUR FIRST TIME USING AN EJECTOR?
WE'RE NOT HUMAN. WE'LL BE ALL RIGHT.
WE ARE NOW WITHIN FIRING RANGE OF THE TARGET.
FIRE.
WHOAAAA!!
VWOOM
ドドドドドド
THOOM THOOM THOOM
THOOM
THOOM

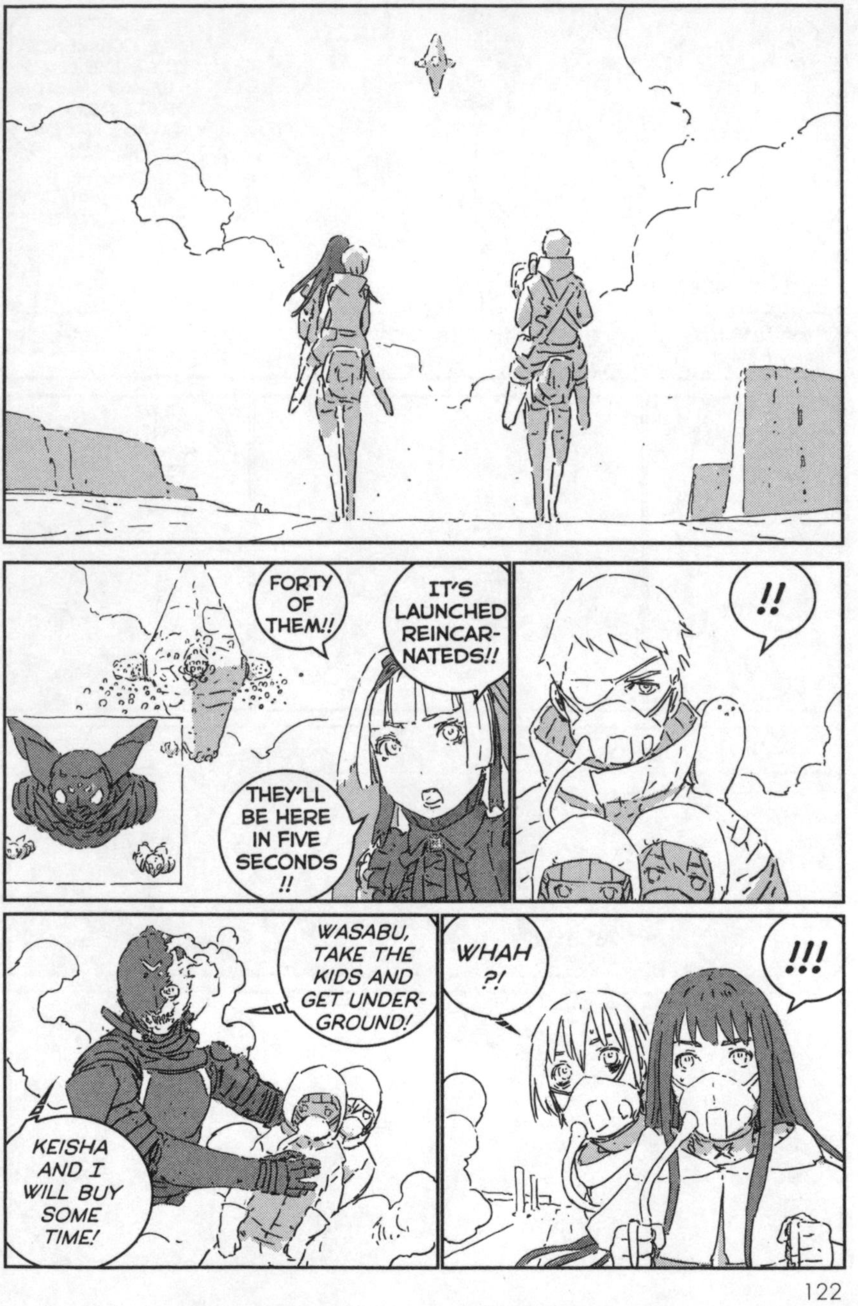
!!
IT'S LAUNCHED REINCARNATEDS!!
FORTY OF THEM!!
THEY'LL BE HERE IN FIVE SECONDS !!
!!!
WHAH ?!
WASABU, TAKE THE KIDS AND GET UNDERGROUND!
KEISHA AND I WILL BUY SOME TIME!

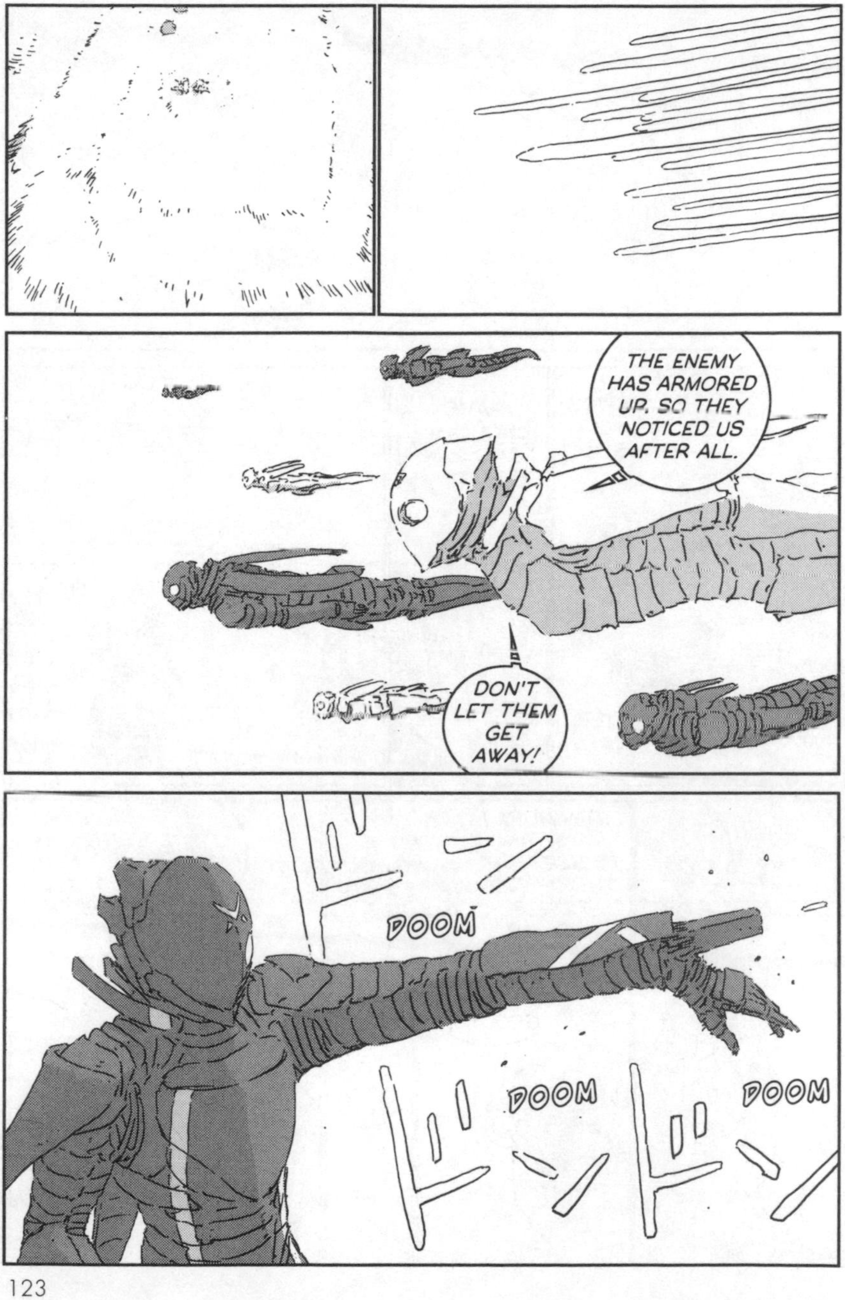
THE ENEMY HAS ARMORED UP. SO THEY NOTICED US AFTER ALL.
DON'T LET THEM GET AWAY!
DOOM
DOOM
ドン
DOOM
ドン

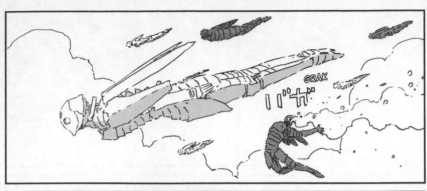

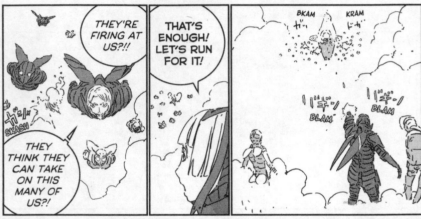

GRAK
BKAM
KRAM
BLAM
BLAM
THAT'S ENOUGH! LET'S RUN FOR IT!
THEY'RE FIRING AT US?!!
SKASH
THEY THINK THEY CAN TAKE ON THIS MANY OF US?!
NOSHIYO! THE ONE WITH THE KIDS FLED UNDERGROUND.
WE'LL GIVE CHASE!
BUT THEY'LL GET THE RED GUY WITHOUT US!
GLORY ISN'T A THING YOU TRY TO WIN IN A RUSH.
IT'S MORE IMPORTANT TO SEE THAT THE OPERATION IS A CLEAR SUCCESS.
LET'S GO!
VWOOSH
RIGHT.

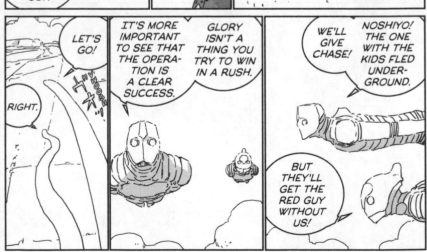

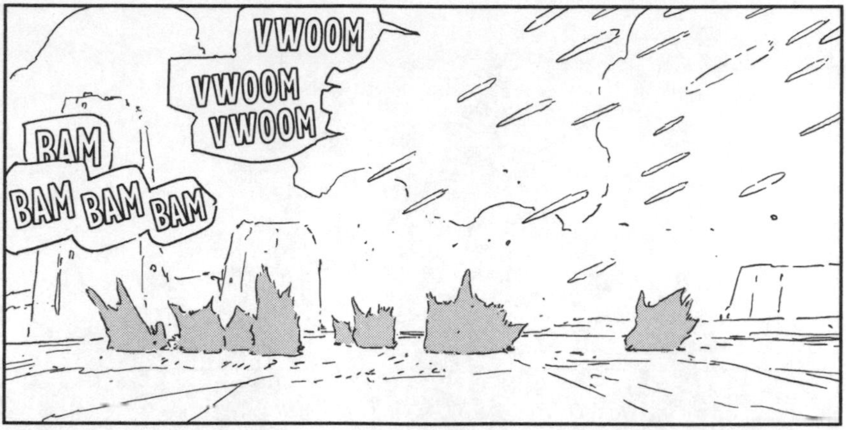
VWOOM
VWOOM
VWOOM
BAM
BAM BAM BAM

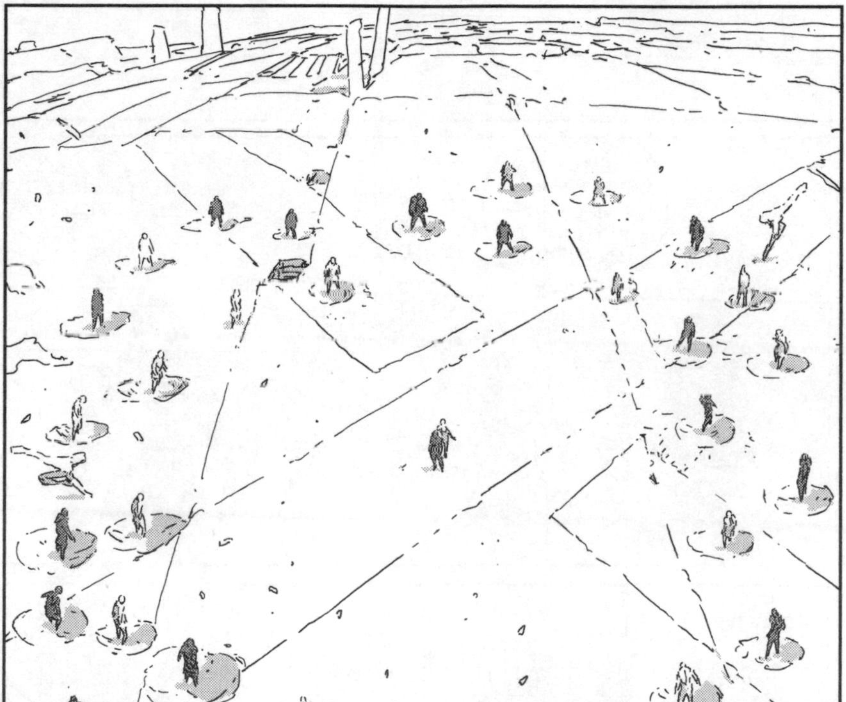

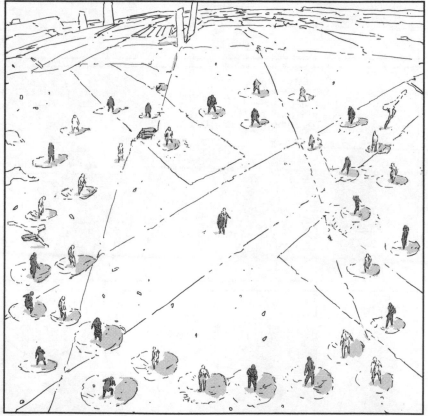

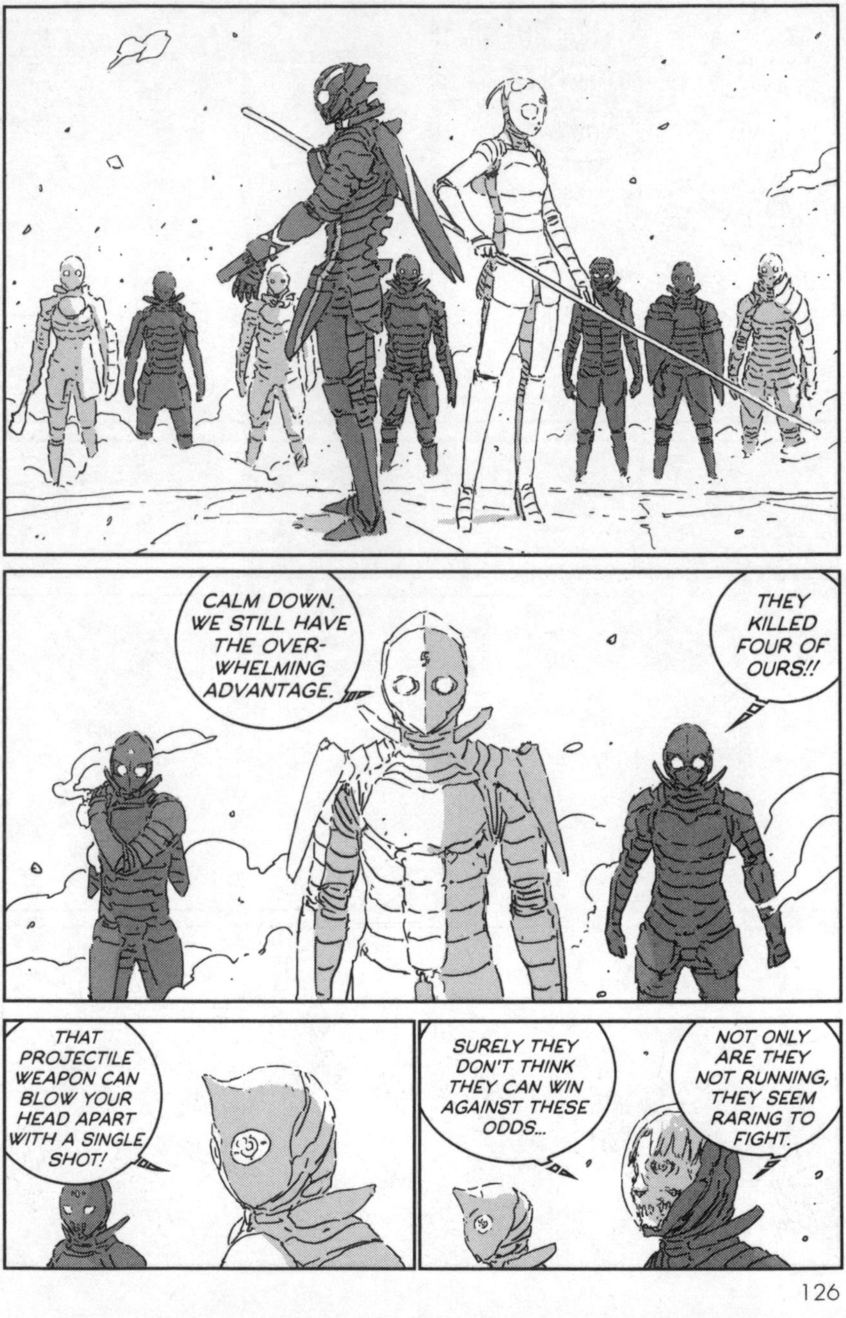
THEY KILLED FOUR OF OURS!!
CALM DOWN. WE STILL HAVE THE OVER-WHELMING ADVANTAGE.
NOT ONLY ARE THEY NOT RUNNING, THEY SEEM RARING TO FIGHT.
SURELY THEY DON'T THINK THEY CAN WIN AGAINST THESE ODDS...
THAT PROJECTILE WEAPON CAN BLOW YOUR HEAD APART WITH A SINGLE SHOT!

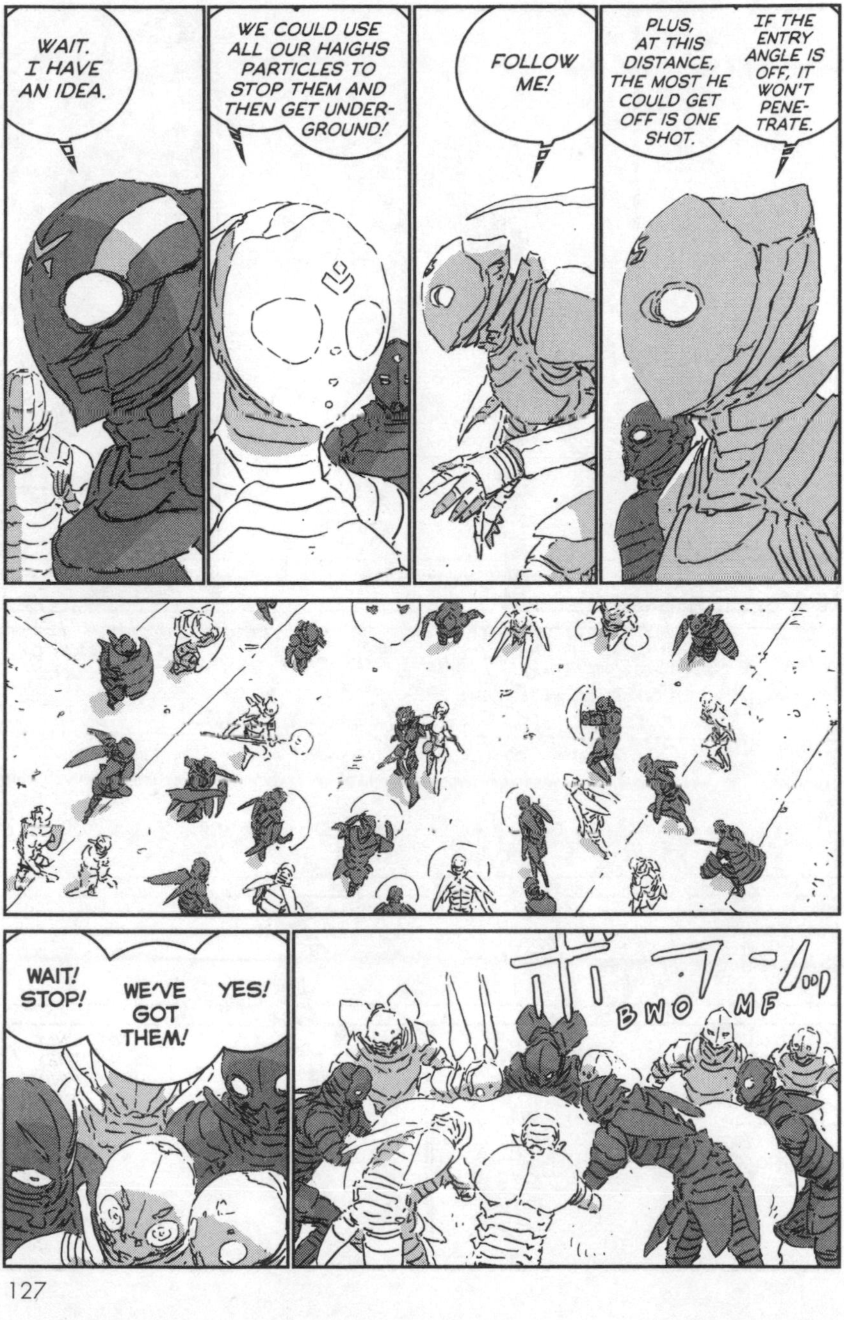
IF THE ENTRY ANGLE IS OFF, IT WON'T PENE-TRATE.
PLUS, AT THIS DISTANCE, THE MOST HE COULD GET OFF IS ONE SHOT.
FOLLOW ME!
WE COULD USE ALL OUR HAIGHS PARTICLES TO STOP THEM AND THEN GET UNDER-GROUND!
WAIT. I HAVE AN IDEA.
BWOMF
YES!
WE'VE GOT THEM!
WAIT! STOP!

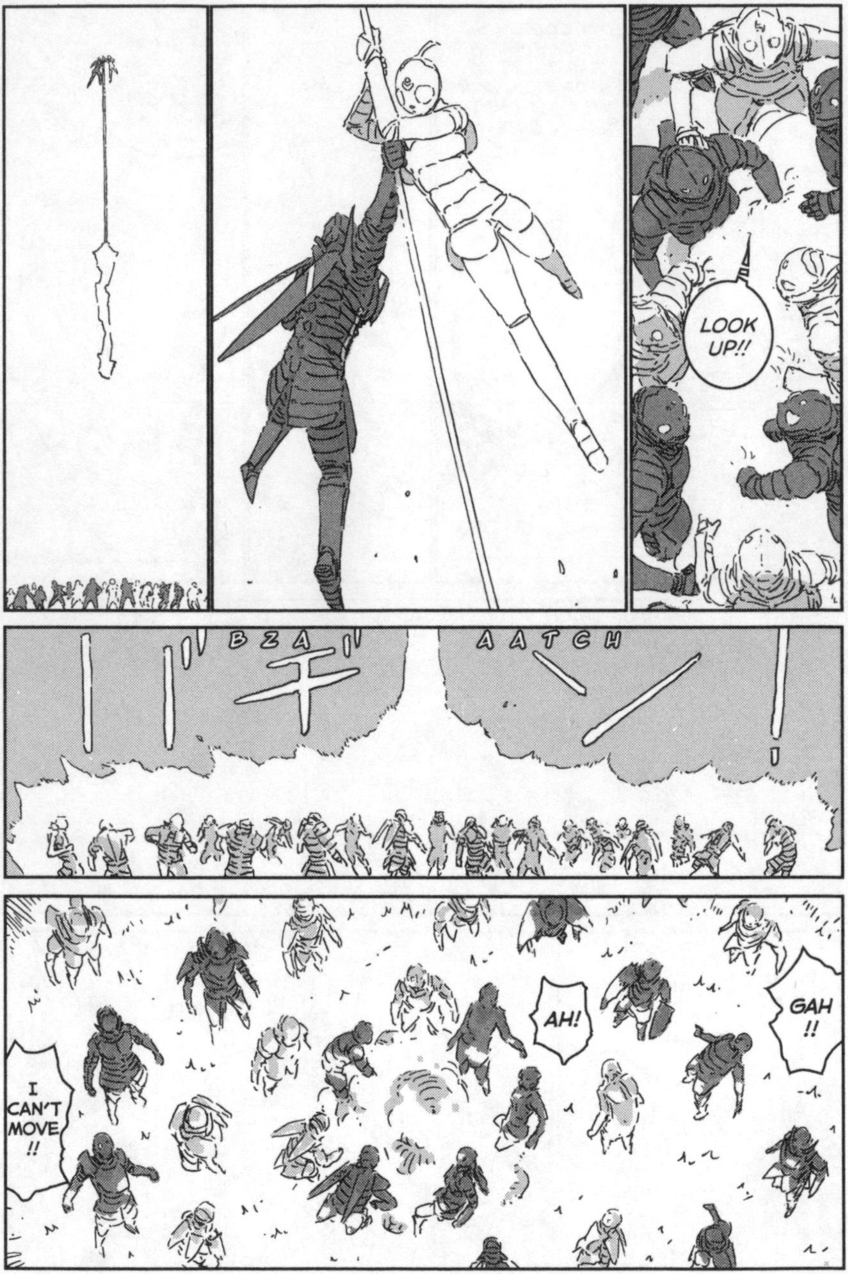
LOOK UP!!
BZA AATCH
GAH !!
AH!
I CAN'T MOVE !!

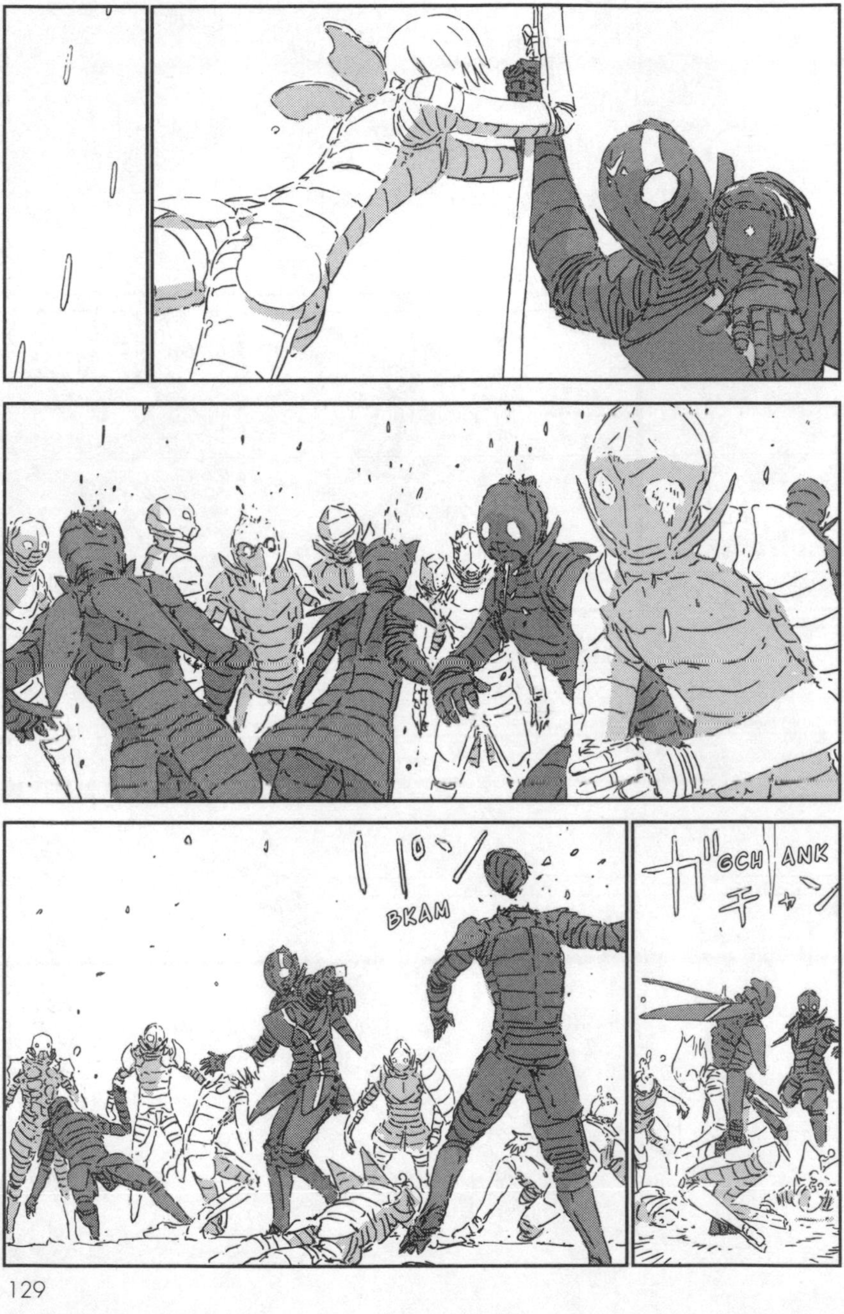
GCH ANK
ガチャン
BKAM

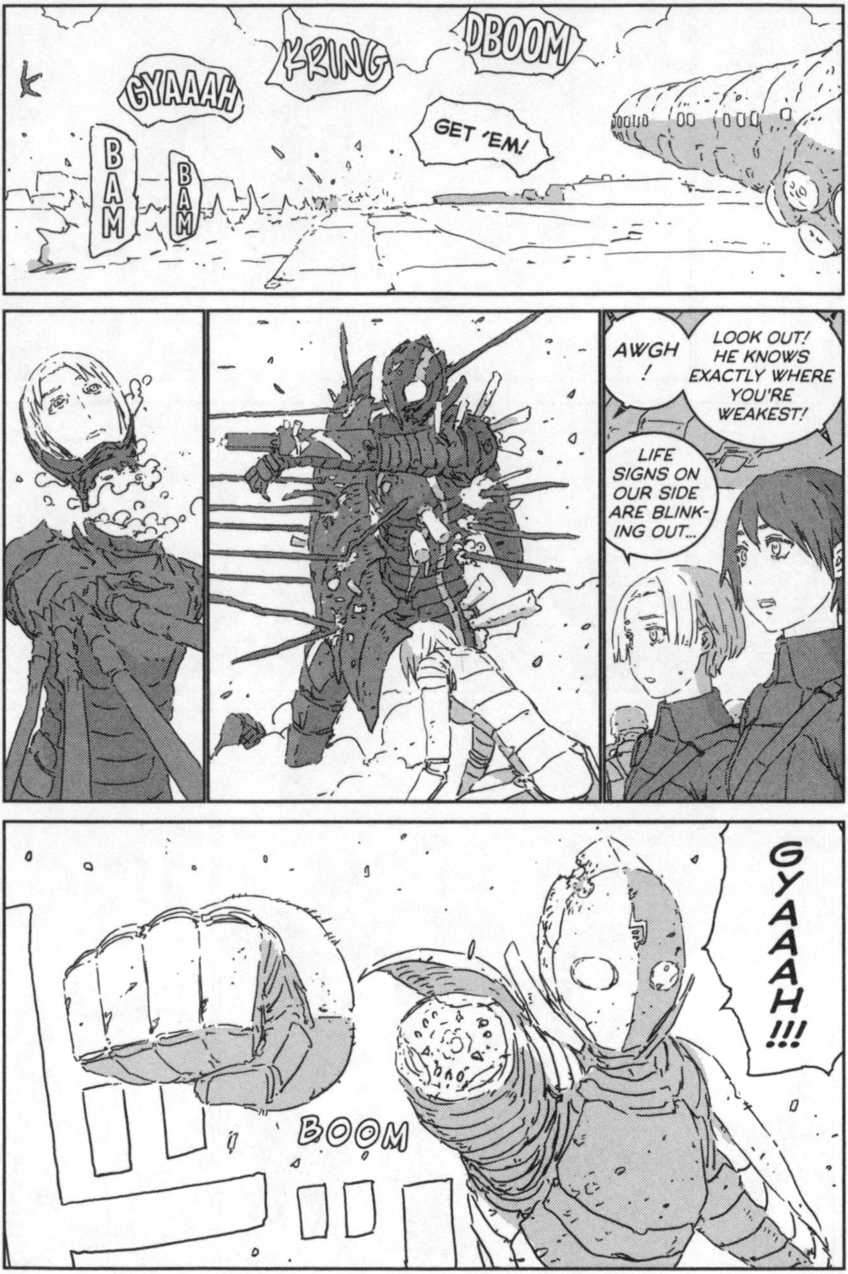
DBOOM
KRING
GYAAAH
GET 'EM!
BAM
BAM
LOOK OUT! HE KNOWS EXACTLY WHERE YOU'RE WEAKEST!
AWGH!
LIFE SIGNS ON OUR SIDE ARE BLINK-ING OUT...
GYAAAH!!!
BOOM

HE THINKS HE'S DODGED IT!
PK AK
KPOW
!
BOBOBOBOBO BOBOBOBOBOBO BOBOBOBOBOBO BOBOBOBOBOBO BOBOBOBOM

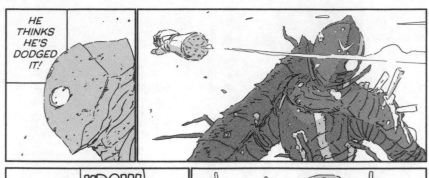

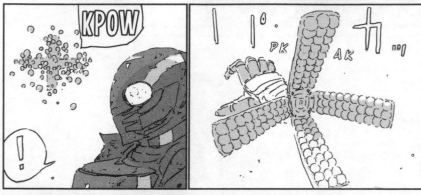

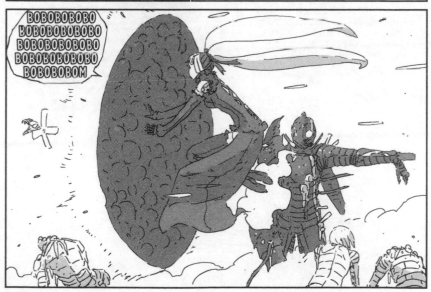

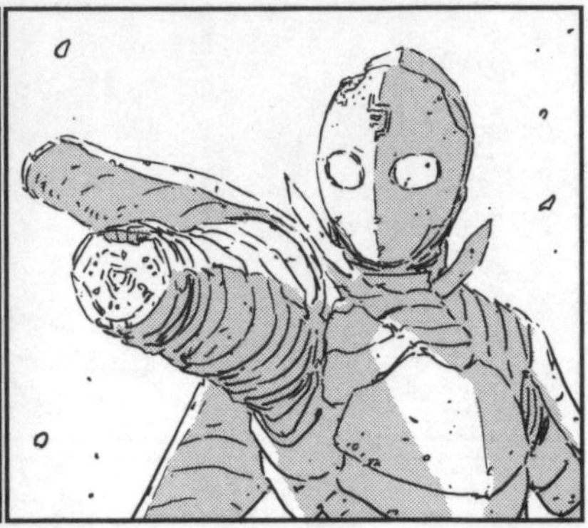
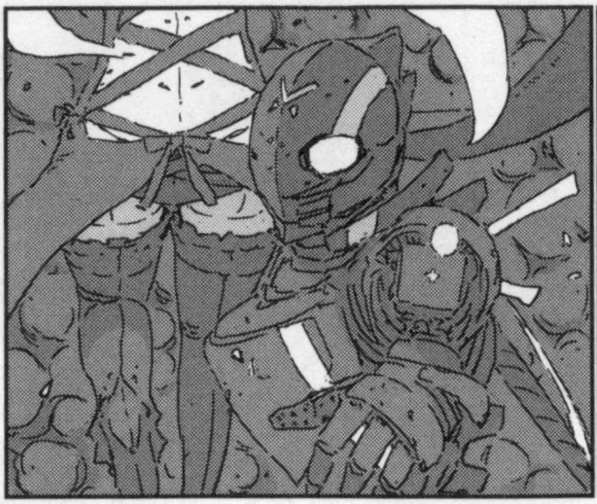
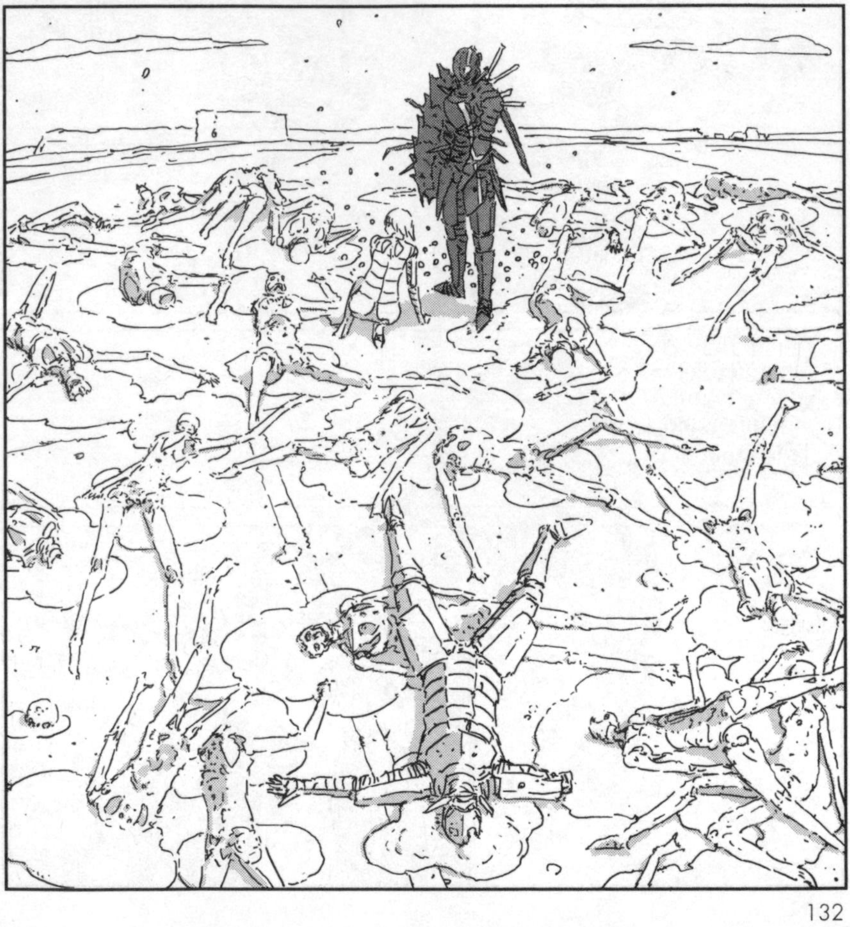

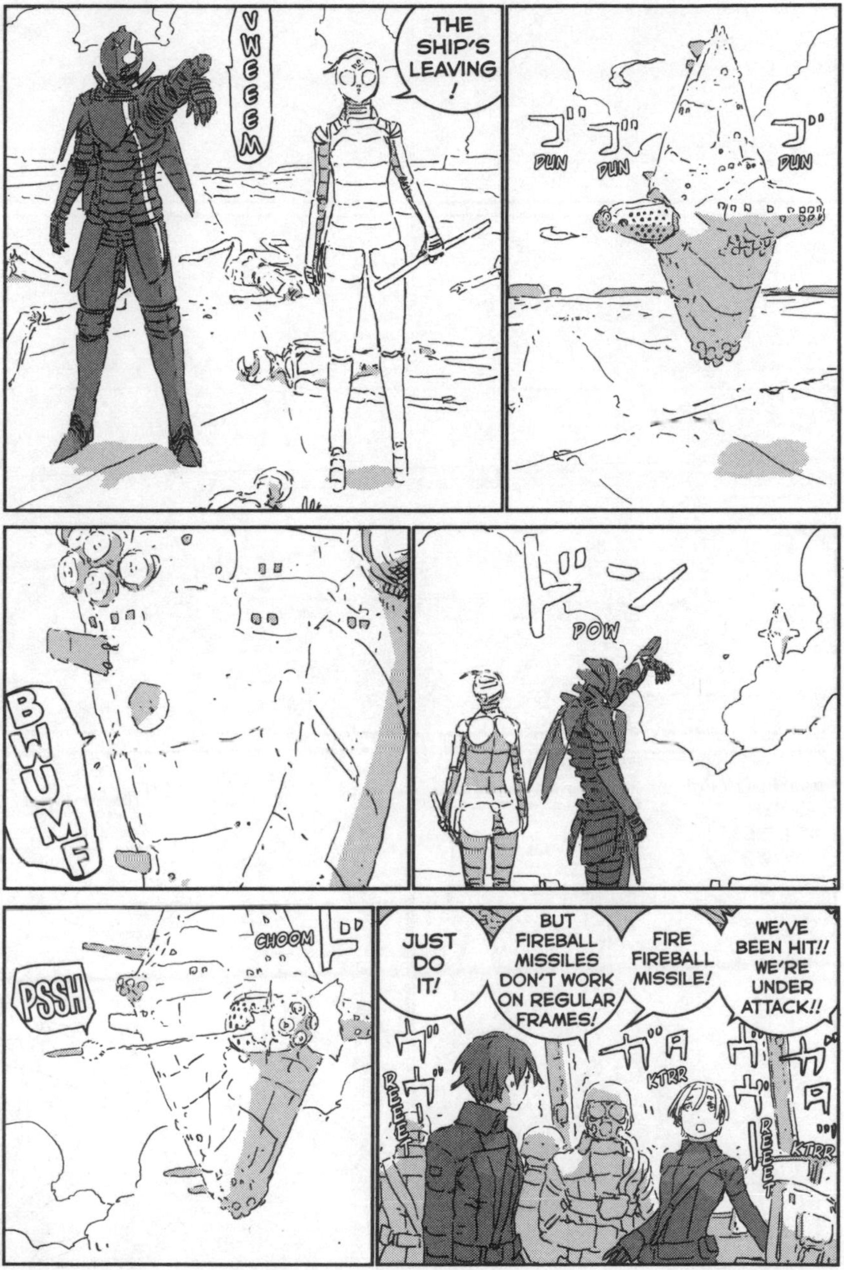
DUN
DUN
DUN
THE SHIP'S LEAVING!
VWEEEM
POW
BWUMF
WE'VE BEEN HIT!! WE'RE UNDER ATTACK!!
FIRE FIREBALL MISSILE!
BUT FIREBALL MISSILES DON'T WORK ON REGULAR FRAMES!
JUST DO IT!
KTRR
REEET
KTRR
REEET
CHOOM
PSSH

ズズズ
ZZZZMMM
WASABU! WHERE ARE YOU NOW?

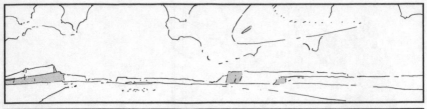

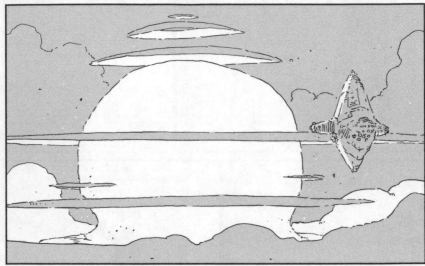

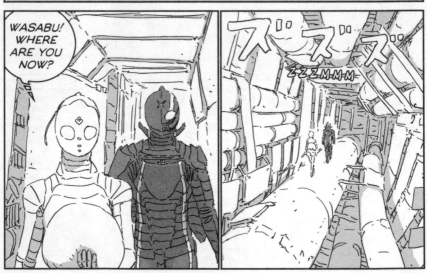

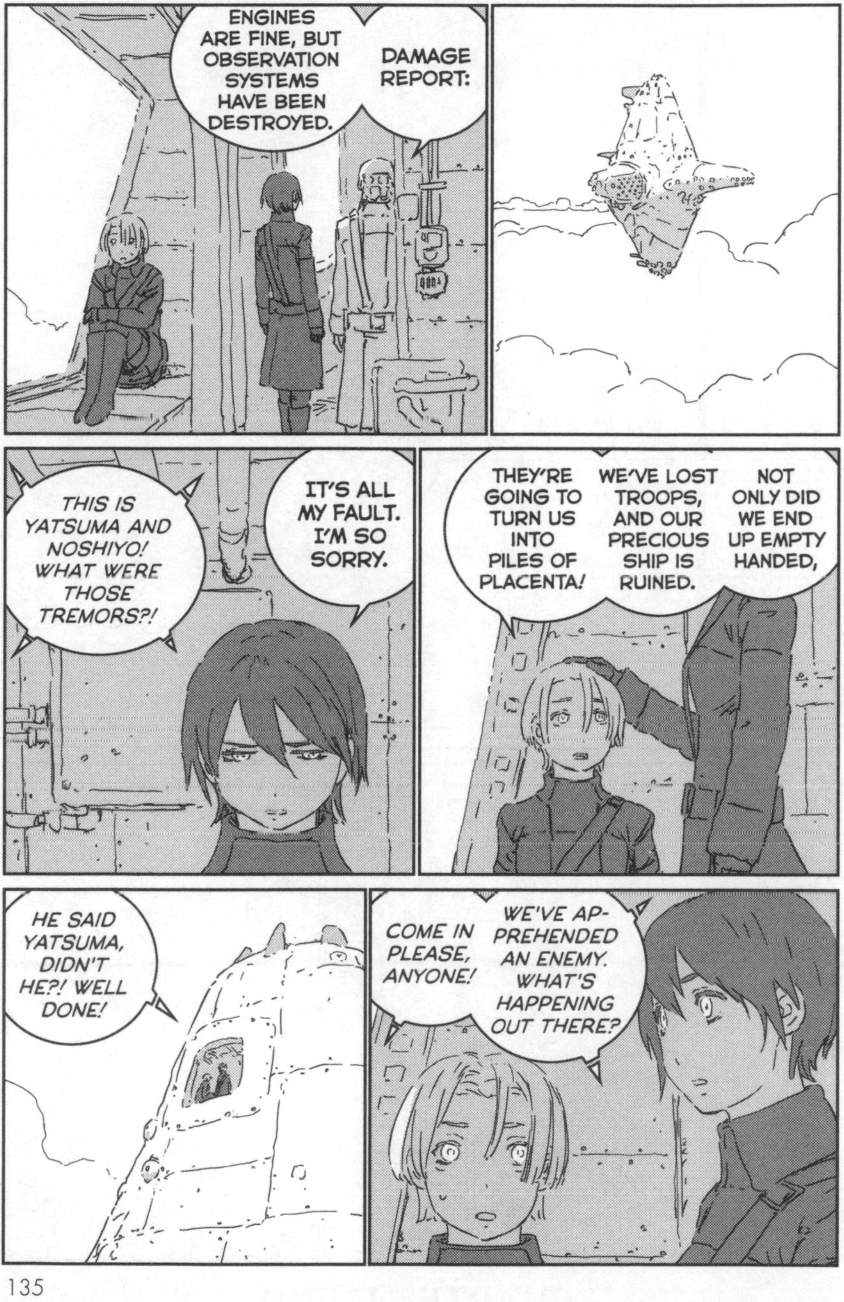
DAMAGE REPORT:
ENGINES ARE FINE, BUT OBSERVATION SYSTEMS HAVE BEEN DESTROYED.
NOT ONLY DID WE END UP EMPTY HANDED,
WE'VE LOST TROOPS, AND OUR PRECIOUS SHIP IS RUINED.
THEY'RE GOING TO TURN US INTO PILES OF PLACENTA!
IT'S ALL MY FAULT. I'M SO SORRY.
THIS IS YATSUMA AND NOSHIYO! WHAT WERE THOSE TREMORS?!
WE'VE AP-PREHENDED AN ENEMY. WHAT'S HAPPENING OUT THERE?
COME IN PLEASE, ANYONE!
HE SAID YATSUMA, DIDN'T HE?! WELL DONE!

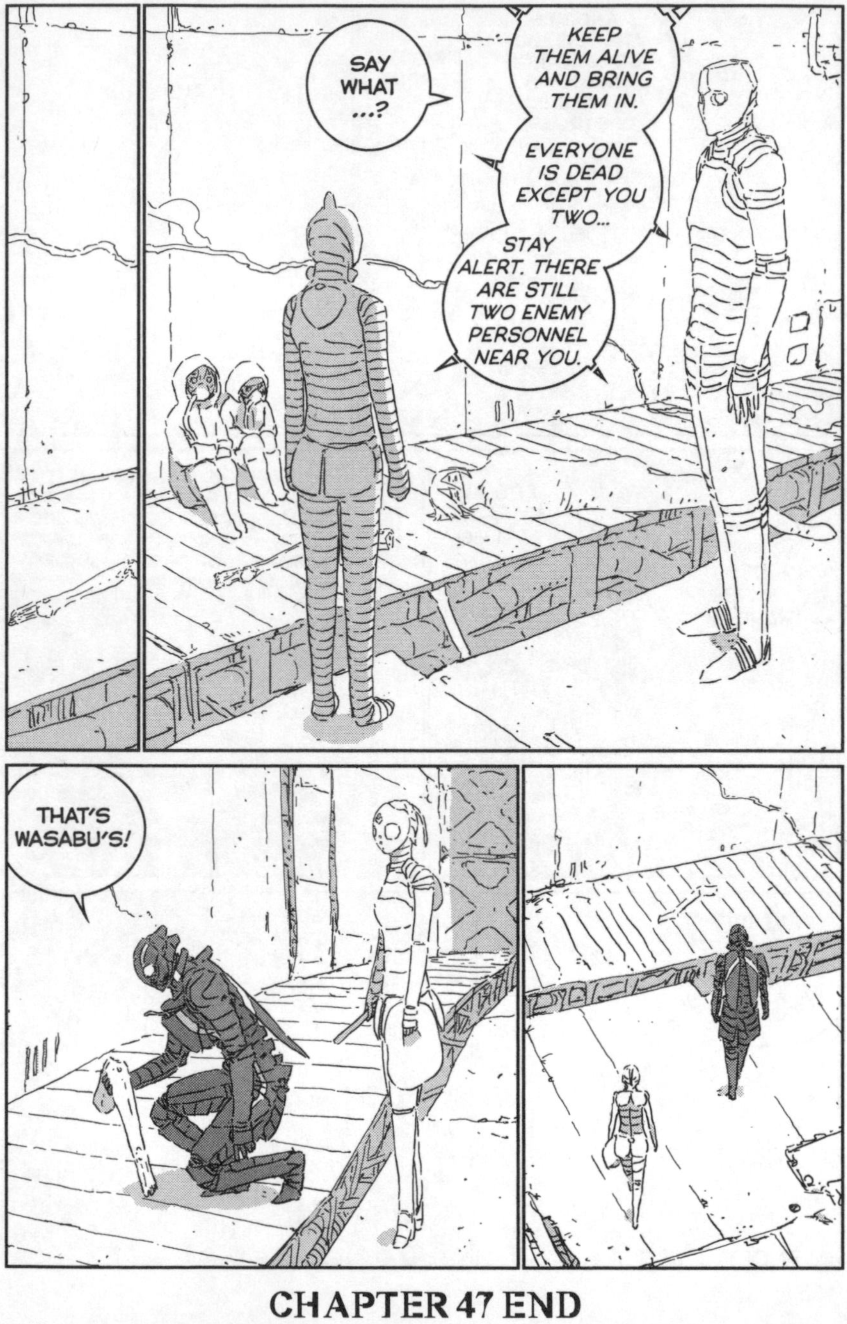
KEEP THEM ALIVE AND BRING THEM IN.
SAY WHAT ...?
EVERYONE IS DEAD EXCEPT YOU TWO...
STAY ALERT. THERE ARE STILL TWO ENEMY PERSONNEL NEAR YOU.
THAT'S WASABU'S!

CHAPTER 47 END

APOSIMZ

CHAPTER 48

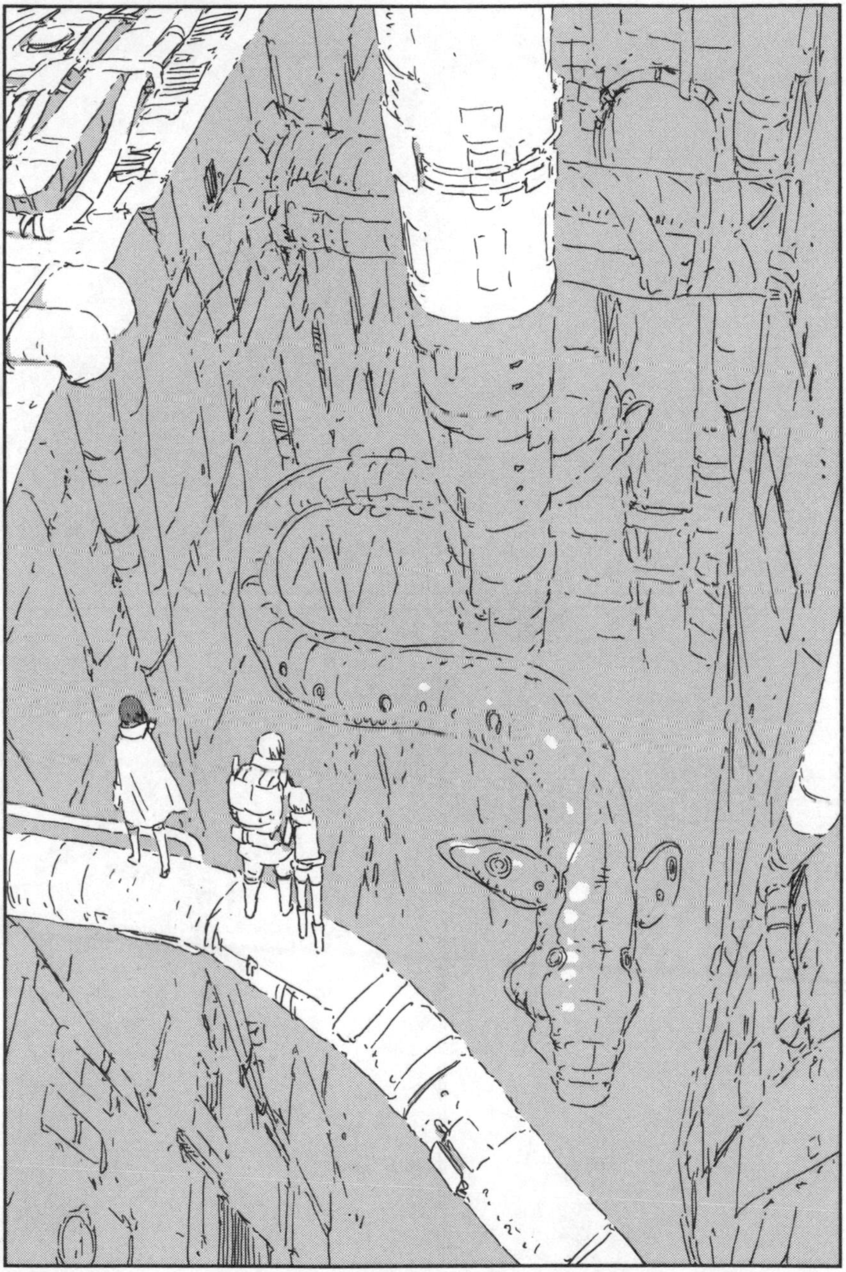

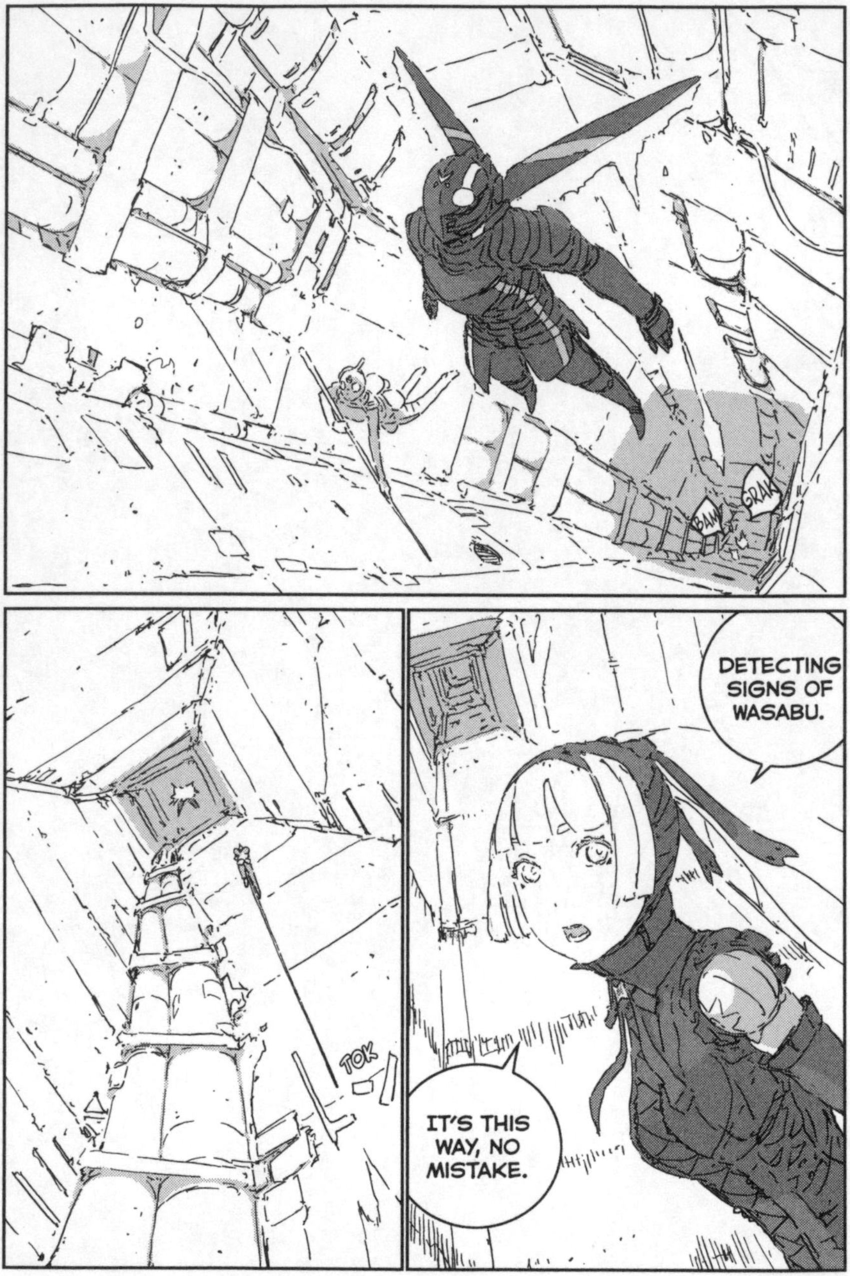
GRAK
BAM
DETECTING SIGNS OF WASABU.
IT'S THIS WAY, NO MISTAKE.
TOK

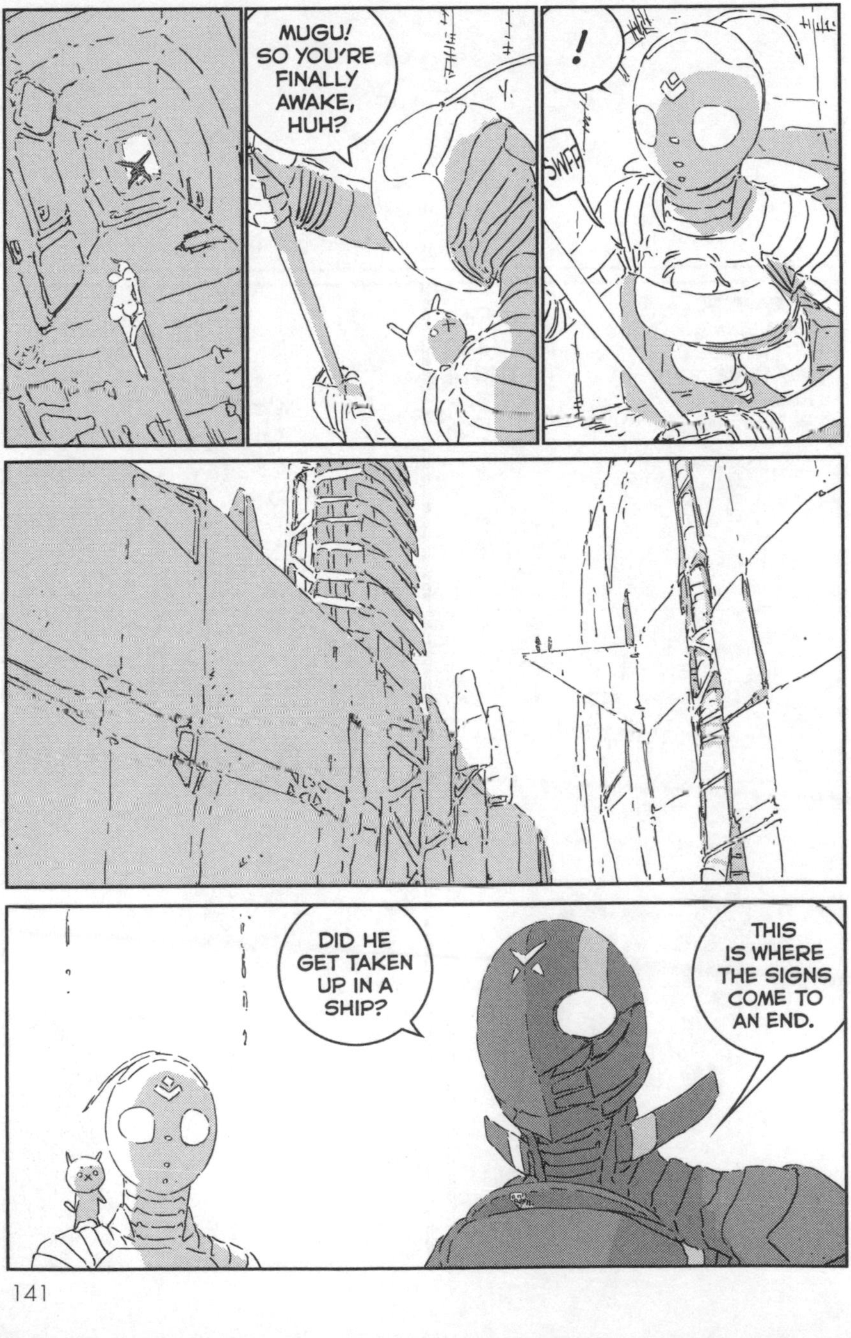
!
SWFF
MUGU! SO YOU'RE FINALLY AWAKE, HUH?
THIS IS WHERE THE SIGNS COME TO AN END.
DID HE GET TAKEN UP IN A SHIP?

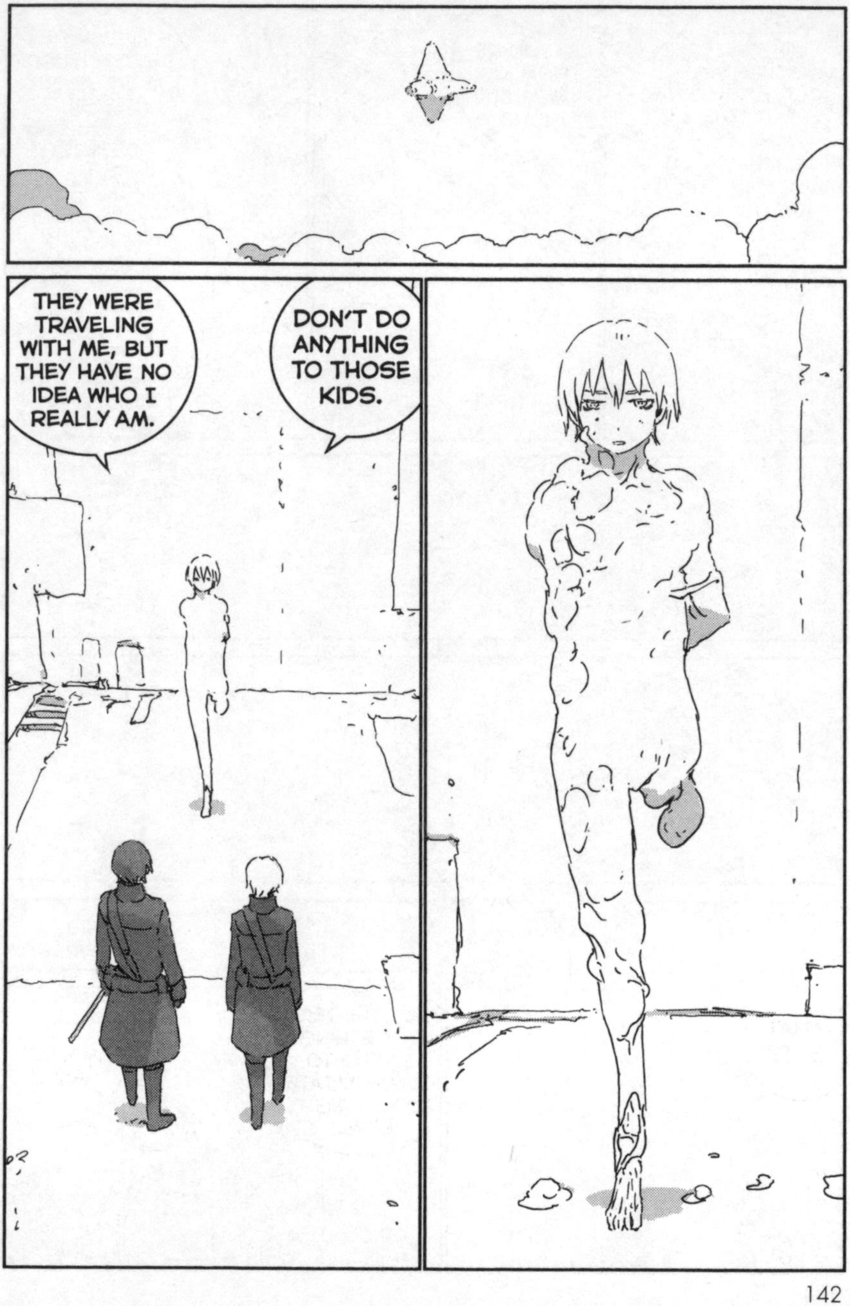
DON'T DO ANYTHING TO THOSE KIDS.
THEY WERE TRAVELING WITH ME, BUT THEY HAVE NO IDEA WHO I REALLY AM.

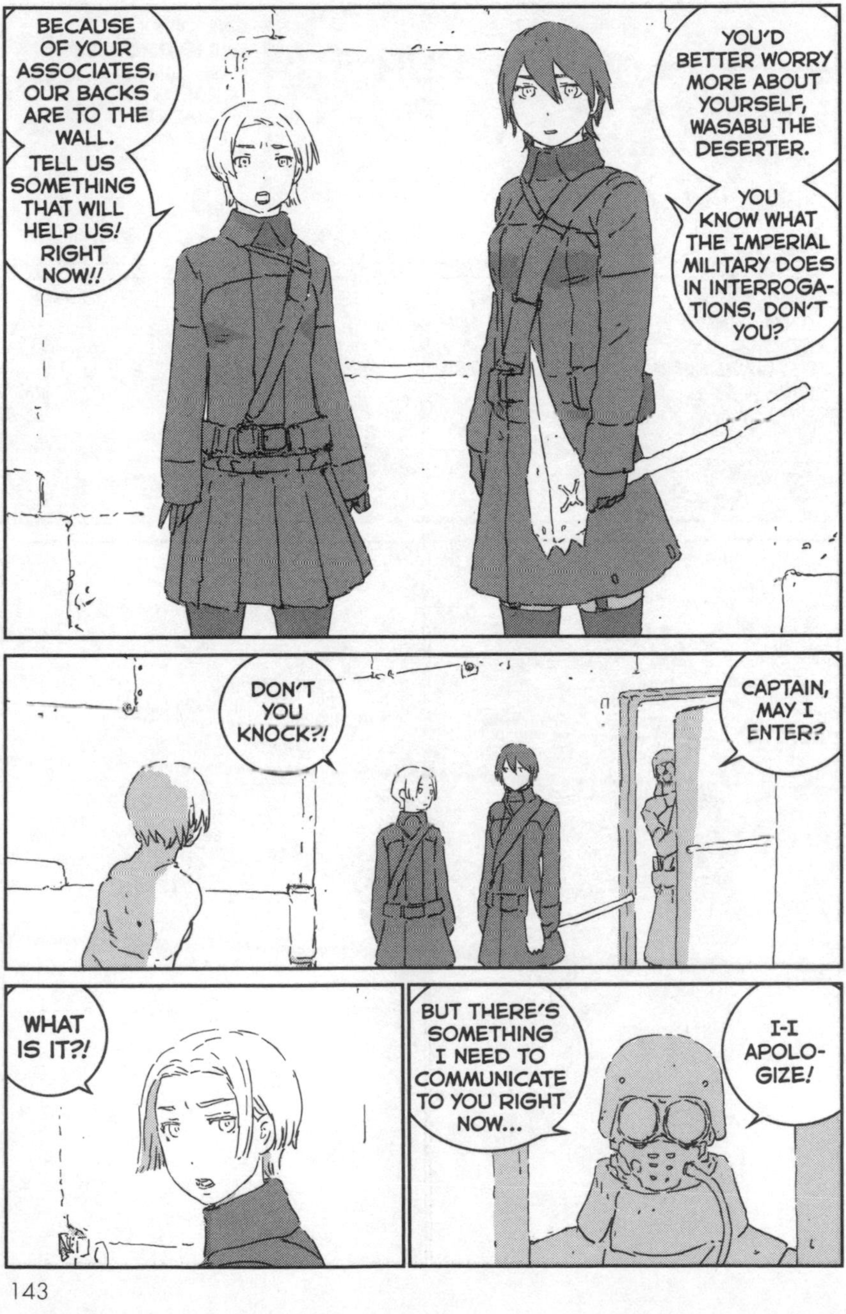
YOU'D BETTER WORRY MORE ABOUT YOURSELF, WASABU THE DESERTER.
YOU KNOW WHAT THE IMPERIAL MILITARY DOES IN INTERROGATIONS, DON'T YOU?
BECAUSE OF YOUR ASSOCIATES, OUR BACKS ARE TO THE WALL.
TELL US SOMETHING THAT WILL HELP US! RIGHT NOW!!
CAPTAIN, MAY I ENTER?
DON'T YOU KNOCK?!
I-I APOLOGIZE!
BUT THERE'S SOMETHING I NEED TO COMMUNICATE TO YOU RIGHT NOW...
WHAT IS IT?!

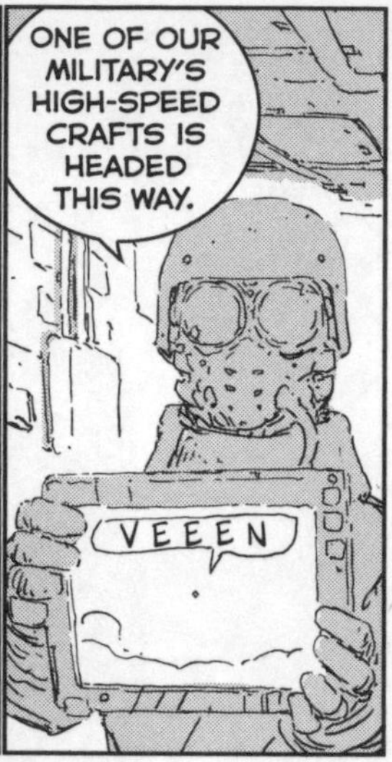
ONE OF OUR MILITARY'S HIGH-SPEED CRAFTS IS HEADED THIS WAY.
VEEEN
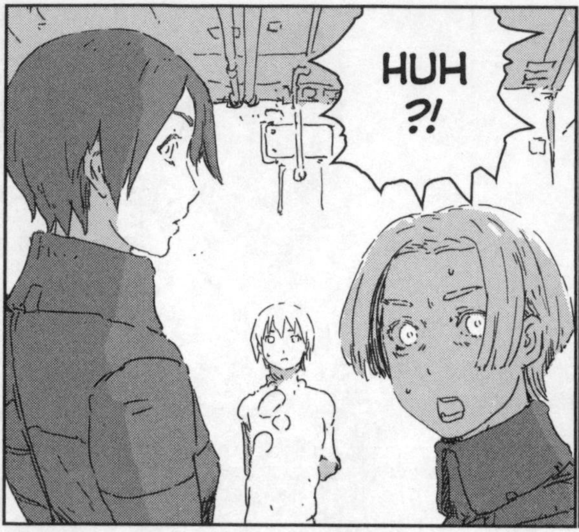
HUH ?!
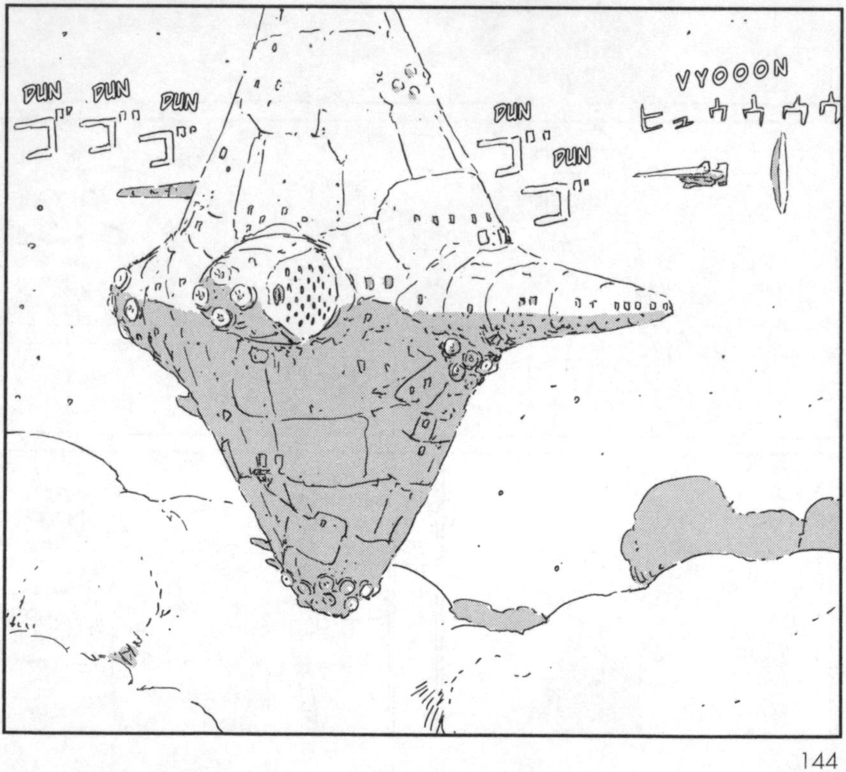
VYOOON
ヒュウウウウ
DUN
ゴ
DUN
ゴ
DUN DUN DUN
ゴゴゴ

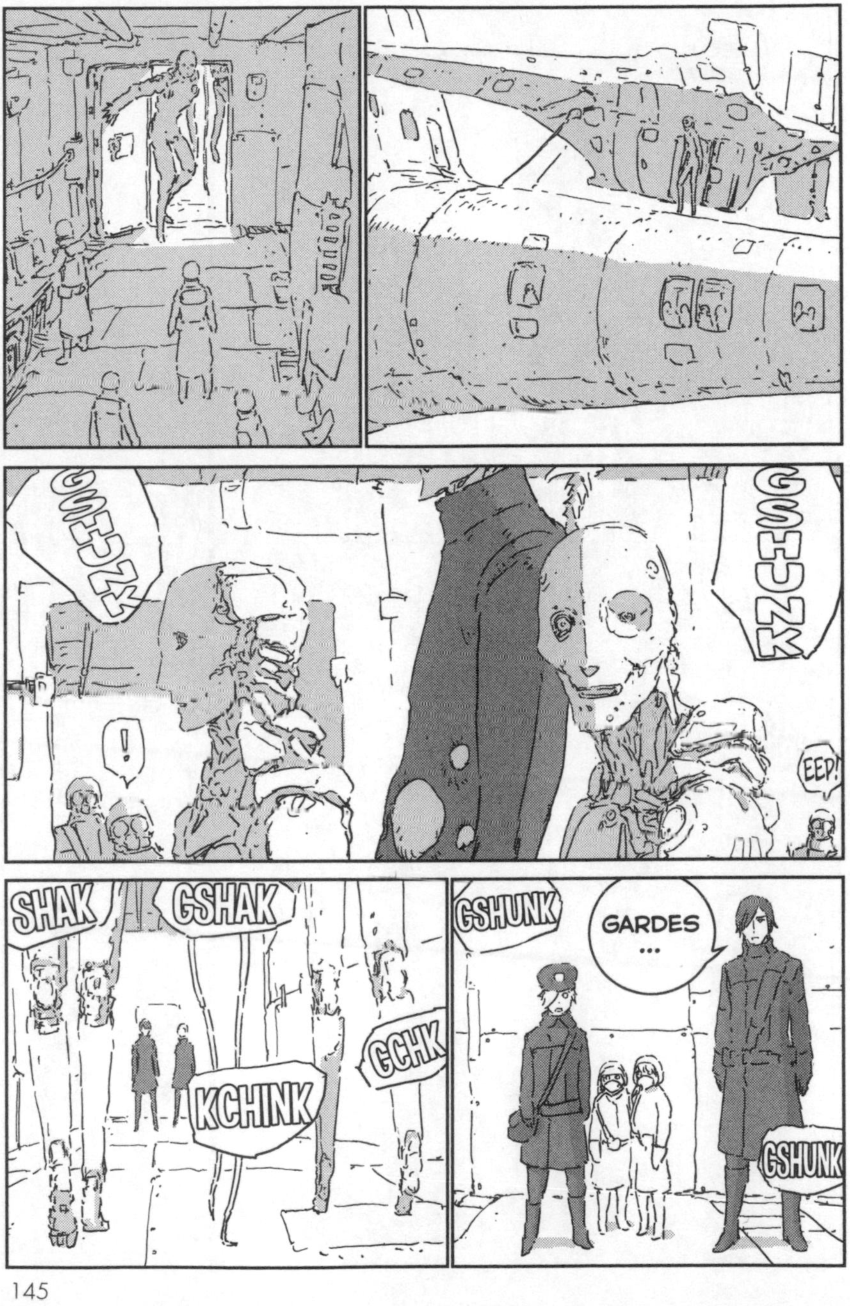
GSHUNK
GSHUNK
EEP!
!
GARDES ...
GSHUNK
GSHUNK
GSHAK
SHAK
GCHK
KCHINK

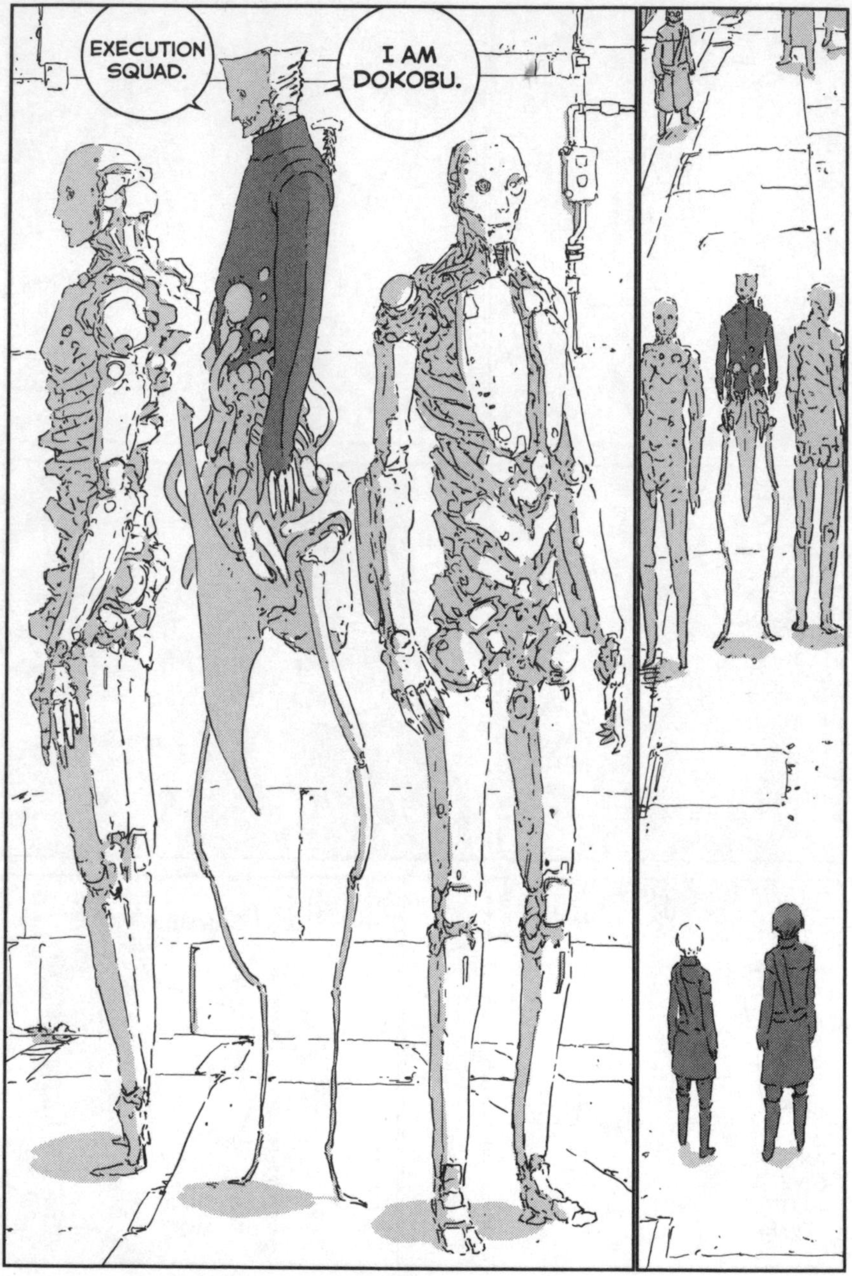
I AM DOKOBU.
EXECUTION SQUAD.

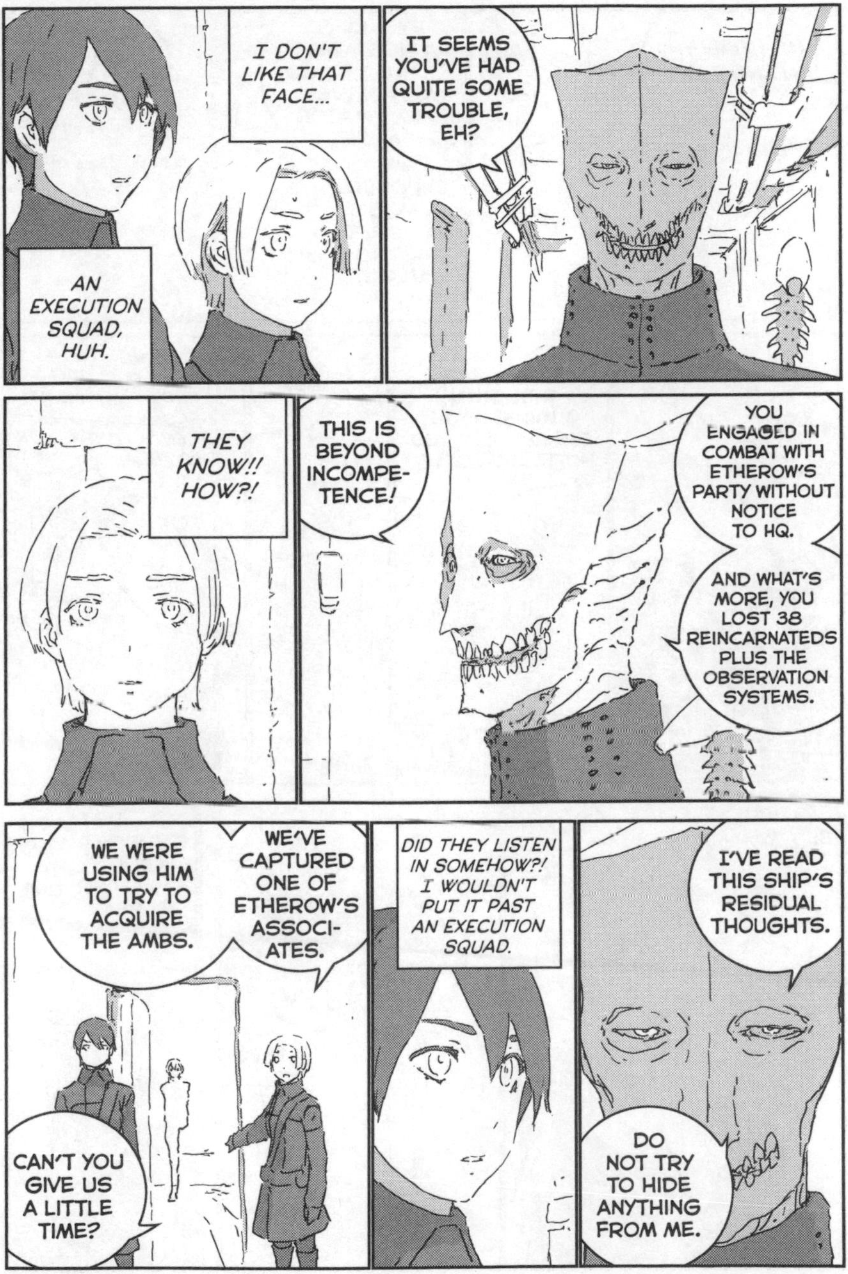
IT SEEMS YOU'VE HAD QUITE SOME TROUBLE, EH?
I DON'T LIKE THAT FACE...
AN EXECUTION SQUAD, HUH.
YOU ENGAGED IN COMBAT WITH ETHEROW'S PARTY WITHOUT NOTICE TO HQ.
AND WHAT'S MORE, YOU LOST 38 REINCARNATEDS PLUS THE OBSERVATION SYSTEMS.
THIS IS BEYOND INCOMPE-TENCE!
THEY KNOW!! HOW?!
I'VE READ THIS SHIP'S RESIDUAL THOUGHTS.
DO NOT TRY TO HIDE ANYTHING FROM ME.
DID THEY LISTEN IN SOMEHOW?! I WOULDN'T PUT IT PAST AN EXECUTION SQUAD.
WE'VE CAPTURED ONE OF ETHEROW'S ASSOCI-ATES.
WE WERE USING HIM TO TRY TO ACQUIRE THE AMBS.
CAN'T YOU GIVE US A LITTLE TIME?

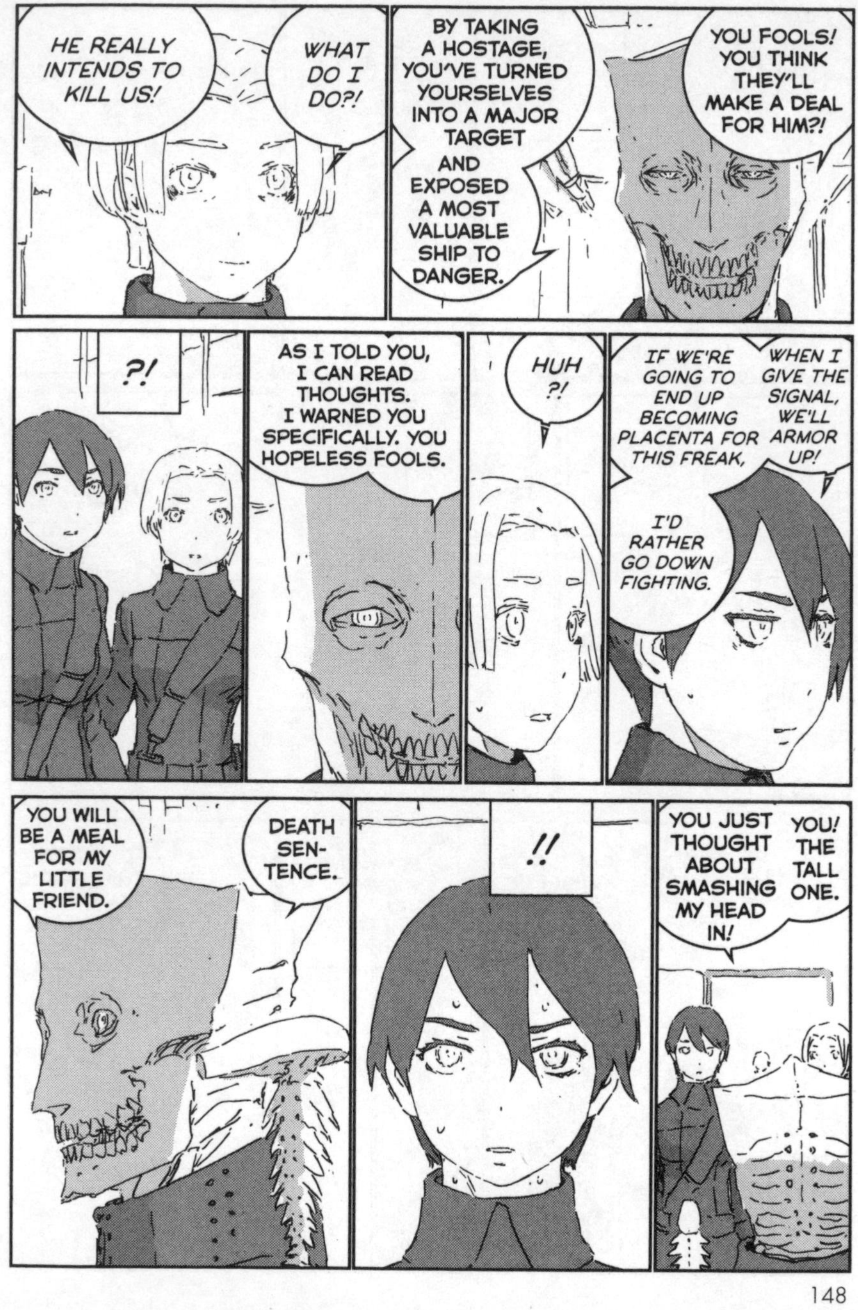
YOU FOOLS! YOU THINK THEY'LL MAKE A DEAL FOR HIM?!
BY TAKING A HOSTAGE, YOU'VE TURNED YOURSELVES INTO A MAJOR TARGET AND EXPOSED A MOST VALUABLE SHIP TO DANGER.
WHAT DO I DO?!
HE REALLY INTENDS TO KILL US!
WHEN I GIVE THE SIGNAL, WE'LL ARMOR UP!
IF WE'RE GOING TO END UP BECOMING PLACENTA FOR THIS FREAK,
I'D RATHER GO DOWN FIGHTING.
HUH ?!
AS I TOLD YOU, I CAN READ THOUGHTS. I WARNED YOU SPECIFICALLY. YOU HOPELESS FOOLS.
?!
YOU! THE TALL ONE.
YOU JUST THOUGHT ABOUT SMASHING MY HEAD IN!
!!
DEATH SEN-TENCE.
YOU WILL BE A MEAL FOR MY LITTLE FRIEND.

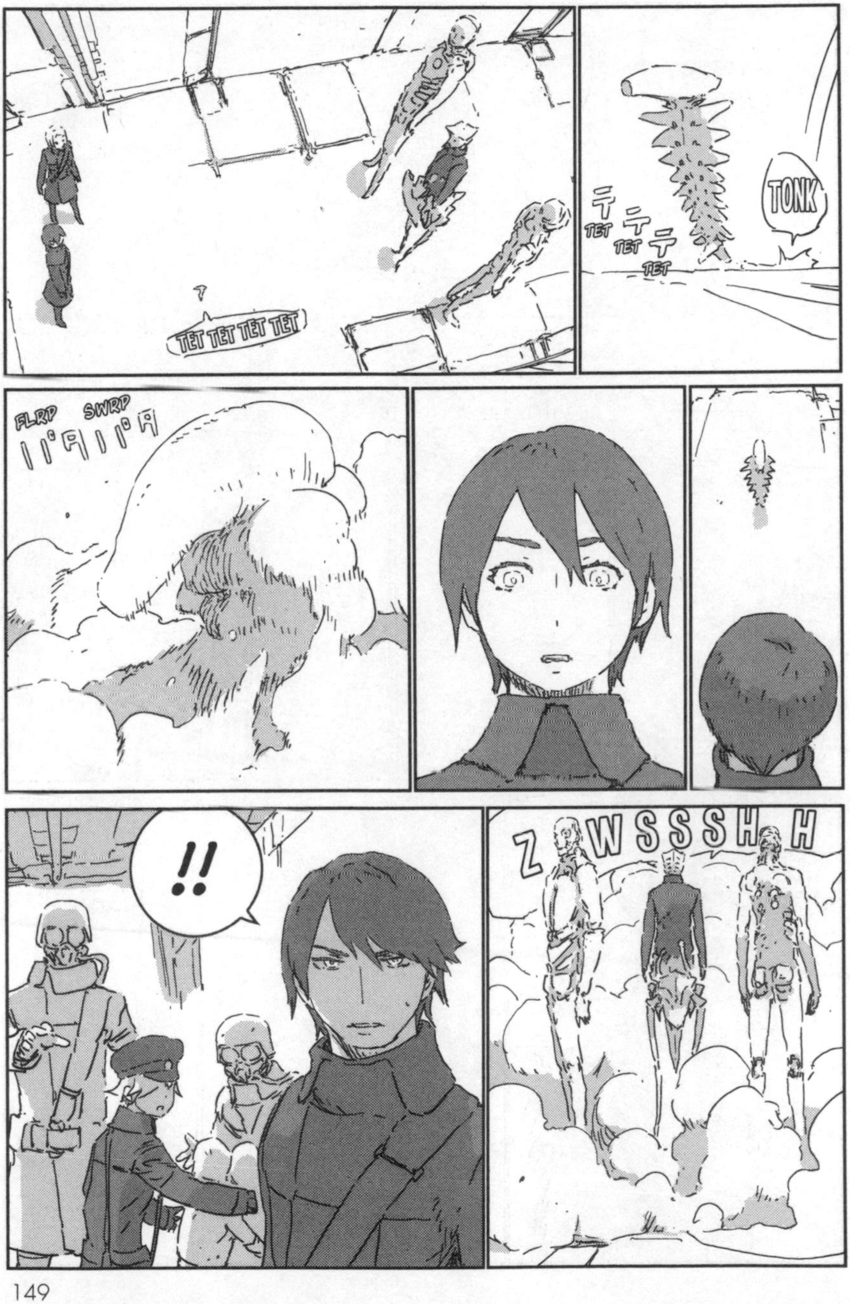
TONK
テ テ テ
TET TET TET
テ
TET TET TET TET
FLRP SWRP
パタパタ
ZWSSSHH H
!!

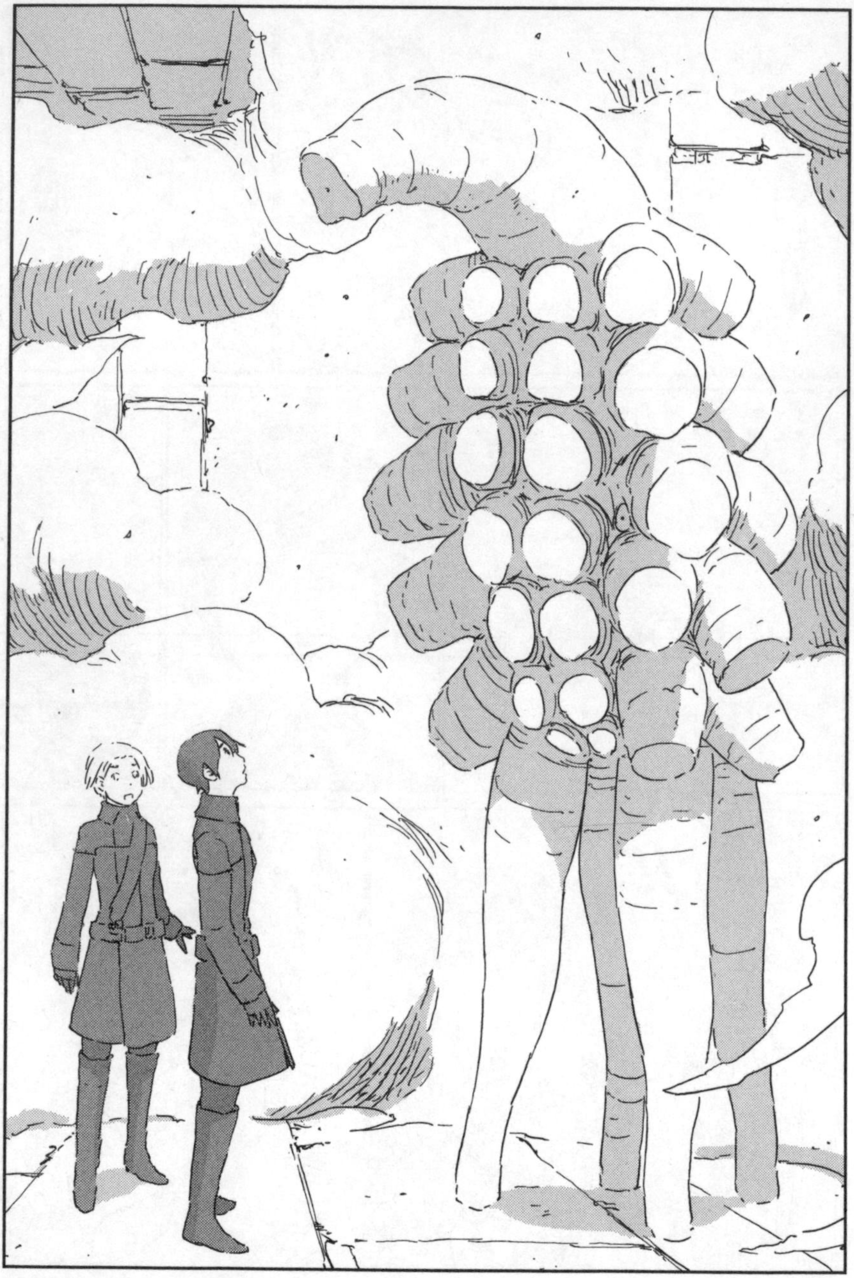

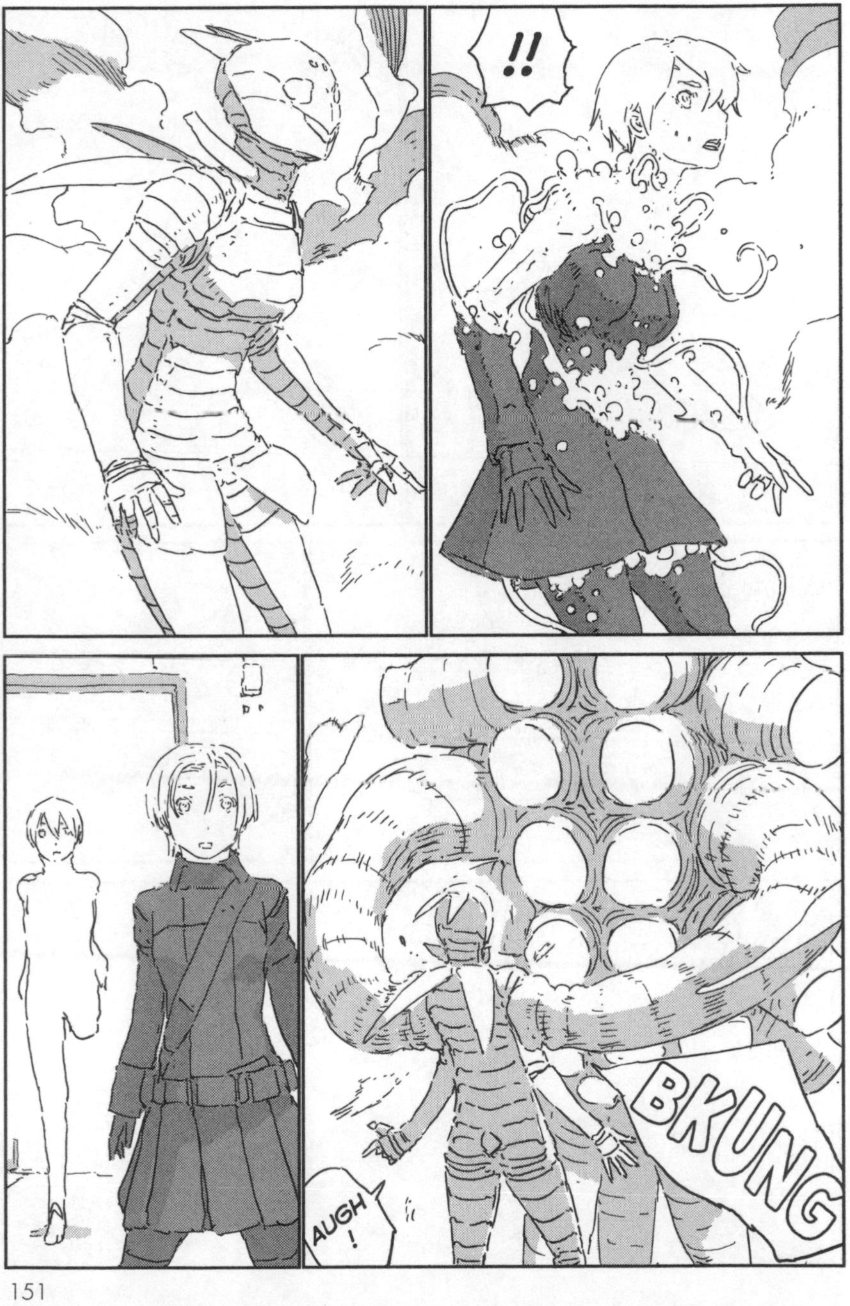
!!
BKUNG
AUGH!

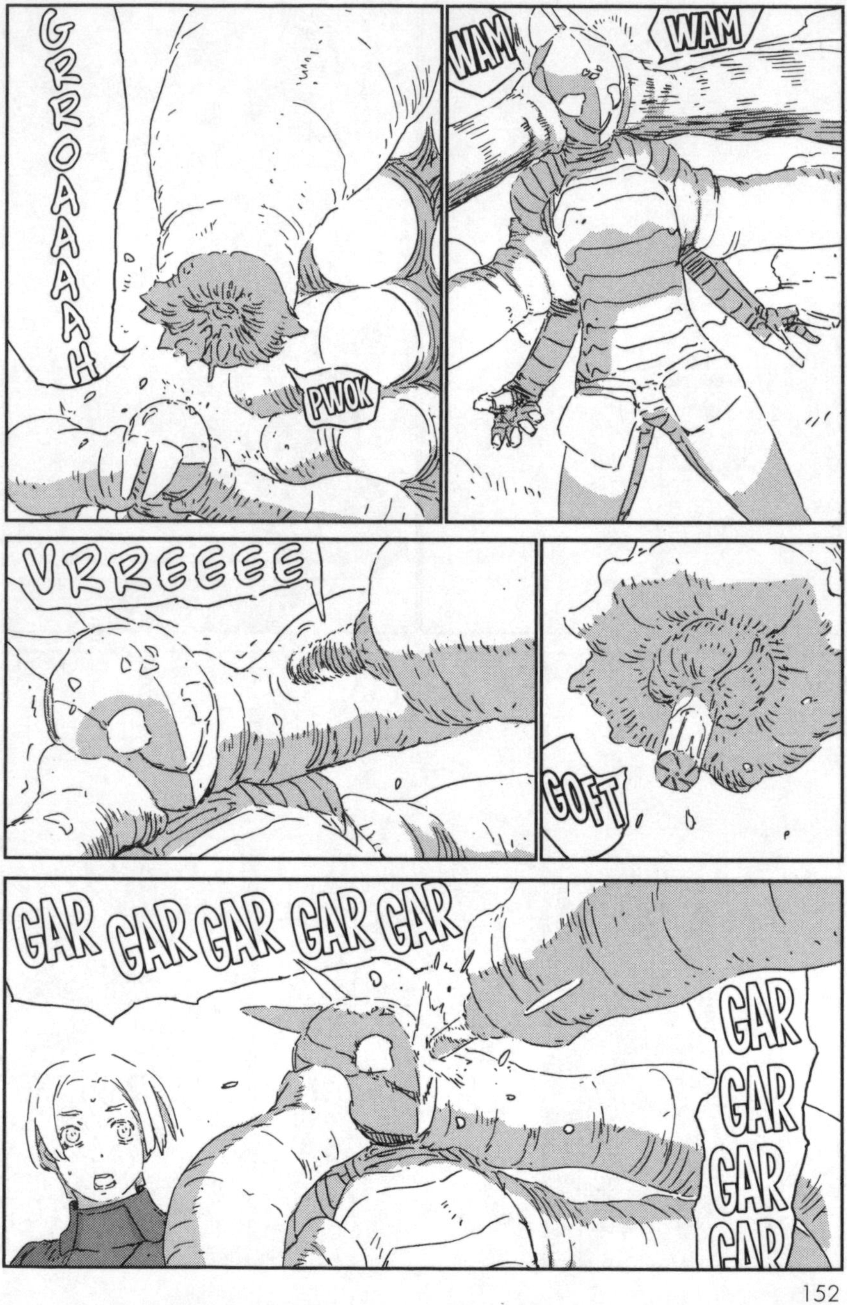
WAM
WAM
GRROAAAAAH
PWOK
GOFT
VRREEEE
GAR GAR GAR GAR GAR
GAR
GAR
GAR
GAR
GAR

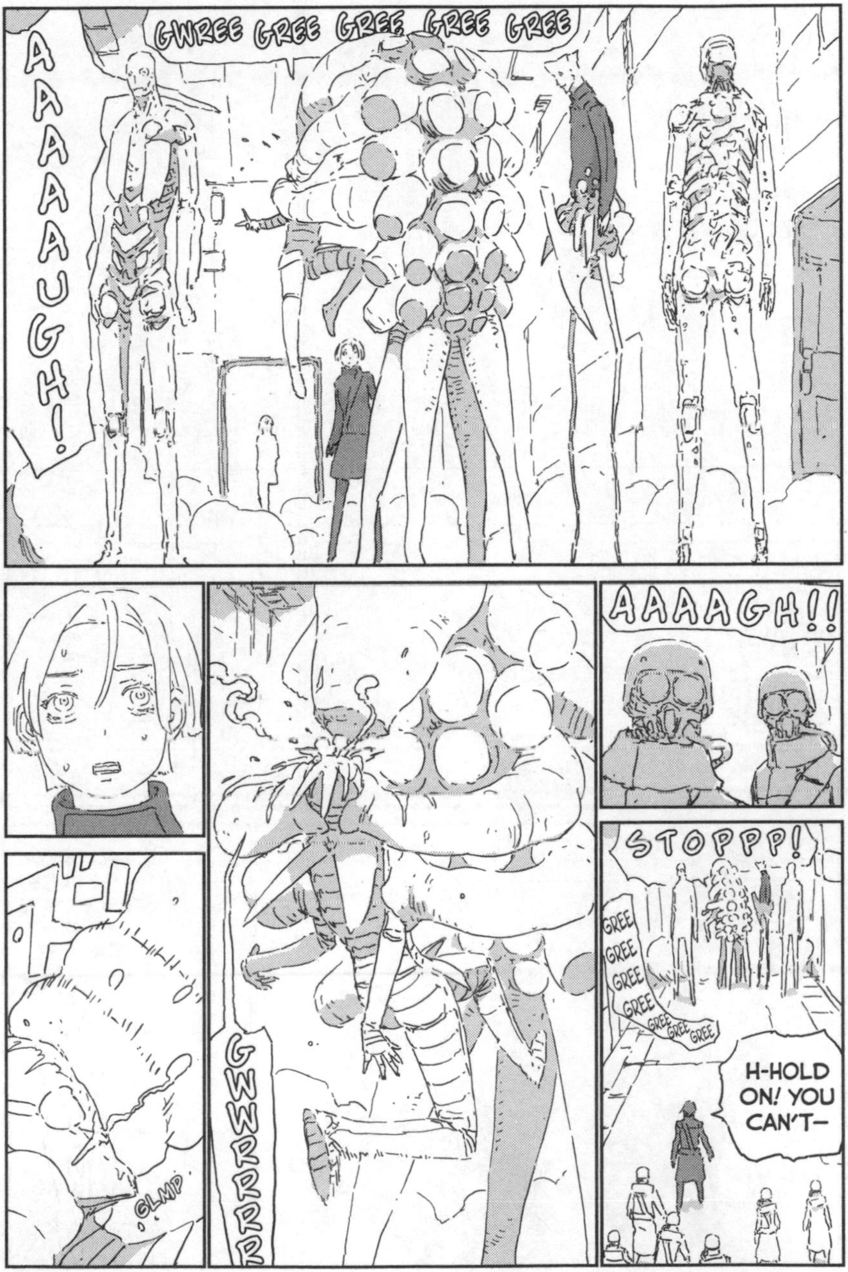
GWREE GREE GREE GREE GREE
AAAAAUGH!
AAAAGH!!
STOPPP!
GREE GREE GREE GREE GREE GREE GREE
H-HOLD ON! YOU CAN'T—
GWWRRRR
GLMP

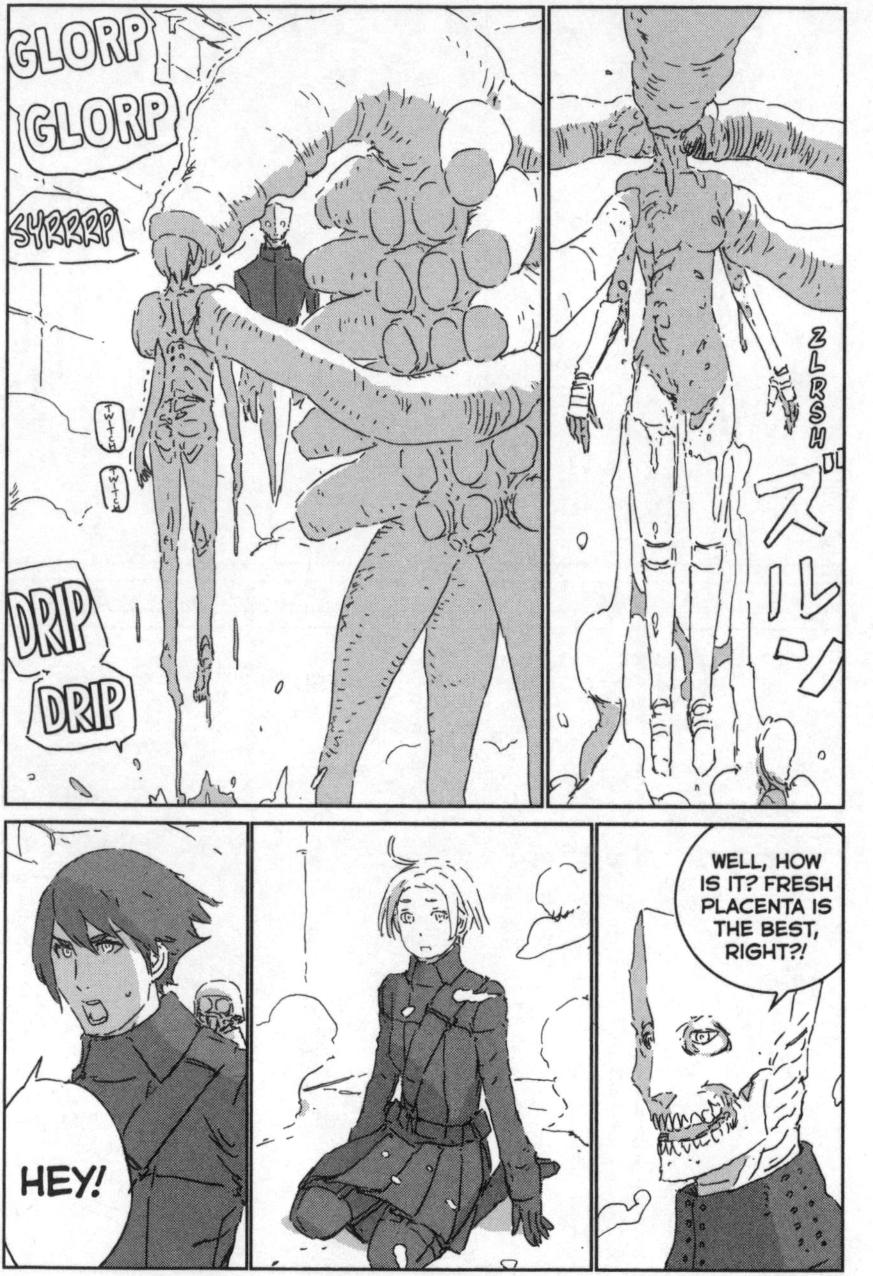
ZLRSH
ズルン
GLORP
GLORP
SYRRRP
TWITCH
TWITCH
DRIP
DRIP
WELL, HOW IS IT? FRESH PLACENTA IS THE BEST, RIGHT?!
HEY!

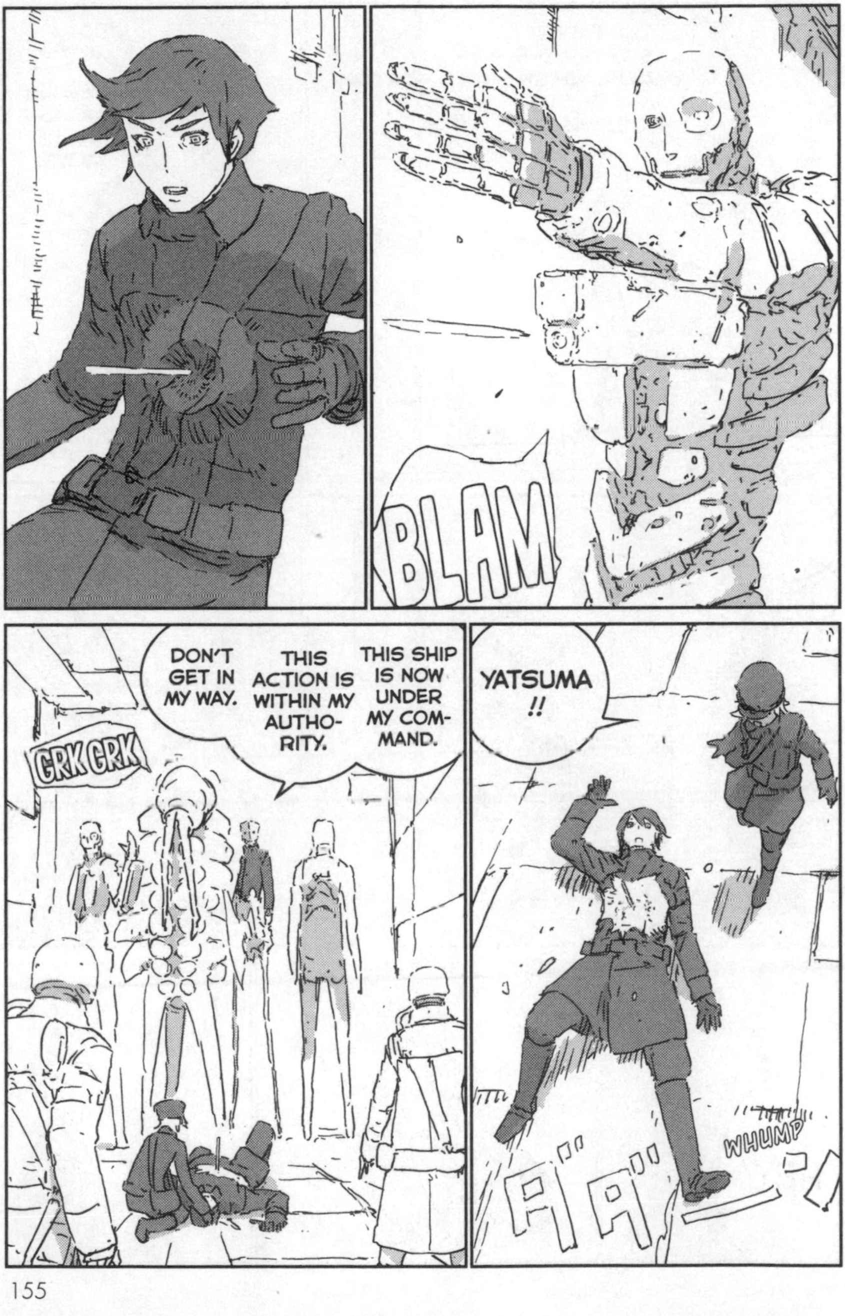
BLAM
YATSUMA !!
WHUMP
DON'T GET IN MY WAY. THIS ACTION IS WITHIN MY AUTHORITY. THIS SHIP IS NOW UNDER MY COMMAND.
GRK GRK

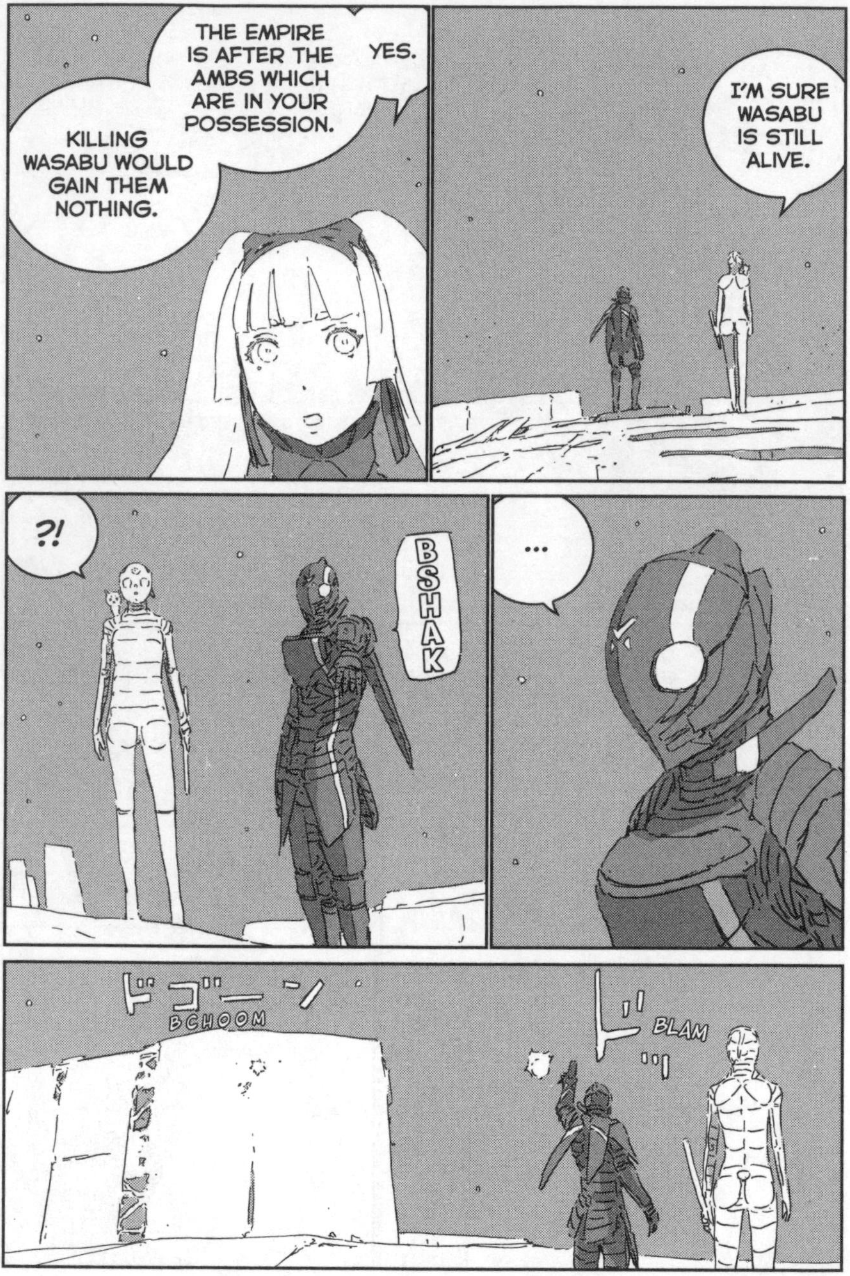
I'M SURE WASABU IS STILL ALIVE.
YES.
THE EMPIRE IS AFTER THE AMBS WHICH ARE IN YOUR POSSESSION.
KILLING WASABU WOULD GAIN THEM NOTHING.
...
BSHAK
?!
BLAM
ドゴーーン
BCHOOM

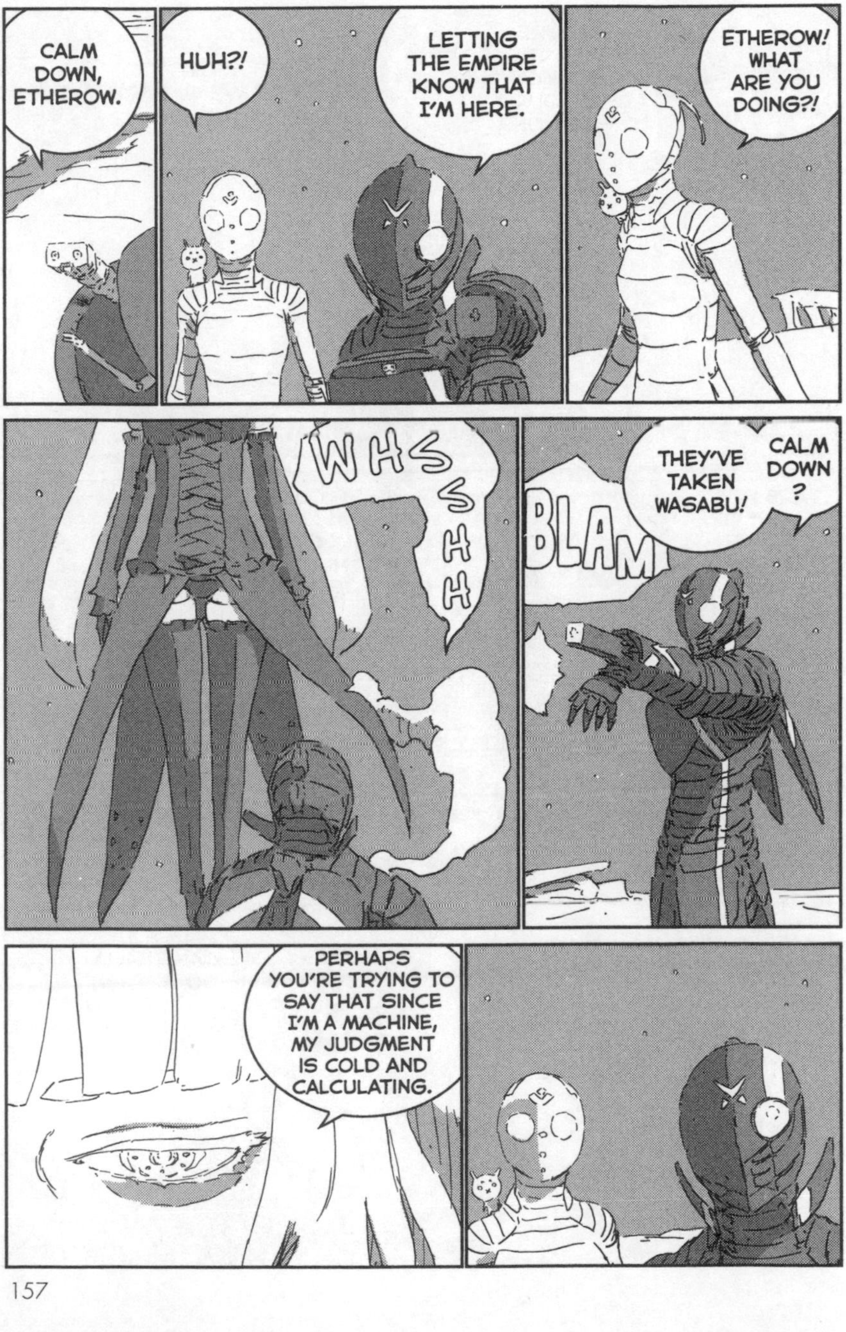
ETHEROW! WHAT ARE YOU DOING?!
LETTING THE EMPIRE KNOW THAT I'M HERE.
HUH?!
CALM DOWN, ETHEROW.
CALM DOWN ?
THEY'VE TAKEN WASABU!
BLAM
WHSSHH
PERHAPS YOU'RE TRYING TO SAY THAT SINCE I'M A MACHINE, MY JUDGMENT IS COLD AND CALCULATING.

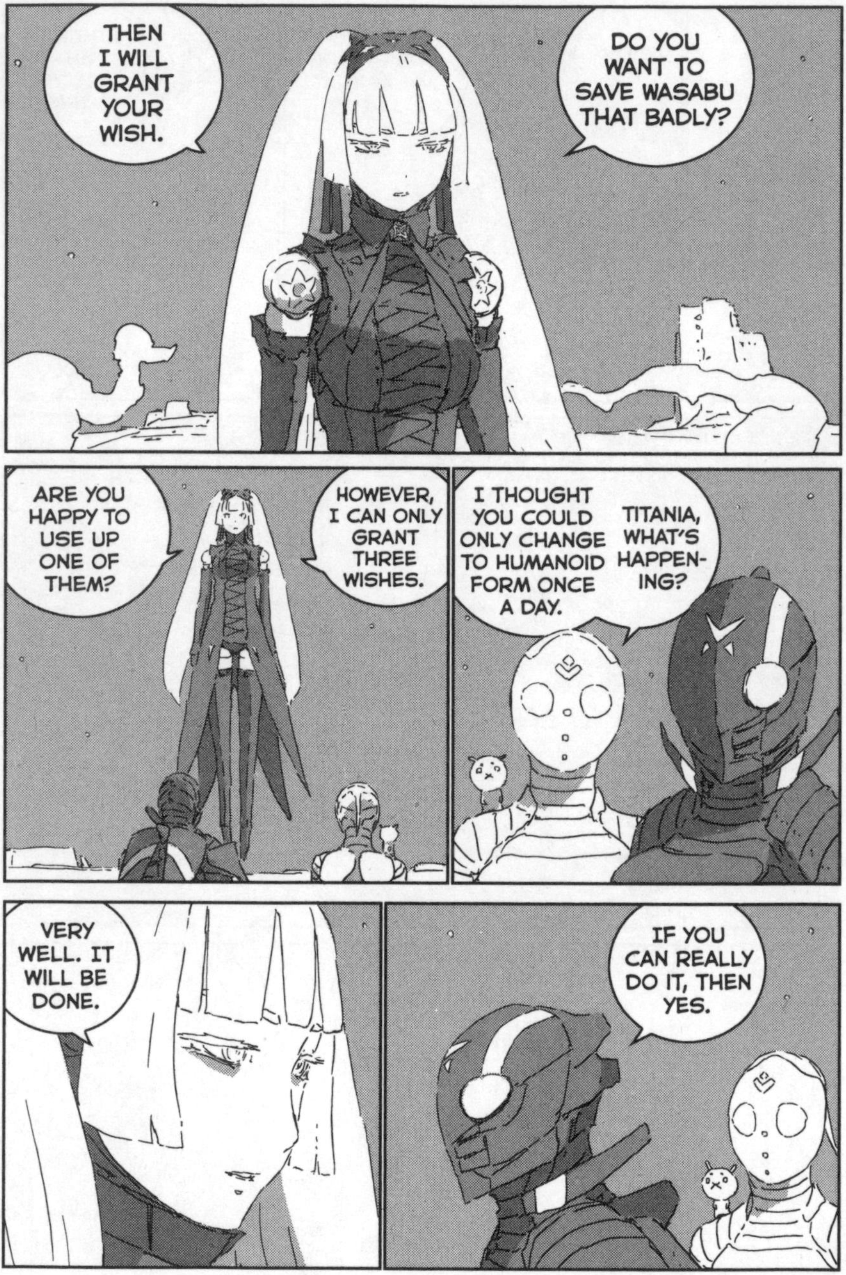
DO YOU WANT TO SAVE WASABU THAT BADLY?
THEN I WILL GRANT YOUR WISH.
TITANIA, WHAT'S HAPPENING?
I THOUGHT YOU COULD ONLY CHANGE TO HUMANOID FORM ONCE A DAY.
HOWEVER, I CAN ONLY GRANT THREE WISHES.
ARE YOU HAPPY TO USE UP ONE OF THEM?
IF YOU CAN REALLY DO IT, THEN YES.
VERY WELL. IT WILL BE DONE.

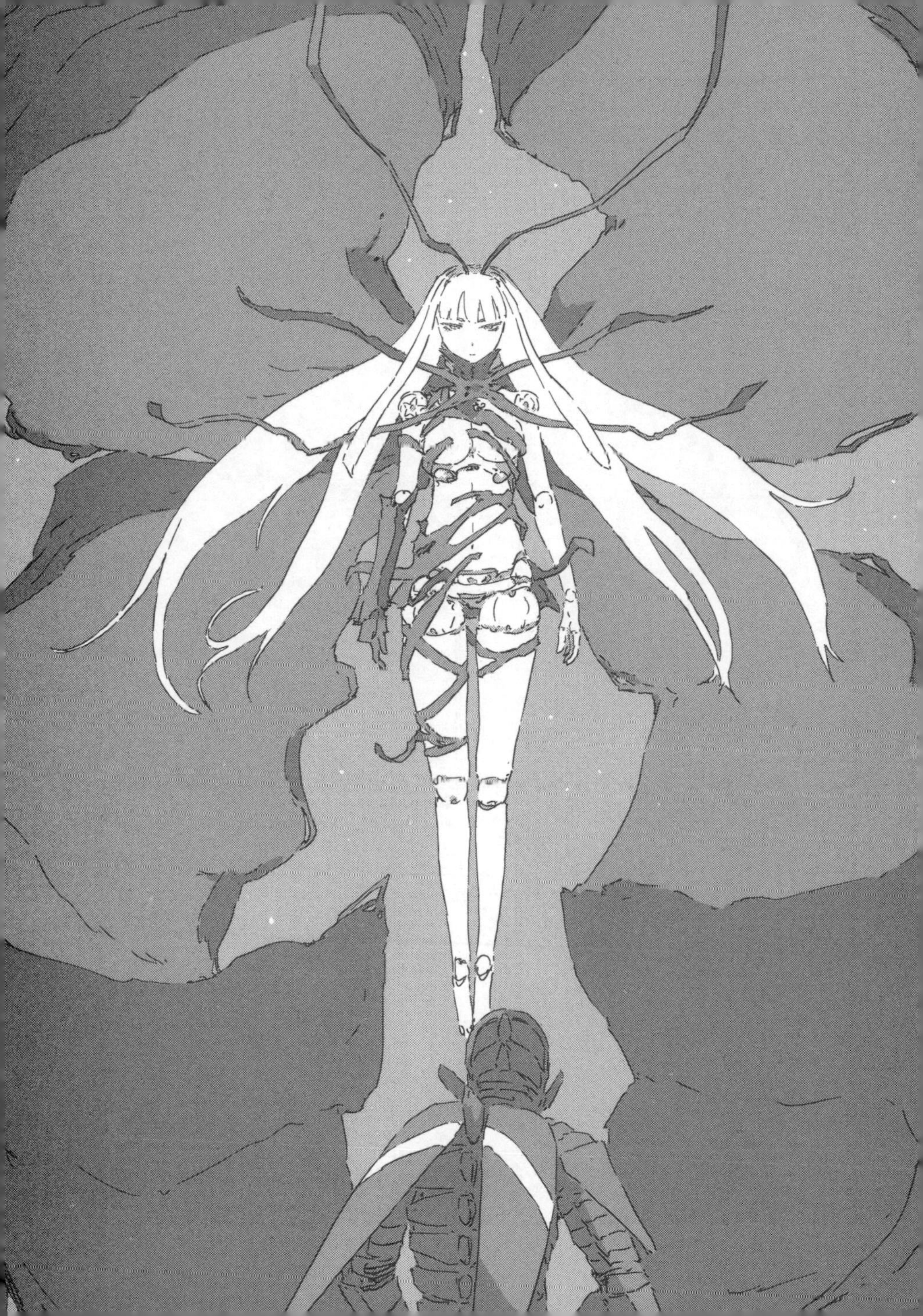

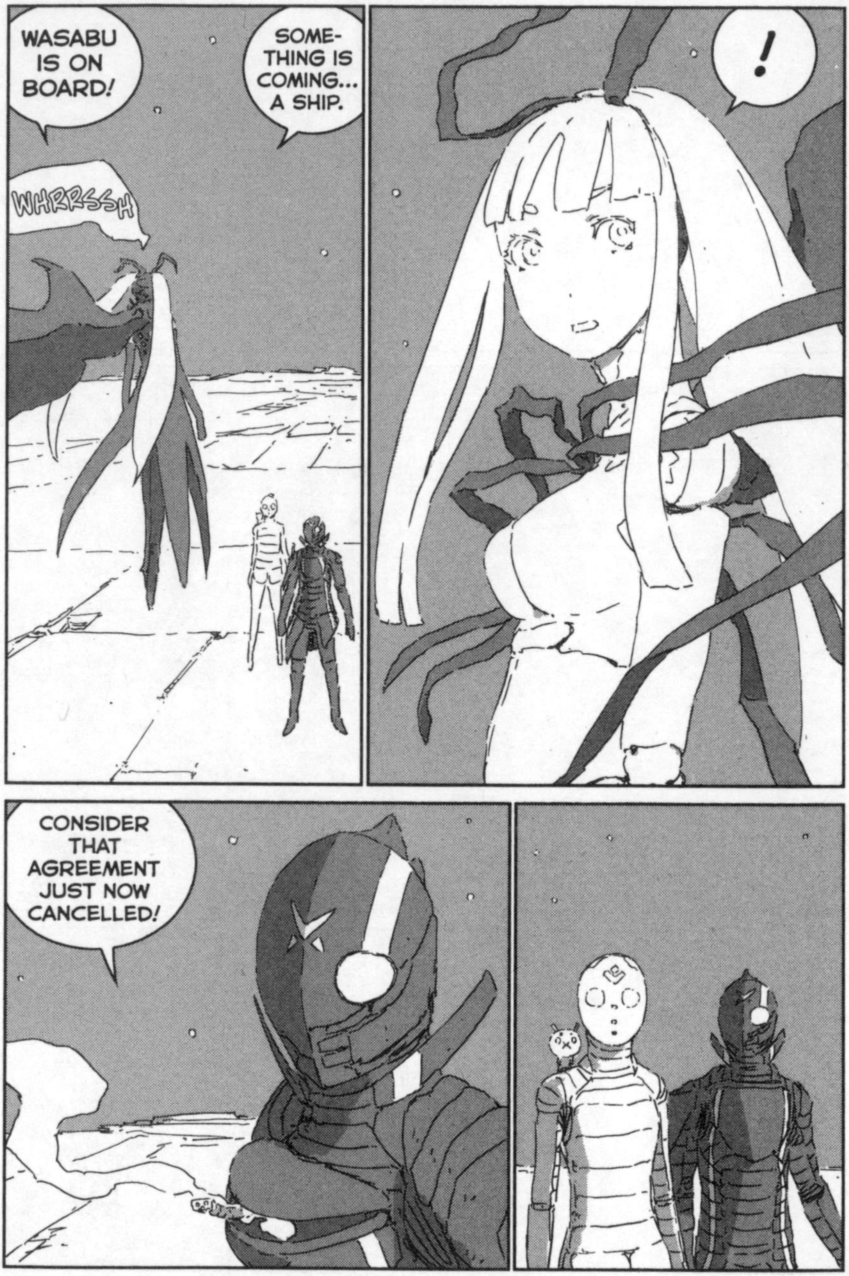
!
SOME-THING IS COMING... A SHIP.
WASABU IS ON BOARD!
WHRRSSH
CONSIDER THAT AGREEMENT JUST NOW CANCELLED!

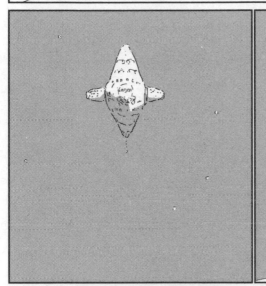

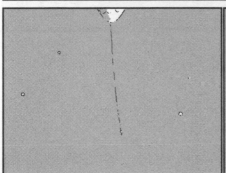

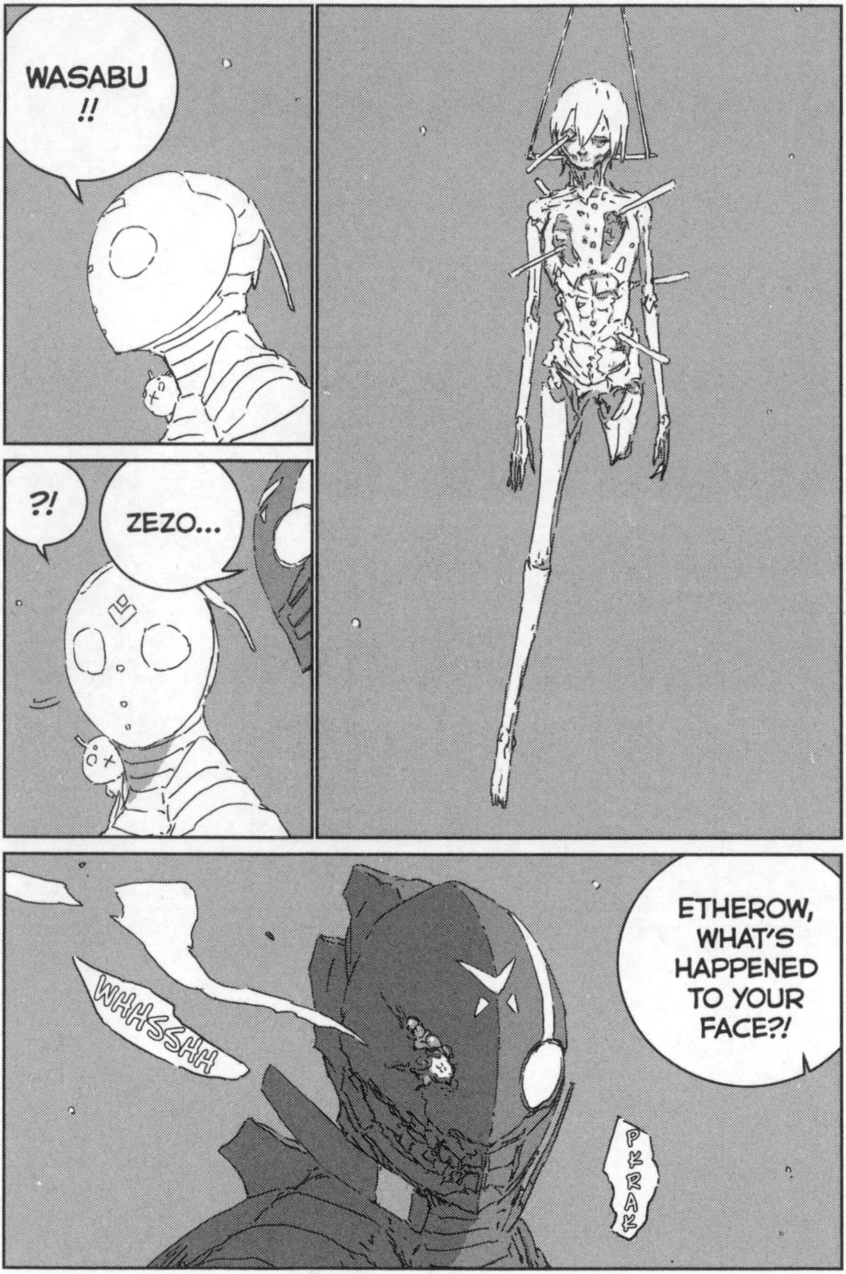
WASABU !!
ZEZO...
?!
ETHEROW, WHAT'S HAPPENED TO YOUR FACE?!
PKRAK
WHHSSHH

CHAPTER 48 END

CONTINUED IN VOLUME 9

APOSIMZ volume 8

A Vertical Comics Edition

Translation: Kumar Sivasubramanian
Production: Grace Lu
Darren Smith

First published in Japan in 2021 by Kodansha, Ltd., Tokyo
Publication for this English edition arranged through Kodansha, Ltd., Tokyo
English language version produced by Vertical Comics,
an imprint of Kodansha USA Publishing, LLC

Translation provided by Vertical Comics, 2022
Published by Kodansha USA Publishing, LLC, New York

Originally published in Japanese as *APOSIMZ 8* by Kodansha, Ltd.
APOSIMZ first serialized in *Monthly Shonen Sirius*, Kodansha, Ltd., 2017-2021

This is a work of fiction.

ISBN: 978-1-64729-061-0

Manufactured in Canada

First Edition

Kodansha USA Publishing, LLC
451 Park Avenue South
7th Floor
New York, NY 10016
www.kodansha.us

Vertical books are distributed through Penguin-Random House Publisher Services.